POEMS

OF

WORDSWORTH

CHOSEN AND EDITED BY

MATTHEW ARNOLD

LONDON
MACMILLAN & CO LTD
NEW YORK · ST MARTIN'S PRESS
1965

43803

—

First Edition printed September 1879
Reprinted with additions November 1879
Reprinted 1880, 1882, 1886, 1888, 1890, 1891, 1893, 1896
1897 (*twice*), 1898, 1900, 1902, 1903, 1904, 1906, 1907, 1908
1909, 1910, 1911, 1912, 1915, 1917, 1919 (*twice*), 1920, 1921
1922, 1924 (*twice*), 1925, 1927, 1929, 1943, 1946, 1947, 1959
1961, 1962, 1963, 1964, 1965

MACMILLAN AND COMPANY LIMITED
St Martin's Street London WC 2
also Bombay Calcutta Madras Melbourne

THE MACMILLAN COMPANY OF CANADA LIMITED
70 Bond Street Toronto 2

ST MARTIN'S PRESS INC
175 Fifth Avenue New York 10 NY

PRINTED IN GREAT BRITAIN

PREFACE.

I REMEMBER hearing Lord Macaulay say, after Words-worth's death, when subscriptions were being collected to found a memorial of him, that ten years earlier more money could have been raised in Cambridge alone, to do honour to Wordsworth, than was now raised all through the country. Lord Macaulay had, as we know, his own heightened and telling way of putting things, and we must always make allowance for it. But probably it is true that Wordsworth has never, either before or since, been so accepted and popular, so established in possession of the minds of all who profess to care for poetry, as he was between the years 1830 and 1840, and at Cambridge. From the very first, no doubt, he had his believers and witnesses. But I have myself heard him declare that, for he knew not how many years, his poetry had never brought him in enough to buy his shoe-strings. The poetry-reading public was very slow to recognise him, and was very easily drawn away from him. Scott effaced him with this public, Byron effaced him.

The death of Byron seemed, however, to make an opening for Wordsworth. Scott, who had for some time ceased to produce poetry himself, and stood before the public as a great novelist ; Scott, too genuine himself not to feel the profound genuineness of Wordsworth, and with an instinctive recognition of his firm hold on nature and of his local truth, always admired him sincerely, and praised him generously. The influence of Coleridge upon young men of ability was then powerful, and was still gathering strength; this influence told entirely in favour of Wordsworth's poetry. Cambridge was a place where Coleridge's influence had great action, and where Wordsworth's poetry, therefore, flourished especially. But even amongst the general public its sale grew large, the eminence of its author was widely recognised, and Rydal Mount became an object of pilgrimage. I remember Wordsworth relating how one of the pilgrims, a clergyman, asked him if he had ever written anything besides the *Guide to the Lakes*. Yes, he answered modestly, he had written verses. Not every pilgrim was a reader, but the vogue was established, and the stream of pilgrims came.

Mr. Tennyson's decisive appearance dates from 1842. One cannot say that he effaced Wordsworth as Scott and Byron had effaced him. The poetry of Wordsworth had been so long before the public, the suffrage of good judges was so steady and so strong in its favour, that by 1842 the verdict of posterity, one may almost say, had been already pronounced, and Wordsworth's English fame was secure. But the vogue, the ear and applause of the great body of poetry-readers, never quite thoroughly perhaps his, he gradually lost more and more, and Mr. Tennyson gained them. Mr. Tennyson drew to himself, and away from Wordsworth, the poetry-reading public, and the new generations. Even in 1850, when Wordsworth died, this diminution of popularity was visible, and occasioned the remark of Lord Macaulay which I quoted at starting.

The diminution has continued. The influence of Coleridge has waned, and Wordsworth's poetry can no longer draw succour from this ally. The poetry has not, however, wanted eulogists; and it may be said to have brought its eulogists luck, for almost every one who has praised Wordsworth's poetry has praised it well. But the public has remained cold, or, at least, undetermined.

Even the abundance of Mr. Palgrave's fine and skilfully chosen specimens of Wordsworth, in the *Golden Treasury*, surprised many readers, and gave offence to not a few. To tenth-rate critics and compilers, for whom any violent shock to the public taste would be a temerity not to be risked, it is still quite permissible to speak of Wordsworth's poetry, not only with ignorance, but with impertinence. On the Continent he is almost unknown.

I cannot think, then, that Wordsworth has, up to this time, at all obtained his deserts. "Glory," said M. Renan the other day, "glory after all is the thing which has the best chance of not being altogether vanity." Wordsworth was a homely man, and himself would certainly never have thought of talking of glory as that which, after all, has the best chance of not being altogether vanity. Yet we may well allow that few things are less vain than *real* glory. Let us conceive of the whole group of civilised nations as being, for intellectual and spiritual purposes, one great confederation, bound to a joint action and working towards a common result ; a confederation whose members have a due knowledge both of the past, out of which they all proceed, and of one another. This was the ideal of Goethe, and it is an ideal which will impose itself upon the thoughts of our modern societies more and more. Then to be recognised by the verdict of such a confederation as a master, or even as a seriously and eminently worthy workman, in one's own line of intellectual or spiritual activity, is indeed glory ; a glory which it would be difficult to rate too highly. For what could be more beneficent, more salutary ? The world is forwarded by having its attention fixed on the best things ; and here is a tribunal, free from all suspicion of national and provincial partiality, putting a stamp on the best things, and recommending them for general honour and acceptance. A nation, again, is furthered by recognition of its real gifts and successes ; it is encouraged to develop them further. And here is an honest verdict, telling us which of our supposed successes are really, in the judgment of the great impartial world, and not in our own private judgment only, successes, and which are not.

It is so easy to feel pride and satisfaction in one's own things, so hard to make sure that one is right in feeling it ! We have a great empire. But so had Nebuchadnezzar. We extol the "unrivalled happiness" of our national civilisation. But then comes a candid friend, and remarks that our upper class is materialised, our middle class vulgarised, and our lower class brutalised. We are proud of our painting, our music. But we find that in the judgment of other people our painting is questionable, and our music non-existent. We are proud of our men of science. And here it turns out that the world is with us ; we find that in the judgment of other people, too, Newton among the dead, and Mr. Darwin among the living, hold as high a place as they hold in our national opinion.

Finally, we are proud of our poets and poetry. Now poetry is nothing less than the most perfect speech of man, that in which he comes nearest to being able to utter the truth. It is no small thing, therefore, to succeed eminently in poetry. And so much is required for duly estimating success here, that about poetry it is perhaps hardest to arrive at a sure general verdict, and takes longest. Meanwhile, our own conviction of the superiority of our national poets is not decisive, is almost certain to be mingled, as we see constantly in English eulogy of Shakspeare, with much of provincial infatuation. And we know what was the opinion current amongst our neighbours the French, people of taste, acuteness, and quick literary tact, not a hundred years ago, about our great poets. The old *Biographie Universelle* notices the pretension of the English to a place for their poets among the chief poets of the world, and says that this is a pretension which to no one but an Englishman can ever seem admissible. And the scornful, disparaging things said by foreigners about Shakspeare and Milton, and about our national over-estimate of them, have been often quoted, and will be in every one's remembrance.

A great change has taken place, and Shakspeare is now generally recognised, even in France, as one of the greatest of poets. Yes, some anti-Gallican cynic will say, the French rank him with Corneille and with Victor Hugo! But let me have the pleasure of quoting a sentence about Shakspeare, which I met with by accident not long ago in the *Correspondant*, a French review which not a dozen English people, I suppose, look at. The writer is praising Shakspeare's prose. With Shakspeare, he says, "prose comes in whenever the subject, being more familiar, is unsuited to the majestic English iambic." And he goes on : "Shakspeare is the king of poetic rhythm and style, as well as the king of the realm of thought ; along with his dazzling prose, Shakspeare has succeeded in giving us the most varied, the most harmonious verse which has ever sounded upon the human ear since the verse of the Greeks." M. Henry Cochin, the writer of this sentence, deserves our gratitude for it ; it would not be easy to praise Shakspeare, in a single sentence, more justly. And when a foreigner and a Frenchman writes thus of Shakspeare, and when Goethe says of Milton, in whom there was so much to repel Goethe rather than to attract him, that "nothing has been ever done so entirely in the sense of the Greeks as *Samson Agonistes*," and that "Milton is in very truth a poet whom we must treat with all reverence," then we understand what constitutes a European recognition of poets and poetry as contradistinguished from a merely national recognition, and that in favour both of Milton and of Shakspeare the judgment of the high court of appeal has finally gone.

I come back to M. Renan's praise of glory, from which I started. Yes, real glory is a most serious thing, glory authenticated by the Amphictyonic Court of final appeal, definitive glory. And even for poets and poetry, long and difficult as may be the process of arriving at the right

award, the right award comes at last, the definitive glory
rests where it is deserved.   Every establishment of such
a real glory is good and wholesome for mankind at large,
good and wholesome for the nation which produced the
poet crowned with it.   To the poet himself it can seldom
do harm, for he, poor man, is in his grave, probably,
long before his glory crowns him.

Wordsworth has been in his grave for some thirty
years, and certainly his lovers and admirers cannot flatter
themselves that this great and steady light of glory as yet
shines over him.   He is not fully recognised at home;
he is not recognised at all abroad.   Yet I firmly believe
that the poetical performance of Wordsworth is, after
that of Shakspeare and Milton, of which all the world
now recognises the worth, undoubtedly the most considerable in our language from the Elizabethan age to the
present time.   Chaucer is anterior; and on other grounds,
too, he cannot well be brought into the comparison.
But taking the roll of our chief poetical names, besides
Shakspeare and Milton, from the age of Elizabeth down-
wards, and going through it,—Spenser, Dryden, Pope,
Gray, Goldsmith, Cowper, Burns, Coleridge, Scott, Camp-
bell, Moore, Byron, Shelley, Keats (I mention those only
who are dead),—I think it certain that Wordsworth's
name deserves to stand, and will finally stand, above
them all.   Several of the poets named have gifts and
excellences which Wordsworth has not.   But taking the
performance of each as a whole, I say that Wordsworth
seems to me to have left a body of poetical work superior
in power, in interest, in the qualities which give enduring
freshness, to that which any one of the others has left.

But this is not enough to say.   I think it certain, further,
that if we take the chief poetical names of the Continent
since the death of Molière, and, omitting Goethe, confront
the remaining names with that of Wordsworth, the result
is the same.   Let us take Klopstock, Lessing, Schiller,
Uhland, Rückert, and Heine for Germany; Filicaia, Al-
fieri, Manzoni, and Leopardi for Italy; Racine, Boileau.

Voltaire, André Chenier, Béranger, Lamartine, Musset, M. Victor Hugo (he has been so long celebrated that although he still lives I may be permitted to name him) for France. Several of these, again, have evidently gifts and excellences to which Wordsworth can make no pretension. But in real poetical achievement it seems to me indubitable that to Wordsworth, here again, belongs the palm. It seems to me that Wordsworth has left behind him a body of poetical work which wears, and will wear, better on the whole than the performance of any one of these personages, so far more brilliant and celebrated, most of them, than the homely poet of Rydal. Wordsworth's performance in poetry is on the whole, in power, in interest, in the qualities which give enduring freshness, superior to theirs.

This is a high claim to make for Wordsworth. But if it is a just claim, if Wordsworth's place among the poets who have appeared in the last two or three centuries is after Shakspeare, Molière, Milton, Goethe, indeed, but before all the rest, then in time Wordsworth will have his due. We shall recognise him in his place, as we recognise Shakspeare and Milton; and not only we ourselves shall recognise him, but he will be recognised by Europe also. Meanwhile, those who recognise him already may do well, perhaps, to ask themselves whether there are not in the case of Wordsworth certain special obstacles which hinder or delay his due recognition by others, and whether these obstacles are not in some measure removable.

The *Excursion* and the *Prelude*, his poems of greatest bulk, are by no means Wordsworth's best work. His best work is in his shorter pieces, and many indeed are there of these which are of first-rate excellence. But in his seven volumes the pieces of high merit are mingled with a mass of pieces very inferior to them; so inferior to them that it seems wonderful how the same poet should have produced both. Shakspeare frequently has lines and passages in a strain quite false, and which are

entirely unworthy of him. But one can imagine his
smiling if one could meet him in the Elysian Fields and tell
him so ; smiling and replying that he knew it perfectly well
himself, and what did it matter? But with Wordsworth
the case is different. Work altogether inferior, work quite
uninspired, flat and dull, is produced by him with evident
unconsciousness of its defects, and he presents it to us
with the same faith and seriousness as his best work. Now
a drama or an epic fill the mind, and one does not look
beyond them ; but in a collection of short pieces the impression made by one piece requires to be continued and
sustained by the piece following. In reading Wordsworth
the impression made by one of his fine pieces is too often
dulled and spoiled by a very inferior piece coming after it.

Wordsworth composed verses during a space of some
sixty years ; and it is no exaggeration to say that within
one single decade of those years, between 1798 and 1808,
almost all his really first-rate work was produced. A
mass of inferior work remains, work done before and
after this golden prime, imbedding the first-rate work
and clogging it, obstructing our approach to it, chilling,
not unfrequently, the high-wrought mood with which we
leave it. To be recognised far and wide as a great poet,
to be possible and receivable as a classic, Wordsworth
needs to be relieved of a great deal of the poetical bag-
gage which now encumbers him. To administer this relief is indispensable, unless he is to continue to be a poet
for the few only, a poet valued far below his real worth
by the world.

There is another thing. Wordsworth classified his
poems not according to any commonly received plan of
arrangement, but according to a scheme of mental
physiology. He has poems of the fancy, poems of the
imagination, poems of sentiment and reflexion, and so
on. His categories are ingenious but far-fetched, and
the result of his employment of them is unsatisfactory.
Poems are separated one from another which possess a
kinship of subject or of treatment far more vital and

deep than the supposed unity of mental origin which was Wordsworth's reason for joining them with others.

The tact of the Greeks in matters of this kind was infallible. We may rely upon it that we shall not improve upon the classification adopted by the Greeks for kinds of poetry ; that their categories of epic, dramatic, lyric, and so forth, have a natural propriety, and should be adhered to. It may sometimes seem doubtful to which of two categories a poem belongs ; whether this or that poem is to be called, for instance, narrative or lyric, lyric or elegiac. But there is to be found in every good poem a strain, a predominant note, which determines the poem as belonging to one of these kinds rather than the other ; and here is the best proof of the value of the classification, and of the advantage of adhering to it. Wordsworth's poems will never produce their due effect until they are freed from their present artificial arrangement, and grouped more naturally.

Disengaged from the quantity of inferior work which now obscures them, the best poems of Wordsworth, I hear many people say, would indeed stand out in great beauty, but they would prove to be very few in number, scarcely more than half-a-dozen. I maintain, on the other hand, that what strikes me with admiration, what establishes in my opinion Wordsworth's superiority, is the great and ample body of powerful work which remains to him, even after all his inferior work has been cleared away. He gives us so much to rest upon, so much which communicates his spirit and engages ours !

This is of very great importance. If it were a comparison of single pieces, or of three or four pieces, by each poet, I do not say that Wordsworth would stand decisively above Gray, or Burns, or Coleridge, or Keats, or Manzoni, or Heine. It is in his ampler body of powerful work that I find his superiority. His good work itself, his work which counts, is not all of it, of course, of equal value. Some kinds of poetry are in themselves lower kinds than

others.   The ballad kind is a lower kind ; the didactic
kind, still more, is a lower kind.   Poetry of this latter
sort, counts, too, sometimes, by its biographical interest
partly, not by its poetical interest pure and simple ; but
then this can only be when the poet producing it has the
power and importance of Wordsworth, a power and importance which he assuredly did not establish by such
didactic poetry alone.   Altogether, it is, I say, by the
great body of powerful and significant work which remains
to him, after every reduction and deduction has been
made, that Wordsworth's superiority is proved.

To exhibit this body of Wordsworth's best work, to
clear away obstructions from around it, and to let it
speak for itself, is what every lover of Wordsworth should
desire.   Until this has been done, Wordsworth, whom
we, to whom he is dear, all of us know and feel to be so
great a poet, has not had a fair chance before the world.
When once it has been done, he will make his way best
not by our advocacy of him, but by his own worth and
power.   We may safely leave him to make his way thus,
we who believe that a superior worth and power in poetry
finds in mankind a sense responsive to it and disposed at
last to recognise it.   Yet at the outset, before he has
been duly known and recognised, we may do Wordsworth
a service, perhaps, by indicating in what his superior
power and worth will be found to consist, and in what
it will not.

Long ago, in speaking of Homer, I said that the noble
and profound application of ideas to life is the most
essential part of poetic greatness.   I said that a great
poet receives his distinctive character of superiority from
his application, under the conditions immutably fixed by
the laws of poetic beauty and poetic truth, from his application, I say, to his subject, whatever it may be, of
the ideas

           "On man, on nature, and on human life,"

which he has acquired for himself.   The line quoted is

Wordsworth's own ; and his superiority arises from his powerful use, in his best pieces, his powerful application to his subject, of ideas "on man, on nature, and on human life."

Voltaire, with his signal acuteness, most truly remarked that "no nation has treated in poetry moral ideas with more energy and depth than the English nation." And he adds : "There, it seems to me, is the great merit of the English poets." Voltaire does not mean, by "treating in poetry moral ideas," the composing moral and didactic poems ;—that brings us but a very little way in poetry. He means just the same thing as was meant when I spoke above "of the noble and profound application of ideas to life ;" and he means the application of these ideas under the conditions fixed for us by the laws of poetic beauty and poetic truth. If it is said that to call these ideas *moral* ideas is to introduce a strong and injurious limitation, I answer that it is to do nothing of the kind, because moral ideas are really so main a part of human life. The question, *how to live,* is itself a moral idea ; and it is the question which most interests every man, and with which, in some way or other, he is perpetually occupied. A large sense is of course to be given to the term *moral.* Whatever bears upon the question, "how to live," comes under it.

> " Nor love thy life, nor hate ; but, what thou liv'st,
> Live well ; how long or short, permit to heaven.

In those fine lines, Milton utters, as every one at once perceives, a moral idea. Yes, but so too, when Keats consoles the forward-bending lover on the Grecian Urn, the lover arrested and presented in immortal relief by the sculptor's hand before he can kiss, with the line,

> " For ever wilt thou love, and she be fair "—

he utters a moral idea. When Shakspeare says, that

> " We are such stuff
> As dreams are made of, and our little life
> Is rounded with a sleep,"

he utters a moral idea.

Voltaire was right in thinking that the energetic and profound treatment of moral ideas, in this large sense, is what distinguishes the English poetry. He sincerely meant praise, not dispraise or hint of limitation; and they err who suppose that poetic limitation is a necessary consequence of the fact, the fact being granted as Voltaire states it. If what distinguishes the greatest poets is their powerful and profound application of ideas to life, which surely no good critic will deny, then to prefix to the term ideas here the term moral makes hardly any difference, because human life itself is in so preponderating a degree moral.

It is important, therefore, to hold fast to this: that poetry is at bottom a criticism of life; that the greatness of a poet lies in his powerful and beautiful application of ideas to life,—to the question: How to live. Morals are often treated in a narrow and false fashion, they are bound up with systems of thought and belief which have had their day, they are fallen into the hands of pedants and professional dealers, they grow tiresome to some of us. We find attraction, at times, even in a poetry of revolt against them; in a poetry which might take for its motto Omar Kheyam's words: "Let us make up in the tavern for the time which we have wasted in the mosque." Or we find attractions in a poetry indifferent to them, in a poetry where the contents may be what they will, but where the form is studied and exquisite. We delude ourselves in either case; and the best cure for our delusion is to let our minds rest upon that great and inexhaustible word *life*, until we learn to enter into its meaning. A poetry of revolt against moral ideas is a poetry of revolt against *life*; a poetry of in-difference towards moral ideas is a poetry of indifference towards *life*.

Epictetus had a happy figure for things like the play of the senses, or literary form and finish, or argument-ative ingenuity, in comparison with "the best and master thing" for us, as he called it, the concern, how to

live. Some people were afraid of them, he said, or they
disliked and undervalued them. Such people were
wrong; they were unthankful or cowardly. But the
things might also be over-prized, and treated as final
when they are not. They bear to life the relation which
inns bear to home. "As if a man, journeying home,
and finding a nice inn on the road, and liking it, were
to stay for ever at the inn! Man, thou hast forgotten
thine object; thy journey was not *to* this, but *through*
this. 'But this inn is taking.' And how many other
inns, too, are taking, and how many fields and meadows!
but as places of passage merely. You have an object,
which is this : to get home, to do your duty to your
family, friends, and fellow-countrymen, to attain inward
freedom, serenity, happiness, contentment. Style takes
your fancy, arguing takes your fancy, and you forget your
home and want to make your abode with them and to
stay with them, on the plea that they are taking. Who
denies that they are taking? but as places of passage, as
inns. And when I say this, you suppose me to be
attacking the care for style, the care for argument. I
am not; I attack the resting in them, the not looking to
the end which is beyond them."

Now, when we come across a poet like Théophile
Gautier, we have a poet who has taken up his abode at
an inn, and never got farther. There may be induce-
ments to this or that one of us, at this or that moment,
to find delight in him, to cleave to him; but after all,
we do not change the truth about him,—we only stay
ourselves in his inn along with him. And when we
come across a poet like Wordsworth, who sings,

> " Of truth, of grandeur, beauty, love and hope.
>   And melancholy fear subdued by faith,
>   Of blessed consolations in distress,
>   Of moral strength and intellectual power,
>   Of joy in widest commonalty spread "—

then we have a poet intent on "the best and master

thing," and who prosecutes his journey home.   We say, for brevity's sake, that he deals with *life*, because he deals with that in which life really consists.   This is what Voltaire means to praise in the English poets,— this dealing with what is really life.   But always it is the mark of the greatest poets that they deal with it ; and to say that the English poets are remarkable for dealing with it, is only another way of saying, what is true, that in poetry the English genius has especially shown its power.

Wordsworth deals with it, and his greatness lies in his dealing with it so powerfully.   I have named a number of celebrated poets above all of whom he, in my opinion, deserves to be placed.   He is to be placed above poets like Voltaire, Dryden, Pope, Lessing, Schiller, because these famous personages, with a thousand gifts and merits, never, or scarcely ever, attain the distinctive accent and utterance of the high and genuine poets—

"Quique pii vates et Phœbo digna locuti,"

at all.   Burns, Keats, Heine, not to speak of others in our list, have this accent ;—who can doubt it ?   And at the same time they have treasures of humour, felicity, passion, for which in Wordsworth we shall look in vain. Where, then, is Wordsworth's superiority ?   It is here ; he deals with more of *life* than they do ; he deals with *life*, as a whole, more powerfully.

No Wordsworthian will doubt this.   Nay, the fervent Wordsworthian will add, as Mr. Leslie Stephen does, that Wordsworth's poetry is precious because his philosophy is sound ; that his " ethical system is as distinctive and capable of exposition as Bishop Butler's ;" that his poetry is informed by ideas which " fall spontaneously into a scientific system of thought."   But we must be on our guard against the Wordsworthians, if we want to secure for Wordsworth his due rank as a poet.   The Wordsworthians are apt to praise him for the wrong things, and to lay far too much stress upon what they

call his philosophy.   His poetry is the reality, his philosophy,—so far, at least, as it may put on the form and
habit of "a scientific system of thought," and the more
that it puts them on,—is the illusion.   Perhaps we shall
one day learn to make this proposition general, and to
say : Poetry is the reality, philosophy the illusion.   But
in Wordsworth's case, at any rate, we cannot do him
justice until we dismiss his formal philosophy.

The *Excursion* abounds with philosophy, and therefore the *Excursion* is to the Wordsworthian what it never
can be to the disinterested lover of poetry,—a satisfactory
work.   "Duty exists," says Wordsworth, in the *Excursion ;* and then he proceeds thus :—

> . . . . "Immutably survive,
> For our support, the measures and the forms,
> Which an abstract Intelligence supplies,
> Whose kingdom is, where time and space are not."

And the Wordsworthian is delighted, and thinks that
here is a sweet union of philosophy and poetry.   But the
disinterested lover of poetry will feel that the lines carry
us really not a step farther than the proposition which
they would interpret ; that they are a tissue of elevated
but abstract verbiage, alien to the very nature of poetry.

Or let us come direct to the centre of Wordsworth's
philosophy, as "an ethical system, as distinctive and
capable of systematical exposition as Bishop Butler's :"—

> . . . . "One adequate support
> For the calamities of mortal life
> Exists, one only ;—an assured belief
> That the procession of our fate, howe'er
> Sad or disturbed, is ordered by a Being
> Of infinite benevolence and power ;
> Whose everlasting purposes embrace
> All accidents, converting them to good."

That is doctrine such as we hear in church too, religious
and philosophic doctrine ; and the attached Wordsworthian loves passages of such doctrine, and brings them

forward in proof of his poet's excellence. But however
true the doctrine may be, it has, as here presented, none
of the characters of *poetic* truth, the kind of truth which
we require from a poet, and in which Wordsworth is
really strong.

Even the "intimations" of the famous Ode, those
corner-stones of the supposed philosophic system of
Wordsworth,—the idea of the high instincts and affections coming out in childhood, testifying of a divine home
recently left, and fading away as our life proceeds,—this
idea, of undeniable beauty as a play of fancy, has itself
not the character of poetic truth of the best kind ; it has
no real solidity. The instinct of delight in Nature and
her beauty had no doubt extraordinary strength in
Wordsworth himself as a child. But to say that universally this instinct is mighty in childhood, and tends to
die away afterwards, is to say what is extremely doubtful.
In many people, perhaps with the majority of educated
persons, the love of nature is nearly imperceptible at ten
years old, but strong and operative at thirty. In general
we may say of these high instincts of early childhood, the
base of the alleged systematic philosophy of Wordsworth,
what Thucydides says of the early achievements of the
Greek race :—" It is impossible to speak with certainty
of what is so remote ; but from all that we can really
investigate, I should say that they were no very great
things."

Finally the "scientific system of thought" in Wordsworth gives us at last such poetry as this, which the
devout Wordsworthian accepts :—

> " O for the coming of that glorious time
> When, prizing knowledge as her noblest wealth
> And best protection, this Imperial Realm,
> While she exacts allegiance, shall admit
> An obligation, on her part, to *teach*
> Them who are born to serve her and obey ;
> Binding herself by statute to secure,
> For all the children whom her soil maintains,
> The rudiments of letters, and inform
> The mind with moral and religious truth."

Wordsworth calls Voltaire dull, and surely the production of these un-Voltairian lines must have been imposed on him as a judgment! One can hear them being quoted at a Social Science Congress; one can call up the whole scene. A great room in one of our dismal provincial towns; dusty air and jaded afternoon daylight; benches full of men with bald heads and women in spectacles; an orator lifting up his face from a manuscript written within and without to declaim these lines of Wordsworth; and in the soul of any poor child of nature who may have wandered in thither, an unutterable sense of lamentation, and mourning, and woe!

"But turn we," as Wordsworth says, "from these bold, bad men," the haunters of Social Science Congresses. And let us be on our guard, too, against the exhibitors and extollers of a "scientific system of thought" in Wordsworth's poetry. The poetry will never be seen aright while they thus exhibit it. The cause of its greatness is simple, and may be told quite simply. Wordsworth's poetry is great because of the extraordinary power with which Wordsworth feels the joy offered to us in nature, the joy offered to us in the simple primary affections and duties; and because of the extraordinary power with which, in case after case, he shows us this joy, and renders it so as to make us share it.

The source of joy from which he thus draws is the truest and most unfailing source of joy accessible to man. It is also accessible universally. Wordsworth brings us word, therefore, according to his own strong and characteristic line, he brings us word

> "Of joy in widest commonalty spread."

Here is an immense advantage for a poet. Wordsworth tells of what all seek, and tells of it at its truest and best source, and yet a source where all may go and draw for it.

Nevertheless, we are not to suppose that everything is precious which Wordsworth, standing even at this perennial and beautiful source, may give us. Wordsworthians are apt to talk as if it must be. They will speak with the same reverence of *The Sailor's Mother*, for example, as of *Lucy Gray*. They do their master harm by such lack of discrimination. *Lucy Gray* is a beautiful success; *The Sailor's Mother* is a failure. To give aright what he wishes to give, to interpret and render successfully, is not always within Wordsworth's own command. It is within no poet's command; here is the part of the Muse, the inspiration, the God, the "not ourselves." In Wordsworth's case, the accident, for so it may almost be called, of inspiration, is of peculiar importance. No poet, perhaps, is so evidently filled with a new and sacred energy when the inspiration is upon him; no poet, when it fails him, is so left "weak as is a breaking wave." I remember hearing him say that "Goethe's poetry was not inevitable enough." The remark is striking and true; no line in Goethe, as Goethe said himself, but its maker knew well how it came there. Wordsworth is right, Goethe's poetry is not inevitable; not inevitable enough. But Wordsworth's poetry, when he is at his best, is inevitable, as inevitable as Nature herself. It might seem that Nature not only gave him the matter for his poem, but wrote his poem for him. He has no style. He was too conversant with Milton not to catch at times his master's manner, and he has fine Miltonic lines; but he has no assured poetic style of his own, like Milton. When he seeks to have a style he falls into ponderosity and pomposity. In the *Excursion* we have his style, as an artistic product of his own creation; and although Jeffrey completely failed to recognise Wordsworth's real greatness, he was yet not wrong in saying of the *Excursion*, as a work of poetic style: "This will never do." And yet magical as is that power, which Wordsworth has not, of assured and possessed poetic style, he has something which is an equivalent for it.

Every one who has any sense for these things feels the

subtle turn, the heightening, which is given to a poet's
verse by his genius for style.   We can feel it in the

> " After life's fitful fever, he sleeps well "—

of Shakspeare ; in the

> . . . . " though fall'n on evil days,
> On evil days though fall'n, and evil tongues "—

of Milton.   It is the incomparable charm of Milton's
power of poetic style which gives such worth to *Paradise
Regained*, and makes a great poem of a work in which
Milton's imagination does not soar high.   Wordsworth
has in constant possession, and at command, no style of
this kind ; but he had too poetic a nature, and had read
the great poets too well, not to catch, as I have already
remarked, something of it occasionally.   We find it not
only in his Miltonic lines ; we find it in such a phrase as
this, where the manner is his own, not Milton's—

> . . . . " the fierce confederate storm
> Of sorrow barricadoed evermore
> Within the walls of cities ;"

although even here, perhaps, the power of style, which
is undeniable, is more properly that of eloquent prose
than the subtle heightening and change wrought by
genuine poetic style.   It is style, again, and the elevation given by style, which chiefly makes the effectiveness
of *Laodameia*.   Still the right sort of verse to choose
from Wordsworth, if we are to seize his true and most
characteristic form of expression, is a line like this from
Michael :—

> "And never lifted up a single stone."

There is nothing subtle in it, no heightening, no study of
poetic style, strictly so called, at all ; yet it is expression
of the highest and most truly expressive kind.

Wordsworth owed much to Burns, and a style of perfect
plainness, relying for effect solely on the weight and

force of that which with entire fidelity it utters, Burns could show him.

> " The poor inhabitant below
>   Was quick to learn and wise to know,
>   And keenly felt the friendly glow
>   And softer flame ;
>   But thoughtless follies laid him low
>   And stain'd his name."

Every one will be conscious of a likeness here to Wordsworth ; and if Wordsworth did great things with this nobly plain manner, we must remember, what indeed he himself would always have been forward to acknowledge, that Burns used it before him.

Still Wordsworth's use of it has something unique and unmatchable. Nature herself seems, I say, to take the pen out of his hand, and to write for him with her own bare, sheer, penetrating power. This arises from two causes : from the profound sincereness with which Wordsworth feels his subject, and also from the profoundly sincere and natural character of his subject itself. He can and will treat such a subject with nothing but the most plain, first-hand, almost austere naturalness. His expression may often be called bald, as, for instance, in the poem of *Resolution and Independence ;* but it is bald as the bare mountain tops are bald, with a baldness which is full of grandeur.

Wherever we meet with the successful balance, in Wordsworth, of profound truth of subject with profound truth of execution, he is unique. His best poems are those which most perfectly exhibit this balance. I have a warm admiration for *Laodameia* and for the great *Ode ;* but if I am to tell the very truth, I find *Laodameia* not wholly free from something artificial, and the great *Ode* not wholly free from something declamatory. If I had to pick out poems of a kind most perfectly to show Wordsworth's unique power, I should rather choose poems such as *Michael, The Fountain, The Highland Reaper.*

And poems with the peculiar and unique beauty which distinguishes these, Wordsworth produced in considerable number ; besides very many other poems of which the worth, although not so rare as the worth of these, is still exceedingly high.

On the whole, then, as I said at the beginning, not only is Wordsworth eminent by reason of the goodness of his best work, but he is eminent also by reason of the great body of good work which he has left to us. With the ancients I will not compare him. In many respects the ancients are far above us, and yet there is something that we demand which they can never give. Leaving the ancients, let us come to the poets and poetry of Christendom. Dante, Shakspeare, Molière, Milton, Goethe, are altogether larger and more splendid luminaries in the poetical heaven than Wordsworth. But I know not where else, among the moderns, we are to find his superiors.

To disengage the poems which show his power, and to present them to the English-speaking public and to the world, is the object of this volume. I by no means say that it contains all which in Wordsworth's poems is interesting. Except in the case of *Margaret*, a story composed separately from the rest of the *Excursion*, and which belongs to a different part of England, I have not ventured on detaching portions of poems, or on giving any piece otherwise than as Wordsworth himself gave it. But, under the conditions imposed by this reserve, the volume contains, I think, everything, or nearly everything, which may best serve him with the majority of lovers of poetry, nothing which may disserve him.

I have spoken lightly of Wordsworthians : and if we are to get Wordsworth recognised by the public and by the world, we must recommend him not in the spirit of a clique, but in the spirit of disinterested lovers of poetry. But I am a Wordsworthian myself. I can read with pleasure and edification *Peter Bell*, and the whole series of *Ecclesiastical Sonnets*, and the address to Mr. Wilkinson's spade, and even the *Thanksgiving Ode;*—everything of Wordsworth, I think, except *Vaudracour and Julia.* It is not for nothing that one has been brought up in the veneration of a man so truly worthy of homage; that one has seen him and heard him, lived in his neighbourhood and been familiar with his country. No Wordsworthian has a tenderer affection for this pure and sage master than I, or is less really offended by his defects. But Wordsworth is something more than the pure and sage master of a small band of devoted followers, and we ought not to rest satisfied until he is seen to be what he is. He is one of the very chief glories of English Poetry; and by nothing is England so glorious as by her poetry. Let us lay aside every weight which hinders our getting him recognised as this, and let our one study be to bring to pass, as widely as possible and as truly as possible, his own word concerning his poems :—"They will co-operate with the benign tendencies in human nature and society, and will, in their degree, be efficacious in making men wiser, better, and happier."

CONTENTS.

CONTENTS.

LYRICAL POEMS.

CONTENTS.

POEMS AKIN TO THE ANTIQUE, AND ODES.

SONNETS.

REFLECTIVE AND ELEGIAC POEMS.

POEMS OF BALLAD FORM

WE ARE SEVEN.

—— A simple child,
That lightly draws its breath,
And feels its life in every limb,
What should it know of death?

I met a little cottage Girl:
She was eight years old, she said;
Her hair was thick with many a curl
That clustered round her head.

She had a rustic, woodland air,
And she was wildly clad:
Her eyes were fair, and very fair;
—Her beauty made me glad.

" Sisters and brothers, little Maid,
How many may you be?"
" How many? Seven in all," she said,
And wondering looked at me.

" And where are they? I pray you tell."
She answered, " Seven are we;
And two of us at Conway dwell,
And two are gone to sea.

" Two of us in the churchyard lie,
    My sister and my brother ;
And, in the churchyard cottage, I
    Dwell near them with my mother."

" You say that two at Conway dwell,
    And two are gone to sea,
Yet ye are seven !—I pray you tell,
    Sweet Maid, how this may be."

Then did the little Maid reply,
" Seven boys and girls are we ;
Two of us in the churchyard lie,
    Beneath the churchyard tree."

" You run about, my little Maid,
    Your limbs they are alive ;
If two are in the churchyard laid,
    Then ye are only five."

" Their graves are green, they may be seen,"
    The little Maid replied,
" Twelve steps or more from my mother's door,
    And they are side by side.

" My stockings there I often knit,
    My kerchief there I hem ;
And there upon the ground I sit—
    I sit and sing to them.

" And often after sunset, Sir,
    When it is light and fair,
I take my little porringer,
    And eat my supper there.

" The first that died was little Jane ;
    In bed she moaning lay,
Till God released her of her pain ;
    And then she went away.

" So in the churchyard she was laid ;
    And, when the grass was dry,
Together round her grave we played,
    My brother John and I.

" And when the ground was white with snow,
    And I could run and slide,
My brother John was forced to go,
    And he lies by her side."

" How many are you, then," said I,
" If they two are in Heaven ?"
    The little Maiden did reply,
" O Master ! we are seven."

" But they are dead ; those two are dead !
    Their spirits are in Heaven !"
'Twas throwing words away : for still
The little Maid would have her will,
    And said, " Nay, we are seven !"

LUCY GRAY;

OR, SOLITUDE.

OFT I had heard of Lucy Gray :
    And, when I crossed the wild,
I chanced to see at break of day
    The solitary Child.

No mate, no comrade Lucy knew ;
She dwelt on a wide moor,
—The sweetest thing that ever grew
Beside a human door !

You yet may spy the fawn at play,
The hare upon the green ;
But the sweet face of Lucy Gray
Will never more be seen.

" To-night will be a stormy night—
You to the town must go ;
And take a lantern, Child, to light
Your mother through the snow."

" That, Father ! will I gladly do :
'Tis scarcely afternoon—
The Minster-clock has just struck two,
And yonder is the Moon."

At this the Father raised his hook,
And snapped a faggot-band ;
He plied his work ;—and Lucy took
The lantern in her hand.

Not blither is the mountain roe :
With many a wanton stroke
Her feet disperse the powdery snow,
That rises up like smoke.

The snow came on before its time :
She wandered up and down ;
And many a hill did Lucy climb ;
But never reached the town.

The wretched parents all that night
Went shouting far and wide ;
But there was neither sound nor sight
To serve them for a guide.

At day-break on a hill they stood
That overlooked the moor ;
And thence they saw the bridge of wood,
A furlong from their door.

They wept—and, turning homeward, cried,
" In Heaven we all shall meet : "
—When in the snow the mother spied
The print of Lucy's feet.

Half breathless from the steep hill's edge
They tracked the footmarks small ;
And through the broken hawthorn-hedge,
And by the long stone-wall ;

And then an open field they crossed :
The marks were still the same ;
They tracked them on, nor ever lost ;
And to the Bridge they came.

They followed from the snowy bank
Those footmarks, one by one,
Into the middle of the plank ;
And further there were none !

—Yet some maintain that to this day
She is a living child ;
That you may see sweet Lucy Gray
Upon the lonesome wild.

O'er rough and smooth she trips along
And never looks behind ;
And sings a solitary song
That whistles in the wind.

ANECDOTE FOR FATHERS,

SHOWING HOW THE PRACTICE OF LYING
MAY BE TAUGHT.

I HAVE a boy of five years old ;
His face is fair and fresh to see ;
His limbs are cast in beauty's mould,
And dearly he loves me.

One morn we strolled on our dry walk,
Our quiet home all full in view,
And held such intermitted talk
As we are wont to do.

My thoughts on former pleasures ran ;
I thought of Kilve's delightful shore,
Our pleasant home when Spring began,
A long, long year before.

A day it was when I could bear
Some fond regrets to entertain ;
With so much happiness to spare,
I could not feel a pain.

The green earth echoed to the feet
Of lambs that bounded through the glade,
From shade to sunshine, and as fleet
From sunshine back to shade.

Birds warbled round me—every trace
Of inward sadness had its charm ;
"Kilve," said I, "was a favoured place,
And so is Liswyn farm."

My Boy was by my side, so slim
And graceful in his rustic dress !
And, as we talked, I questioned him,
In very idleness.

"Now tell me, had you rather be,"
I said, and took him by the arm,
"On Kilve's smooth shore, by the green sea.
Or here at Liswyn farm ?"

In careless mood he looked at me,
While still I held him by the arm,
And said, "At Kilve I'd rather be
Than here at Liswyn farm."

"Now, little Edward, say why so ;
My little Edward, tell me why."—
"I cannot tell, I do not know."—
"Why, this is strange," said I ;

"For, here are woods, and green hills warm :
There surely must some reason be
Why you would change sweet Liswyn farm
For Kilve by the green sea."

At this, my Boy hung down his head,
He blushed with shame, nor made reply ;
And five times to the child I said,
"Why, Edward, tell me why ?"

His head he raised—there was in sight,
It caught his eye, he saw it plain—
Upon the house-top, glittering bright,
A broad and gilded Vane.

Then did the Boy his tongue unlock ;
And thus to me he made reply :
" At Kilve there was no weather-cock,
And that's the reason why."

O dearest, dearest Boy ! my heart
For better lore would seldom yearn,
Could I but teach the hundredth part
Of what from thee I learn.

ALICE FELL ;

OR, POVERTY.

THE post-boy drove with fierce career,
For threatening clouds the moon had drowned ·
When, as we hurried on, my ear
Was smitten with a startling sound.

As if the wind blew many ways,
I heard the sound,—and more and more ;
It seemed to follow with the chaise,
And still I heard it as before.

At length I to the boy called out ;
He stopped his horses at the word,
But neither cry, nor voice, nor shout,
Nor aught else like it, could be heard.

The boy then smacked his whip, and fast
The horses scampered through the rain ;
But, hearing soon upon the blast
The cry, I bade him halt again.

Forthwith alighting on the ground,
" Whence comes," said I, " this piteous moan ?"
And there a little Girl I found,
Sitting behind the chaise, alone.

" My cloak !" no other word she spake,
But loud and bitterly she wept,
As if her innocent heart would break ;
And down from off her seat she leapt.

" What ails you, child ?"—she sobbed " Look here !"
I saw it in the wheel entangled,
A weather-beaten rag as e'er
From any garden scare-crow dangled.

There, twisted between nave and spoke,
It hung, nor could at once be freed ;
But our joint pains unloosed the cloak,
A miserable rag indeed !

" And whither are you going, child,
To-night along these lonesome ways ?"
" To Durham," answered she half wild—
" Then come with me into the chaise."

Insensible to all relief
Sat the poor girl, and forth did send
Sob after sob, as if her grief
Could never, never have an end.

" My child, in Durham do you dwell?"
    She checked herself in her distress,
And said, " My name is Alice Fell;
    I'm fatherless and motherless.

" And I to Durham, Sir, belong."
    Again, as if the thought would choke
Her very heart, her grief grew strong;
    And all was for her tattered cloak!

The chaise drove on; our journey's end
    Was nigh; and sitting by my side,
As if she had lost her only friend
    She wept, nor would be pacified.

Up to the tavern-door we post;
    Of Alice and her grief I told;
And I gave money to the host,
    To buy a new cloak for the old.

" And let it be of duffil grey,
    As warm a cloak as man can sell!"
Proud creature was she the next day,
    The little orphan, Alice Fell!

THE PET LAMB.

A PASTORAL.

THE dew was falling fast, the stars began to blink;
I heard a voice; it said, " Drink, pretty Creature, drink!"
And, looking o'er the hedge, before me I espied
A snow-white mountain Lamb with a Maiden at its side.

No other sheep were near, the Lamb was all alone,
And by a slender cord was tethered to a stone ;
With one knee on the grass did the little Maiden kneel,
While to that mountain Lamb she gave its evening meal.

The Lamb, while from her hand he thus his supper took,
Seemed to feast with head and ears ; and his tail with
    pleasure shook.
" Drink, pretty Creature, drink," she said in such a tone
That I almost received her heart into my own.

'Twas little Barbara Lewthwaite, a Child of beauty rare !
I watched them with delight, they were a lovely pair.
Now with her empty can the Maiden turned away :
But ere ten yards were gone her footsteps did she stay.

Towards the Lamb she looked ; and from that shady place
I unobserved could see the workings of her face :
If Nature to her tongue could measured numbers bring,
Thus, thought I, to her Lamb that little Maid might sing :

"What ails thee, Young One ? what ? Why pull so at thy
    cord ?
Is it not well with thee ? well both for bed and board ?
Thy plot of grass is soft, and green as grass can be ;
Rest, little Young One, rest ; what is't that aileth thee ?

" What is it thou wouldst seek ? What is wanting to thy
    heart ?
Thy limbs are they not strong ?   And beautiful thou art :
This grass is tender grass ; these flowers they have no peers ;
And that green corn all day is rustling in thy ears !

"If the Sun be shining hot, do but stretch thy woollen chain,
This beech is standing by, its covert thou canst gain ;
For rain and mountain storms ! the like thou needest not
    fear—
The rain and storm are things that scarcely can come here.

"Rest, little Young One, rest; thou hast forgot the day
When my Father found thee first in places far away;
Many flocks were on the hills, but thou wert owned by
none,
And thy mother from thy side for evermore was gone.

"He took thee in his arms, and in pity brought thee home:
A blessed day for thee! then whither wouldst thou roam?
A faithful Nurse thou hast; the dam that did thee yean
Upon the mountain tops no kinder could have been.

"Thou knowest that twice a day I have brought thee in
this can
Fresh water from the brook, as clear as ever ran;
And twice in the day, when the ground is wet with dew,
I bring thee draughts of milk, warm milk it is and new.

"Thy limbs will shortly be twice as stout as they are now,
Then I'll yoke thee to my cart like a pony in the plough;
My playmate thou shalt be; and when the wind is cold
Our hearth shall be thy bed, our house shall be thy fold.

"It will not, will not rest!—Poor Creature, can it be
That 'tis thy mother's heart which is working so in thee?
Things that I know not of belike to thee are dear,
And dreams of things which thou canst neither see nor hear.

"Alas, the mountain tops that look so green and fair!
I've heard of fearful winds and darkness that come there;
The little brooks that seem all pastime and all play,
When they are angry, roar like lions for their prey.

"Here thou needest not dread the raven in the sky;
Night and day thou art safe,—our cottage is hard by.
Why bleat so after me? Why pull so at thy chain?
Sleep—and at break of day I will come to thee again!'

—As homeward through the lane I went with lazy feet,
This song to myself did I oftentimes repeat ;
And it seemed, as I retraced the ballad line by line,
That but half of it was hers, and one half of it was *mine.*

Again, and once again, did I repeat the song ;
"Nay," said I, "more than half to the *Damsel* must
    belong,
For she looked with such a look, and she spake with such
    a tone,
That I almost received her heart into my own."

THE CHILDLESS FATHER.

"Up, Timothy, up with your staff and away !
Not a soul in the village this morning will stay ;
The Hare has just started from Hamilton's grounds,
And Skiddaw is glad with the cry of the hounds."

—Of coats and of jackets grey, scarlet, and green,
On the slopes of the pastures all colours were seen ;
With their comely blue aprons, and caps white as snow,
The girls on the hills made a holiday show.

Fresh sprigs of green box-wood, not six months before,
Filled the funeral basin[1] at Timothy's door ;
A coffin through Timothy's threshold had past ;
One Child did it bear, and that Child was his last.

[1] In several parts of the North of England when a funeral takes place, a basin full of Sprigs of Box-wood is placed at the door of the house from which the coffin is taken up, and each person who attends the funeral ordinarily takes a Sprig of this Box-wood, and throws it into the grave of the deceased.

Now fast up the dell came the noise and the fray,
The horse and the horn, and the hark! hark away!
Old Timothy took up his staff, and he shut
With a leisurely motion the door of his hut.

Perhaps to himself at that moment he said,
"The key I must take, for my Ellen is dead."
But of this in my ears not a word did he speak,
And he went to the chase with a tear on his cheek.

THE REVERIE OF POOR SUSAN.

At the corner of Wood Street, when daylight appears,
Hangs a Thrush that sings loud, it has sung for three years:
Poor Susan has passed by the spot, and has heard
In the silence of morning the song of the Bird.

'Tis a note of enchantment; what ails her? She sees
A mountain ascending, a vision of trees;
Bright volumes of vapour through Lothbury glide,
And a river flows on through the vale of Cheapside.

Green pastures she views in the midst of the dale,
Down which she so often has tripped with her pail;
And a single small Cottage, a nest like a dove's,
The one only dwelling on earth that she loves.

She looks, and her heart is in heaven: but they fade,
The mist and the river, the hill and the shade:
The stream will not flow, and the hill will not rise,
And the colours have all passed away from her eyes.

POWER OF MUSIC.

An Orpheus! an Orpheus!—yes, Faith may grow bold,
And take to herself all the wonders of old ;—
Near the stately Pantheon you'll meet with the same
In the street that from Oxford hath borrowed its name.

His station is there ;—and he works on the crowd,
He sways them with harmony merry and loud ;
He fills with his power all their hearts to the brim—
Was aught ever heard like his Fiddle and him ?

What an eager assembly ! what an empire is this !
The weary have life, and the hungry have bliss ;
The mourner is cheered, and the anxious have rest ;
And the guilt-burthened soul is no longer opprest.

As the Moon brightens round her the clouds of the night,
So he, where he stands, is a centre of light ;
It gleams on the face, there, of dusky-browed Jack,
And the pale-visaged Baker's, with basket on back.

That errand-bound 'Prentice was passing in haste—
What matter ! he's caught—and his time runs to waste—
The Newsman is stopped, though he stops on the fret,
And the half-breathless Lamplighter—he's in the net !

The Porter sits down on the weight which he bore ;
The Lass with her barrow wheels hither her store ;—
If a thief could be here he might pilfer at ease ;
She sees the Musician, 'tis all that she sees !

He stands, backed by the wall ;—he abates not his din ;
His hat gives him vigour, with boons dropping in,
From the old and the young, from the poorest ; and there
The one-pennied Boy has his penny to spare.

O blest are the hearers, and proud be the hand
Of the pleasure it spreads through so thankful a band ;
I am glad for him, blind as he is !—all the while
If they speak 'tis to praise, and they praise with a smile.

That tall Man, a giant in bulk and in height,
Not an inch of his body is free from delight ;
Can he keep himself still, if he would ? oh, not he !
The music stirs in him like wind through a tree.

Mark that Cripple who leans on his crutch ; like a tower
That long has leaned forward, leans hour after hour !—
That Mother, whose spirit in fetters is bound,
While she dandles the Babe in her arms to the sound.

Now, coaches and chariots ! roar on like a stream ;
Here are twenty souls happy as souls in a dream :
They are deaf to your murmurs—they care not for you,
Nor what ye are flying, nor what ye pursue !

STAR-GAZERS.

WHAT crowd is this ? what have we here ! we must not
    pass it by ;
A Telescope upon its frame, and pointed to the sky :
Long is it as a barber's pole, or mast of little boat,
Some little pleasure-skiff, that doth on Thames's waters
    float.

The Showman chooses well his place, 'tis Leicester's
  busy Square ;
And is as happy in his night, for the heavens are blue and
  fair ;
Calm, though impatient, is the crowd ; each stands ready
  with the fee,
Impatient till his moment comes—what an insight must
  it be !

Yet, Showman, where can lie the cause ? Shall thy im-
  plement have blame,
A boaster, that when he is tried, fails, and is put to shame ?
Or is it good as others are, and be their eyes in fault ?
Their eyes, or minds ? or, finally, is yon resplendent Vault ?

Is nothing of that radiant pomp so good as we have here ?
Or gives a thing but small delight that never can be dear ?
The silver moon with all her vales, and hills of mightiest
  fame,
Doth she betray us when they're seen ? or are they but a
  name ?

Or is it rather that Conceit rapacious is and strong,
And bounty never yields so much but it seems to do her
  wrong ?
Or is it, that when human souls a journey long have had
And are returned into themselves, they cannot but be sad ?

Or must we be constrained to think that these spectators
  rude,
Poor in estate, of manners base, men of the multitude,
Have souls which never yet have risen, and therefore pro-
  strate lie ?
No, no, this cannot be—Men thirst for power and majesty !

Does, then, a deep and earnest thought the blissful mind
    employ
Of him who gazes, or has gazed ? a grave and steady joy,
That doth reject all show of pride, admits no outward sign,
Because not of this noisy world, but silent and divine !

Whatever be the cause, 'tis sure that they who pry and pore
Seem to meet with little gain, seem less happy than before :
One after one they take their turn, nor have I one espied
That doth not slackly go away, as if dissatisfied.

NARRATIVE POEMS

RUTH.

WHEN Ruth was left half desolate,
Her father took another mate;
And Ruth, not seven years old,
A slighted child, at her own will
Went wandering over dale and hill,
In thoughtless freedom bold.

And she had made a pipe of straw,
And from that oaten pipe could draw
All sounds of winds and floods;
Had built a bower upon the green,
As if she from her birth had been
An infant of the woods.

Beneath her father's roof, alone
She seemed to live; her thoughts her own;
Herself her own delight;
Pleased with herself, nor sad, nor gay;
And, passing thus the livelong day,
She grew to woman's height.

There came a Youth from Georgia's shore—
A military casque he wore,
With splendid feathers drest;
He brought them from the Cherokees;
The feathers nodded in the breeze,
And made a gallant crest.

From Indian blood you deem him sprung :
Ah no ! he spake the English tongue,
And bore a soldier's name ;
And, when America was free
From battle and from jeopardy,
He 'cross the ocean came.

With hues of genius on his cheek
In finest tones the Youth could speak :
—While he was yet a boy,
The moon, the glory of the sun,
And streams that murmur as they run,
Had been his dearest joy.

He was a lovely Youth ! I guess
The panther in the wilderness
Was not so fair as he ;
And, when he chose to sport and play,
No dolphin ever was so gay
Upon the tropic sea.

Among the Indians he had fought
And with him many tales he brought
Of pleasure and of fear ;
Such tales as told to any maid
By such a youth, in the green shade,
Were perilous to hear.

He told of girls—a happy rout !
Who quit their fold with dance and shout,
Their pleasant Indian town,
To gather strawberries all day long ;
Returning with a choral song
When daylight is gone down.

He spake of plants divine and strange
That every hour their blossoms change,
Ten thousand lovely hues!
With budding, fading, faded flowers
They stand the wonder of the bowers
From morn to evening dews.

He told of the magnolia, spread
High as a cloud, high over head!
The cypress and her spire;
—Of flowers that with one scarlet gleam
Cover a hundred leagues, and seem
To set the hills on fire.

The Youth of green savannahs spake,
And many an endless, endless lake,
With all its fairy crowds
Of islands, that together lie
As quietly as spots of sky
Among the evening clouds.

And then he said, "How sweet it were
A fisher or a hunter there,
A gardener in the shade,
Still wandering with an easy mind
To build a household fire, and find
A home in every glade!

"What days and what sweet years! Ah me!
Our life were life indeed, with thee
So passed in quiet bliss,
And all the while," said he, "to know
That we were in a world of woe,
On such an earth as this!"

And then he sometimes interwove
Fond thoughts about a father's love:
" For there," said he, " are spun
Around the heart such tender ties,
That our own children to our eyes
Are dearer than the sun.

" Sweet Ruth ! and could you go with me
My helpmate in the woods to be,
Our shed at night to rear ;
Or run, my own adopted bride,
A sylvan huntress at my side,
And drive the flying deer !

" Beloved Ruth !"—No more he said.
The wakeful Ruth at midnight shed
A solitary tear :
She thought again—and did agree
With him to sail across the sea,
And drive the flying deer.

" And now, as fitting is and right,
We in the church our faith will plight
A husband and a wife."
Even so they did ; and I may say
That to sweet Ruth that happy day
Was more than human life.

Through dream and vision did she sink,
Delighted all the while to think
That on those lonesome floods,
And green savannahs, she should share
His board with lawful joy, and bear
His name in the wild woods.

But, as you have before been told,
This Stripling, sportive, gay, and bold,
And with his dancing crest
So beautiful, through savage lands
Had roamed about, with vagrant bands
Of Indians in the West.

The wind, the tempest roaring high,
The tumult of a tropic sky,
Might well be dangerous food
For him, a Youth to whom was given
So much of earth—so much of Heaven,
And such impetuous blood.

Whatever in those climes he found
Irregular in sight or sound
Did to his mind impart
A kindred impulse, seemed allied
To his own powers, and justified
The workings of his heart.

Nor less, to feed voluptuous thought,
The beauteous forms of nature wrought
Fair trees and lovely flowers ;
The breezes their own languor lent ;
The stars had feelings, which they sent
Into those gorgeous bowers.

Yet, in his worst pursuits, I ween
That sometimes there did intervene
Pure hopes of high intent :
For passions linked to forms so fair
And stately, needs must have their share
Of noble sentiment.

But ill he lived, much evil saw,
With men to whom no better law
Nor better life was known ;
Deliberately, and undeceived,
Those wild men's vices he received,
And gave them back his own.

His genius and his moral frame
Were thus impaired, and he became
The slave of low desires :
A man who without self-control
Would seek what the degraded soul
Unworthily admires.

And yet he with no feigned delight
Had wooed the Maiden, day and night
Had loved her, night and morn :
What could he less than love a maid
Whose heart with so much nature played?
So kind and so forlorn !

Sometimes, most earnestly, he said,
" O Ruth ! I have been worse than dead ;
False thoughts, thoughts bold and vain,
Encompassed me on every side
When first, in confidence and pride,
I crossed the Atlantic Main.

" It was a fresh and glorious world,
A banner bright that was unfurled
Before me suddenly :
I looked upon those hills and plains,
And seemed as if let loose from chains,
To live at liberty.

" But wherefore speak of this ? For now,
Sweet Ruth ! with thee, I know not how,
    I feel my spirit burn—
Even as the east when day comes forth ;
And, to the west, and south, and north,
    The morning doth return."

Full soon that purer mind was gone ;
No hope, no wish remained, not one,—
    They stirred him now no more ;
New objects did new pleasure give,
And once again he wished to live
    As lawless as before.

Meanwhile, as thus with him it fared,
They for the voyage were prepared,
    And went to the sea-shore ;
But, when they thither came, the Youth
Deserted his poor Bride, and Ruth
    Could never find him more.

" God help thee, Ruth !"—Such pains she had,
That she in half a year was mad,
    And in a prison housed ;
And there she sang tumultuous songs,
By recollection of her wrongs
    To fearful passion roused.

Yet sometimes milder hours she knew,
Nor wanted sun, nor rain, nor dew,
    Nor pastimes of the May,
—They all were with her in her cell ;
And a wild brook with cheerful knell
    Did o'er the pebbles play.

When Ruth three seasons thus had lain,
There came a respite to her pain ;
She from her prison fled ;
But of the vagrant none took thought ;
And where it liked her best she sought
Her shelter and her bread.

Among the fields she breathed again ·
The master-current of her brain
Ran permanent and free ;
And, coming to the banks of Tone,
There did she rest ; and dwell alone
Under the greenwood tree.

The engines of her pain, the tools
That shaped her sorrow, rocks and pools,
And airs that gently stir
The vernal leaves, she loved them still.
Nor ever taxed them with the ill
Which had been done to her.

A barn her *winter* bed supplies ;
But, till the warmth of summer skies
And summer days is gone,
(And all do in this tale agree)
She sleeps beneath the greenwood tree,
And other home hath none.

An innocent life, yet far astray !
And Ruth will, long before her day,
Be broken down and old :
Sore aches she needs must have ! but less
Of mind, than body's wretchedness,
From damp, and rain, and cold.

If she is prest by want of food,
She from her dwelling in the wood
Repairs to a road-side;
And there she begs at one steep place
Where up and down with easy pace
The horsemen-travellers ride.

That oaten pipe of hers is mute,
Or thrown away; but with a flute
Her loneliness she cheers:
This flute, made of a hemlock stalk,
At evening in his homeward walk
The Quantock woodman hears.

I, too, have passed her on the hills
Setting her little water-mills
By spouts and fountains wild—
Such small machinery as she turned
Ere she had wept, ere she had mourned,
A young and happy child!

Farewell! and when thy days are told
Ill-fated Ruth! in hallowed mould
Thy corpse shall buried be;
For thee a funeral bell shall ring,
And all the congregation sing
A Christian psalm for thee.

SIMON LEE,

THE OLD HUNTSMAN,

WITH AN INCIDENT IN WHICH HE WAS CONCERNED.

In the sweet shire of Cardigan,
Not far from pleasant Ivor-hall,
An Old Man dwells, a little man,
'Tis said he once was tall.
Full five-and-thirty years he lived
A running Huntsman merry;
And still the centre of his cheek
Is blooming as a cherry.

No man like him the horn could sound,
And hill and valley rang with glee
When Echo bandied, round and round,
The halloo of Simon Lee.
In those proud days, he little cared
For husbandry or tillage;
To blither tasks did Simon rouse
The sleepers of the village.

He all the country could outrun,
Could leave both man and horse behind;
And often, ere the chase was done,
He reeled and was stone-blind.
And still there's something in the world
At which his heart rejoices;
For when the chiming hounds are out,
He dearly loves their voices!

But, oh the heavy change !—bereft
Of health, strength, friends, and kindred, see !
Old Simon to the world is left
In liveried poverty.
His Master's dead,—and no one now
Dwells in the Hall of Ivor ;
Men, dogs, and horses, all are dead ;
He is the sole survivor.

And he is lean and he is sick ;
His body, dwindled and awry,
Rests upon ankles swoln and thick ;
His legs are thin and dry.
One prop he has, and only one,
His Wife, an aged woman,
Lives with him, near the waterfall,
Upon the village Common.

Beside their moss-grown hut of clay,
Not twenty paces from the door,
A scrap of land they have, but they
Are poorest of the poor.
This scrap of land he from the heath
Enclosed when he was stronger ;
But what avails it now, the land
Which he can till no longer ?

Oft, working by her husband's side,
Ruth does what Simon cannot do ;
For she, with scanty cause for pride,
Is stouter of the two.
And though you with your utmost skill
From labour could not wean them,
Alas ! 'tis very little—all
Which they can do between them.

Few months of life has he in store,
As he to you will tell,
For still, the more he works, the more
Do his weak ankles swell.
My gentle Reader, I perceive
How patiently you've waited,
And now I fear that you expect
Some tale will be related.

O Reader! had you in your mind
Such stores as silent thought can bring,
O gentle Reader! you would find
A tale in everything.
What more I have to say is short,
And you must kindly take it:
It is no tale; but, should you *think*,
Perhaps a tale you'll make it.

One summer-day I chanced to see
This Old Man doing all he could
To unearth the root of an old tree,
A stump of rotten wood.
The mattock totter'd in his hand;
So vain was his endeavour,
That at the root of the old tree
He might have worked for ever.

" You're overtasked, good Simon Lee,
Give me your tool," to him I said;
And at the word right gladly he
Received my proffered aid.
I struck, and with a single blow
The tangled root I severed,
At which the poor Old Man so long
And vainly had endeavoured.

The tears into his eyes were brought,
And thanks and praises seemed to run
So fast out of his heart, I thought
They never would have done.
—I've heard of hearts unkind, kind deeds
With coldness still returning ;
Alas ! the gratitude of men
Hath oftener left me mourning.

FIDELITY.

A BARKING sound the Shepherd hears,
A cry as of a dog or fox ;
He halts—and searches with his eyes
Among the scattered rocks ;
And now at distance can discern
A stirring in a brake of fern ;
And instantly a dog is seen,
Glancing through that covert green.

The Dog is not of mountain breed ;
Its motions, too, are wild and shy ;
With something, as the Shepherd thinks,
Unusual in its cry :
Nor is there any one in sight
All round, in hollow or on height ;
Nor shout, nor whistle strikes his ear ;
What is the Creature doing here ?

It was a cove, a huge recess,
That keeps, till June, December's snow ;
A lofty precipice in front,
A silent tarn[1] below !
Far in the bosom of Helvellyn,
Remote from public road or dwelling,
Pathway, or cultivated land ;
From trace of human foot or hand.

There sometimes doth a leaping fish
Send through the tarn a lonely cheer ;
The crags repeat the raven's croak,
In symphony austere ;
Thither the rainbow comes—the cloud—
And mists that spread the flying shroud ;
And sunbeams ; and the sounding blast,
That, if it could, would hurry past ;
But that enormous barrier binds it fast.

Not free from boding thoughts, a while
The Shepherd stood : then makes his way
Towards the Dog, o'er rocks and stones,
As quickly as he may ;
Nor far had gone before he found
A human skeleton on the ground ;
The appalled discoverer with a sigh
Looks round, to learn the history.

From those abrupt and perilous rocks
The Man had fallen, that place of fear !
At length upon the Shepherd's mind
It breaks, and all is clear :
He instantly recalled the name,
And who he was, and whence he came ;
Remembered, too, the very day
On which the traveller passed this way.

---

[1] Tarn is a *small* Mere or Lake, mostly high up in the mountains.

But hear a wonder, for whose sake
This lamentable tale I tell!
A lasting monument of words
This wonder merits well.
The Dog, which still was hovering nigh,
Repeating the same timid cry,
This Dog, had been through three months' space
A dweller in that savage place.

Yes, proof was plain that, since the day
When this ill-fated traveller died,
The Dog had watched about the spot,
Or by his Master's side:
How nourished here through such long time
He knows, who gave that love sublime;
And gave that strength of feeling, great
Above all human estimate.

INCIDENT

CHARACTERISTIC OF A FAVOURITE DOG.

ON his morning rounds the Master
Goes to learn how all things fare;
Searches pasture after pasture,
Sheep and cattle eyes with care;
And for silence or for talk,
He hath comrades in his walk;
Four dogs, each pair of different breed,
Distinguished two for scent, and two for speed.

See a hare before him started !
—Off they fly in earnest chase ;
Every dog is eager-hearted,
All the four are in the race :
And the hare whom they pursue,
Hath an instinct what to do ;
Her hope is near : no turn she makes ;
But, like an arrow, to the river takes.

Deep the river was, and crusted
Thinly by a one night's frost ;
But the nimble Hare hath trusted
To the ice, and safely crost ;
She hath crost, and without heed
All are following at full speed,
When, lo ! the ice, so thinly spread,
Breaks—and the Greyhound, DART, is over head !

Better fate have PRINCE and SWALLOW—
See them cleaving to the sport !
MUSIC has no heart to follow,
Little MUSIC, she stops short.
She hath neither wish nor heart,
Hers is now another part :
A loving creature she, and brave !
And fondly strives her struggling friend to save.

From the brink her paws she stretches,
Very hands as you would say !
And afflicting moans she fetches,
As he breaks the ice away.
For herself she hath no fears,—
Him alone she sees and hears,—
Makes efforts and complainings ; nor gives o'er
Until her Fellow sank, and re-appeared no more.

HART-LEAP WELL.

art-Leap Well is a small spring of water, about five miles from Richmond in Yorkshire, and near the side of the road that leads from Richmond to Askrigg. Its name is derived from a remarkable Chase, the memory of which is preserved by the monuments spoken of in the second Part of the following Poem, which monuments do now exist as I have there described them.

The Knight had ridden down from Wensley Moor
With the slow motion of a summer's cloud ;
He turned aside towards a vassal's door,
And "Bring another horse !" he cried aloud.

"Another horse !"—That shout the vassal heard
And saddled his best steed, a comely gray ;
Sir Walter mounted him ; he was the third
Which he had mounted on that glorious day.

Joy sparkled in the prancing courser's eyes ;
The Horse and Horseman are a happy pair ;
But, though Sir Walter like a falcon flies,
There is a doleful silence in the air.

A rout this morning left Sir Walter's Hall,
That as they galloped made the echoes roar ;
But horse and man are vanished, one and all ;
Such race, I think, was never seen before.

Sir Walter, restless as a veering wind,
Calls to the few tired dogs that yet remain :
Blanch, Swift, and Music, noblest of their kind,
Follow, and up the weary mountain strain.

The Knight hallooed, he cheered and chid them on
With suppliant gestures and upbraidings stern ;
But breath and eyesight fail ; and, one by one,
The dogs are stretched among the mountain fern.

Where is the throng, the tumult of the race ?
The bugles that so joyfully were blown ?
—This Chase it looks not like an earthly Chase ;
Sir Walter and the Hart are left alone.

The poor Hart toils along the mountain side ;
I will not stop to tell how far he fled,
Nor will I mention by what death he died ;
But now the Knight beholds him lying dead.

Dismounting, then, he leaned against a thorn ;
He had no follower, Dog, nor Man, nor Boy :
He neither cracked his whip, nor blew his horn,
But gazed upon the spoil with silent joy.

Close to the thorn on which Sir Walter leaned,
Stood his dumb partner in this glorious feat ;
Weak as a lamb the hour that it is yeaned ;
And white with foam as if with cleaving sleet.

Upon his side the Hart was lying stretched :
His nostril touched a spring beneath a hill,
And with the last deep groan his breath had fetched
The waters of the spring were trembling still.

And now, too happy for repose or rest,
(Never had living man such joyful lot !)
Sir Walter walked all round, north, south, and west,
And gazed and gazed upon that darling spot.

And climbing up the hill—(it was at least
Nine roods of sheer ascent) Sir Walter found
Three several hoof-marks which the hunted Beast
Had left imprinted on the grassy ground.

Sir Walter wiped his face, and cried, "Till now
Such sight was never seen by living eyes :
Three leaps have borne him from this lofty brow,
Down to the very fountain where he lies.

" I'll build a Pleasure-house upon this spot,
And a small Arbour, made for rural joy ;
'Twill be the traveller's shed, the pilgrim's cot,
A place of love for damsels that are coy.

" A cunning artist will I have to frame
A basin for that Fountain in the dell !
And they who do make mention of the same,
From this day forth, shall call it HART-LEAP WELL.

" And, gallant Stag ! to make thy praises known,
Another monument shall here be raised ;
Three several Pillars, each a rough-hewn stone,
And planted where thy hoofs the turf have grazed.

" And, in the summer-time when days are long,
I will come hither with my Paramour ;
And with the dancers and the minstrel's song
We will make merry in that pleasant Bower.

" Till the foundations of the mountains fail
My Mansion with its Arbour shall endure ;—
The joy of them who till the fields of Swale,
And them who dwell among the woods of Ure !"

C 2

Then home he went, and left the Hart, stone-dead,
With breathless nostrils stretched above the spring.
—Soon did the Knight perform what he had said,
And far and wide the fame thereof did ring.

Ere thrice the Moon into her port had steered,
A Cup of stone received the living Well ;
Three Pillars of rude stone Sir Walter reared,
And built a House of Pleasure in the dell.

And near the Fountain, flowers of stature tall
With trailing plants and trees were intertwined,—
Which soon composed a little sylvan Hall,
A leafy shelter from the sun and wind.

And thither, when the summer-days were long,
Sir Walter led his wondering Paramour ;
And with the dancers and the minstrel's song
Made merriment within that pleasant Bower.

The Knight, Sir Walter, died in course of time,
And his bones lie in his paternal vale.—
But there is matter for a second rhyme,
And I to this would add another tale.

PART SECOND.

THE moving accident is not my trade :
To freeze the blood I have no ready arts :
'Tis my delight, alone in summer shade,
To pipe a simple song for thinking hearts.

As I from Hawes to Richmond did repair,
It chanced that I saw standing in a dell
Three Aspens at three corners of a square ;
And one, not four yards distant, near a Well.

What this imported I could ill divine :
And, pulling now the rein my horse to stop,
I saw three Pillars standing in a line,
The last stone-Pillar on a dark hill-top.

The trees were gray, with neither arms nor head ;
Half-wasted the square Mound of tawny green ;
So that you just might say, as then I said,
" Here in old time the hand of man hath been."

I looked upon the hill both far and near,
More doleful place did never eye survey ;
It seemed as if the spring-time came not here,
And Nature here were willing to decay.

I stood in various thoughts and fancies lost,
When one, who was in shepherd's garb attired,
Came up the hollow :—Him did I accost,
And what this place might be I then inquired.

The Shepherd stopped, and that same story told
Which in my former rhyme I have rehearsed.
" A jolly place," said he, " in times of old !
But something ails it now ; the spot is curst.

" You see these lifeless stumps of aspen wood—
Some say that they are beeches, others elms—
These were the Bower ; and here a Mansion stood,
The finest palace of a hundred realms !

" The Arbour does its own condition tell ;
You see the Stones, the Fountain, and the Stream ;
But as to the great Lodge ! you might as well
Hunt half a day for a forgotten dream.

" There's neither dog nor heifer, horse nor sheep,
　　Will wet his lips within that Cup of stone ;
　And oftentimes, when all are fast asleep,
　　This water doth send forth a dolorous groan.

" Some say that here a murder has been done,
　　And blood cries out for blood : but, for my part,
　I've guessed, when I've been sitting in the sun,
　　That it was all for that unhappy Hart.

" What thoughts must through the Creature's brain have
　　　　past !
　Even from the topmost stone, upon the steep,
　Are but three bounds—and look, Sir, at this last—
　　—O Master ! it has been a cruel leap.

" For thirteen hours he ran a desperate race ;
　　And in my simple mind we cannot tell
　What cause the Hart might have to love this place,
　　And come and make his deathbed near the Well.

" Here on the grass perhaps asleep he sank,
　　Lulled by the Fountain in the summer-tide ;
　This water was perhaps the first he drank
　　When he had wandered from his mother's side.

" In April here beneath the scented thorn
　　He heard the birds their morning carols sing ;
　And he, perhaps, for aught we know, was born
　　Not half a furlong from that self-same spring.

" Now, here is neither grass nor pleasant shade ;
　　The sun on drearier hollow never shone ;
　So will it be, as I have often said,
　　Till Trees, and Stones, and Fountain, all are gone."

" Gray-headed Shepherd, thou hast spoken well ;
  Small difference lies between thy creed and mine :
  This Beast not unobserved by Nature fell ;
  His death was mourned by sympathy divine.

" The Being, that is in the clouds and air,
  That is in the green leaves among the groves,
  Maintains a deep and reverential care
  For the unoffending creatures whom he loves.

" The Pleasure-house is dust :—behind, before,
  This is no common waste, no common gloom ;
  But Nature, in due course of time, once more
  Shall here put on her beauty and her bloom.

" She leaves these objects to a slow decay,
  That what we are, and have been, may be known ;
  But, at the coming of the milder day,
  These monuments shall all be overgrown.

" One lesson, Shepherd, let us two divide,
  Taught both by what she shows, and what conceals
  Never to blend our pleasure or our pride
  With sorrow of the meanest thing that feels."

THE FORCE OF PRAYER ;

OR,

THE FOUNDING OF BOLTON PRIORY.

A TRADITION.

" What is good for a bootless bene ? "
  With these dark words begins my Tale ;
  And their meaning is, whence can comfort spring
  When Prayer is of no avail ?

"What is good for a bootless bene?"
    The Falconer to the Lady said ;
And she made answer "ENDLESS SORROW!"
    For she knew that her son was dead.

She knew it by the Falconer's words,
    And from the look of the Falconer's eye ;
And from the love which was in her soul
    For her youthful Romilly.

—Young Romilly through Barden woods
    Is ranging high and low ;
And holds a Greyhound in a leash,
    To let slip upon buck or doe.

The Pair have reached that fearful chasm,
    How tempting to bestride !
For lordly Wharf is there pent in
    With rocks on either side.

This Striding-place is called THE STRID,
    A name which it took of yore :
A thousand years hath it borne that name,
    And shall a thousand more.

And hither is young Romilly come,
    And what may now forbid
That he, perhaps for the hundredth time,
    Shall bound across THE STRID?

He sprang in glee,—for what cared he
That the river was strong, and the rocks were steep?
But the Greyhound in the leash hung back,
    And checked him in his leap.

The Boy is in the arms of Wharf,
And strangled by a merciless force ;
For never more was young Romilly seen
Till he rose a lifeless corse.

Now there is stillness in the Vale,
And deep, unspeaking sorrow :
Wharf shall be to pitying hearts
A name more sad than Yarrow.

If for a lover the Lady wept,
A solace she might borrow
From death, and from the passion of death ;—
Old Wharf might heal her sorrow.

She weeps not for the wedding-day
Which was to be to-morrow :
Her hope was a further-looking hope,
And hers is a Mother's sorrow.

He was a Tree that stood alone,
And proudly did its branches wave ;
And the root of this delightful Tree
Was in her Husband's grave !

Long, long in darkness did she sit,
And her first words were, "Let there be
In Bolton, on the Field of Wharf,
A stately Priory !"

The stately Priory was reared ;
And Wharf, as he moved along,
To Matins joined a mournful voice,
Nor failed at Even-song.

And the Lady prayed in heaviness
That looked not for relief!
But slowly did her succour come,
And a patience to her grief.

Oh! there is never sorrow of heart
That shall lack a timely end,
If but to God we turn, and ask
Of Him to be our Friend!

THE AFFLICTION OF MARGARET.

WHERE art thou, my beloved Son,
Where art thou, worse to me than dead?
Oh find me, prosperous or undone!
Or, if the grave be now thy bed,
Why am I ignorant of the same
That I may rest; and neither blame
Nor sorrow may attend thy name?

Seven years, alas! to have received
No tidings of an only child;
To have despaired, and have believed,
And be for evermore beguiled;
Sometimes with thoughts of very bliss!
I catch at them, and then I miss;
Was ever darkness like to this?

He was among the prime in worth,
An object beauteous to behold;
Well born, well bred; I sent him forth
Ingenuous, innocent, and bold:
If things ensued that wanted grace,
As hath been said, they were not base;
And never blush was on my face.

Ah! little doth the Young-one dream,
When full of play and childish cares,
What power is in his wildest scream,
Heard by his Mother unawares!
He knows it not, he cannot guess:
Years to a mother bring distress;
But do not make her love the less.

Neglect me! no, I suffered long
From that ill thought; and, being blind,
Said, "Pride shall help me in my wrong:
Kind mother have I been, as kind
As ever breathed:" and that is true;
I've wet my path with tears like dew,
Weeping for him when no one knew.

My Son, if thou be humbled, poor,
Hopeless of honour and of gain,
Oh! do not dread thy mother's door;
Think not of me with grief and pain;
I now can see with better eyes;
And worldly grandeur I despise,
And fortune with her gifts and lies.

Alas! the fowls of Heaven have wings,
And blasts of Heaven will aid their flight;
They mount—how short a voyage brings
The wanderers back to their delight!
Chains tie *us* down by land and sea;
And wishes, vain as mine, may be
All that is left to comfort thee.

Perhaps some dungeon hears thee groan,
Maimed, mangled by inhuman men;
Or thou upon a desert thrown
Inheritest the Lion's den;
Or hast been summoned to the deep,
Thou, Thou and all thy mates, to keep
An incommunicable sleep.

I look for Ghosts ; but none will force
Their way to me :—'tis falsely said
That there was ever intercourse
Between the living and the dead ;
For, surely, then I should have sight
Of Him I wait for day and night,
With love and longings infinite.

My apprehensions come in crowds ;
I dread the rustling of the grass ;
The very shadows of the clouds
Have power to shake me as they pass :
I question things, and do not find
One that will answer to my mind ;
And all the world appears unkind.

Beyond participation lie
My troubles, and beyond relief :
If any chance to heave a sigh,
They pity me, and not my grief.
Then come to me, my Son, or send
Some tidings that my woes may end ;
I have no other earthly friend !

THE COMPLAINT

OF A FORSAKEN INDIAN WOMAN.

[When a Northern Indian, from sickness, is unable to continue his journey with his companions, he is left behind, covered over with Deer-skins, and is supplied with water, food, and fuel, if the situation of the place will afford it. He is informed of the track which his companions intend to pursue, and if he is unable to follow, or overtake them, he perishes alone in the Desert; unless he should have the good fortune to fall in with some other Tribes of Indians. The females are equally, or still more, exposed to the same fate. See that very interesting work, Hearne's *Journey from Hudson's Bay to the Northern Ocean.* In the high Northern Latitudes, as the same writer informs us, when the Northern Lights vary their position in the air, they make a rustling and a crackling noise, as alluded to in the following poem.]

BEFORE I see another day,
Oh let my body die away !
In sleep I heard the northern gleams ;
The stars were mingled with my dreams ;
In rustling conflict through the skies,
I heard, I saw the flashes drive,
And yet they are upon my eyes,
And yet I am alive ;
Before I see another day,
Oh let my body die away.

My fire is dead : it knew no pain ;
Yet is it dead, and I remain.
All stiff with ice the ashes lie ;
And they are dead, and I will die.
When I was well, I wished to live,
For clothes, for warmth, for food, and fire ;
But they to me no joy can give,
No pleasure now, and no desire.
Then here contented will I lie !
Alone I cannot fear to die.

Alas ! ye might have dragged me on
Another day, a single one !
Too soon I yielded to despair ;
Why did ye listen to my prayer ?
When ye were gone my limbs were stronger ;
And oh how grievously I rue,
That, afterwards, a little longer,
My Friends, I did not follow you !
For strong and without pain I lay,
My Friends, when ye were gone away.

My Child ! they gave thee to another,
A woman who was not thy mother.
When from my arms my Babe they took,
On me how strangely did he look !
Through his whole body something ran,
A most strange working did I see ;
—As if he strove to be a man,
That he might pull the sledge for me :
And then he stretched his arms, how wild !
Oh mercy ! like a helpless child.

My little joy ! my little pride !
In two days more I must have died.
Then do not weep and grieve for me ;
I feel I must have died with thee.
O wind, that o'er my head art flying
The way my Friends their course did bend,
I should not feel the pain of dying,
Could I with thee a message send ;
Too soon, my Friends, ye went away ;
For I had many things to say.

I'll follow you across the snow ;
Ye travel heavily and slow ;
In spite of all my weary pain
I'll look upon your tents again.
—My fire is dead, and snowy white
The water which beside it stood ;
The wolf has come to me to-night
And he has stolen away my food.
For ever left alone am I,
Then wherefore should I fear to die.

SONG

AT THE FEAST OF BROUGHAM CASTLE,

UPON THE RESTORATION OF LORD CLIFFORD, THE
SHEPHERD, TO THE ESTATES AND HONOURS OF
HIS ANCESTORS.

HIGH in the breathless Hall the Minstrel sate,
And Eamont's murmur mingled with the Song.—
The words of ancient time I thus translate,
A festal Strain that hath been silent long.

"From Town to Town, from Tower to Tower,
The Red Rose is a gladsome Flower.
Her thirty years of winter past,
The Red Rose is revived at last ;
She lifts her head for endless spring,
For everlasting blossoming :
Both Roses flourish, Red and White.
In love and sisterly delight
The two that were at strife are blended,
And all old troubles now are ended.—
Joy ! joy to both ! but most to her
Who is the flower of Lancaster !
Behold her how She smiles to-day
On this great throng, this bright array !
Fair greeting doth she send to all
From every corner of the Hall ;
But, chiefly from above the Board
Where sits in state our rightful Lord,
A Clifford to his own restored !

"They came with banner, spear, and shield ;
And it was proved in Bosworth-field.

Not long the Avenger was withstood—
Earth helped him with the cry of blood :
St. George was for us, and the might
Of blessed Angels crowned the right.
Loud voice the Land has uttered forth,
We loudest in the faithful North :
Our fields rejoice, our mountains ring,
Our streams proclaim a welcoming ;
Our strong-abodes and castles see
The glory of their loyalty.

" How glad is Skipton at this hour—
Though she is but a lonely Tower !
To vacancy and silence left ;
Of all her guardian sons bereft—
Knight, Squire, or Yeoman, Page or Groom
We have them at the feast of Brougham.
How glad Pendragon—though the sleep
Of years be on her !—She shall reap
A taste of this great pleasure, viewing
As in a dream her own renewing.
Rejoiced is Brough, right glad I deem
Beside her little humble Stream ;
And she that keepeth watch and ward
Her statelier Eden's course to guard ;
They both are happy at this hour,
Though each is but a lonely Tower :—
But here is perfect joy and pride
For one fair house by Eamont's side,
This day distinguished without peer
To see her Master and to cheer—
Him, and his Lady Mother dear !

" Oh ! it was a time forlorn
When the fatherless was born—

Give her wings that she may fly,
Or she sees her infant die !
Swords that are with slaughter wild
Hunt the Mother and the Child.
Who will take them from the light ?
—Yonder is a man in sight—
Yonder is a house—but where ?
No, they must not enter there.
To the caves, and to the brooks,
To the clouds of Heaven she looks ;
She is speechless, but her eyes
Pray in ghostly agonies.
Blissful Mary, Mother mild,
Maid and Mother undefiled,
Save a Mother and her Child !

"Now who is he that bounds with joy
On Carrock's side, a Shepherd Boy ?
No thoughts hath he but thoughts that pass
Light as the wind along the grass.
Can this be He who hither came
In secret, like a smothered flame ?
O'er whom such thankful tears were shed
For shelter, and a poor man's bread !
God loves the Child ; and God hath willed
That those dear words should be fulfilled,
The Lady's words, when forced away
The last she to her Babe did say,
'My own, my own, thy fellow-guest
I may not be ; but rest thee, rest,
For lowly Shepherd's life is best !'

"Alas ! when evil men are strong
No life is good, no pleasure long,
The Boy must part from Mosedale's groves,
And leave Blencathara's rugged coves,

And quit the flowers that summer brings
To Glenderamakin's lofty springs;
Must vanish, and his careless cheer
Be turned to heaviness and fear.
—Give Sir Lancelot Threlkeld praise !
Hear it, good man, old in days !
Thou Tree of covert and of rest !
For this young Bird that is distrest ;
Among thy branches safe he lay,
And he was free to sport and play,
When falcons were abroad for prey.

"A recreant Harp that sings of fear
And heaviness in Clifford's ear !
I said, when evil men are strong,
No life is good, no pleasure long,
A weak and cowardly untruth !
Our Clifford was a happy Youth,
And thankful through a weary time,
That brought him up to manhood's prime.
—Again he wanders forth at will,
And tends a flock from hill to hill ;
His garb is humble ; ne'er was seen
Such garb with such a noble mien ;
Among the shepherd-grooms no mate
Hath he, a Child of strength and state :
Yet lacks not friends for solemn glee,
And a cheerful company,
That learned of him submissive ways
And comforted his private days.
To his side the Fallow-deer
Came, and rested without fear ;
The Eagle, lord of land and sea,
Stooped down to pay him fealty ;

And both the undying fish that swim
Through Bowscale Tarn did wait on him;
The Pair were servants of his eye
In their immortality;
They moved about in open sight,
To and fro, for his delight.
He knew the rocks which Angels haunt
On the mountains visitant;
He hath kenned them taking wing:
And the caves where Faeries sing
He hath entered; and been told
By Voices how men lived of old.
Among the Heavens his eye can see
Face of thing that is to be;
And, if men report him right,
He could whisper words of might.
—Now another day is come,
Fitter hope, and nobler doom;
He hath thrown aside his Crook,
And hath buried deep his Book;
Armour rusting in his Halls
On the blood of Clifford calls;—
'Quell the Scot,' exclaims the Lance—
Bear me to the heart of France,
Is the longing of the Shield—
Tell thy name, thou trembling Field;
Field of death, where'er thou be,
Groan thou with our victory!
Happy day, and mighty hour,
When our Shepherd, in his power,
Mailed and horsed, with lance and sword,
To his Ancestors restored
Like a re-appearing Star,
Like a glory from afar,
First shall head the Flock of War!"

Alas ! the fervent Harper did not know
That for a tranquil Soul the Lay was framed,
Who, long compelled in humble walks to go,
Was softened into feeling, soothed, and tamed.

Love had he found in huts where poor men lie ;
His daily teachers had been woods and rills,
The silence that is in the starry sky,
The sleep that is among the lonely hills.

In him the savage virtue of the Race,
Revenge, and all ferocious thoughts were dead :
Nor did he change ; but kept in lofty place
The wisdom which adversity had bred.

Glad were the Vales, and every cottage hearth ;
The Shepherd Lord was honoured more and more ;
And, ages after he was laid in earth,
" The Good Lord Clifford " was the name he bore.

THE LEECH-GATHERER;

OR,

RESOLUTION AND INDEPENDENCE.

THERE was a roaring in the wind all night ;
The rain came heavily and fell in floods ;
But now the sun is rising calm and bright ;
The birds are singing in the distant woods ;
Over his own sweet voice the Stock-dove broods ;
The Jay makes answer as the Magpie chatters ;
And all the air is filled with pleasant noise of waters.

All things that love the sun are out of doors ;
The sky rejoices in the morning's birth ;
The grass is bright with rain-drops ;—on the moors
The Hare is running races in her mirth ;
And with her feet she from the plashy earth
Raises a mist ; that, glittering in the sun,
Runs with her all the way, wherever she doth run.

I was a traveller then upon the moor ;
I saw the Hare that raced about with joy ;
I heard the woods and distant waters roar ;
Or heard them not, as happy as a boy :
The pleasant season did my heart employ :
My old remembrances went from me wholly :
And all the ways of men, so vain and melancholy!

But, as it sometimes chanceth, from the might
Of joy in minds that can no further go,
As high as we have mounted in delight
In our dejection do we sink as low,
To me that morning did it happen so ;
And fears and fancies thick upon me came ;
Dim sadness—and blind thoughts, I knew not, nor could
name.

I heard the Sky-lark warbling in the sky ;
And I bethought me of the playful Hare :
Even such a happy child of earth am I ;
Even as these blissful creatures do I fare ;
Far from the world I walk, and from all care ;
But there may come another day to me—
Solitude, pain of heart, distress, and poverty.

My whole life I have lived in pleasant thought,
As if life's business were a summer mood :
As if all needful things would come unsought
To genial faith, still rich in genial good :
But how can He expect that others should
Build for him, sow for him, and at his call
Love him, who for himself will take no heed at all ?

I thought of Chatterton, the marvellous Boy,
The sleepless Soul that perished in his pride ;
Of Him who walked in glory and in joy
Following his plough, along the mountain-side :
By our own spirits are we deified ;
We Poets in our youth begin in gladness ;
But thereof comes in the end despondency and madness.

Now, whether it were by peculiar grace,
A leading from above, a something given,
Yet it befel, that, in this lonely place,
When I with these untoward thoughts had striven,
Beside a pool bare to the eye of heaven
I saw a Man before me unawares :
The oldest man he seemed that ever wore grey
    hairs.

As a huge Stone is sometimes seen to lie
Couched on the bald top of an eminence ;
Wonder to all who do the same espy,
By what means it could thither come, and whence
So that it seems a thing endued with sense :
Like a Sea-beast crawled forth, that on a shelf
Of rock or sand reposeth, there to sun itself ;

Such seemed this Man, not all alive nor dead,
Nor all asleep—in his extreme old age :
His body was bent double, feet and head
Coming together in life's pilgrimage ;
As if some dire constraint of pain, or rage
Of sickness felt by him in times long past,
A more than human weight upon his frame had cast.

Himself he propped, his body, limbs, and face,
Upon a long grey Staff of shaven wood :
And, still as I drew near with gentle pace,
Upon the margin of that moorish flood
Motionless as a Cloud the Old-man stood ;
That heareth not the loud winds when they call ;
And moveth all together, if it move at all.

At length, himself unsettling, he the Pond
Stirred with his Staff, and fixedly did look
Upon the muddy water, which he conned,
As if he had been reading in a book :
And now a stranger's privilege I took ;
And, drawing to his side, to him did say,
" This morning gives us promise of a glorious day."

A gentle answer did the Old-man make,
In courteous speech which forth he slowly drew :
And him with further words I thus bespake,
" What occupation do you there pursue ?
This is a lonesome place for one like you."
He answered, while a flash of mild surprise
Broke from the sable orbs of his yet vivid eyes.

His words came feebly, from a feeble chest,
But each in solemn order followed each,
With something of a lofty utterance drest—
Choice word and measured phrase, above the reach
Of ordinary men ; a stately speech ;
Such as grave livers do in Scotland use,
Religious men, who give to God and Man their dues.

He told, that to these waters he had come
To gather Leeches, being old and poor :
Employment hazardous and wearisome !
And he had many hardships to endure ;
From pond to pond he roamed, from moor to moor ;
Housing, with God's good help, by choice or chance ;
And in this way he gained an honest maintenance.

The Old-man still stood talking by my side ;
But now his voice to me was like a stream
Scarce heard ; nor word from word could I divide ;
And the whole Body of the Man did seem
Like one whom I had met with in a dream ;
Or like a man from some far region sent,
To give me human strength, by apt admonishment.

My former thoughts returned : the fear that kills ;
And hope that is unwilling to be fed ;
Cold, pain, and labour, and all fleshly ills ;
And mighty Poets in their misery dead.
—Perplexed, and longing to be comforted,
My question eagerly did I renew,
" How is it that you live, and what is it you do ? "

He with a smile did then his words repeat ;
And said, that, gathering Leeches, far and wide
He travelled ; stirring thus about his feet
The waters of the Pools where they abide.
" Once I could meet with them on every side ;
But they have dwindled long by slow decay ;
Yet still I persevere, and find them where I may."

While he was talking thus, the lonely place,
The Old-man's shape, and speech, all troubled me :
In my mind's eye I seemed to see him pace
About the weary moors continually,
Wandering about alone and silently.
While I these thoughts within myself pursued,
He, having made a pause, the same discourse renewed.

And soon with this he other matter blended,
Cheerfully uttered, with demeanour kind,
But stately in the main ; and when he ended,
I could have laughed myself to scorn to find
In that decrepit Man so firm a mind.
" God," said I, " be my help and stay secure ;
I'll think of the Leech-gatherer on the lonely moor !"

THE BROTHERS.[1]

' THESE Tourists, Heaven preserve us ! needs must live
A profitable life : some glance along,
Rapid and gay, as if the earth were air,
And they were butterflies to wheel about
Long as the summer lasted : some, as wise,
Perched on the forehead of a jutting crag,
Pencil in hand and book upon the knee,
Will look and scribble, scribble on and look
Until a man might travel twelve stout miles,
Or reap an acre of his neighbour's corn.
But, for that moping Son of Idleness,
Why can he tarry *yonder ?*—In our churchyard
Is neither epitaph nor monument,
Tombstone nor name—only the turf we tread
And a few natural graves." To Jane, his wife,
Thus spake the homely Priest of Ennerdale.
It was a July evening ; and he sate
Upon the long stone-seat beneath the eaves
Of his old cottage,—as it chanced, that day,
Employed in winter's work. Upon the stone
His Wife sate near him, teasing matted wool,
While, from the twin cards toothed with glittering wire,
He fed the spindle of his youngest Child,
Who turned her large round wheel in the open air
With back and forward steps. Towards the field
In which the Parish Chapel stood alone,

---

1 This Poem was intended to conclude a series of pastorals, the
scene of which was laid among the mountains of Cumberland and
Westmoreland. I mention this to apologise for the abruptness with
which the poem begins.

D

Girt round with a bare ring of mossy wall,
While half an hour went by, the Priest had sent
Many a long look of wonder : and at last,
Risen from his seat beside the snow-white ridge
Of carded wool which the old man had piled
He laid his implements with gentle care,
Each in the other locked ; and, down the path
That from his cottage to the churchyard led,
He took his way, impatient to accost
The Stranger, whom he saw still lingering there.

'Twas one well known to him in former days,
A Shepherd-lad ;—who ere his sixteenth year
Had left that calling, tempted to entrust
His expectations to the fickle winds
And perilous waters,—with the mariners
A fellow mariner,—and so had fared
Through twenty seasons ; but he had been reared
Among the mountains, and he in his heart
Was half a Shepherd on the stormy seas.
Oft in the piping shrouds had Leonard heard
The tones of waterfalls, and inland sounds
Of caves and trees :—and, when the regular wind
Between the tropics filled the steady sail,
And blew with the same breath through days and weeks
Lengthening invisibly its weary line
Along the cloudless Main, he, in those hours
Of tiresome indolence, would often hang
Over the vessel's side, and gaze and gaze ;
And, while the broad green wave and sparkling foam
Flashed round him images and hues that wrought
In union with the employment of his heart,
He, thus by feverish passion overcome,
Even with the organs of his bodily eye,
Below him, in the bosom of the deep,

Saw mountains,—saw the forms of sheep that grazed
On verdant hills—with dwellings among trees,
And shepherds clad in the same country gray
Which he himself had worn.[1]

      And now, at last,
From perils manifold, with some small wealth
Acquired by traffic 'mid the Indian Isles,
To his paternal home he is returned,
With a determined purpose to resume
The life he had lived there; both for the sake
Of many darling pleasures, and the love
Which to an only brother he has borne
In all his hardships, since that happy time
When, whether it blew foul or fair, they two
Were brother Shepherds on their native hills.
—They were the last of all their race; and now,
When Leonard had approached his home, his heart
Failed in him; and, not venturing to enquire
Tidings of one whom he so dearly loved,
Towards the churchyard he had turned aside;
That, as he knew in what particular spot
His family were laid, he thence might learn
If still his Brother lived, or to the file
Another grave was added.—He had found
Another grave,—near which a full half-hour
He had remained; but, as he gazed, there grew
Such a confusion in his memory,
That he began to doubt; and hope was his
That he had seen this heap of turf before,—
That it was not another grave; but one
He had forgotten. He had lost his path,
As up the vale, that afternoon, he walked

[1] This description of the Calenture is sketched from an imperfect
recollection of an admirable one in prose, by Mr. Gilbert, author of
"The Hurricane."

Through fields which once had been well known to
     him:
And oh what joy the recollection now
Sent to his heart! He lifted up his eyes,
And, looking round, imagined that he saw
Strange alteration wrought on every side
Among the woods and fields, and that the rocks,
And everlasting hills themselves were changed.

     By this the Priest, who down the field had come,
Unseen by Leonard, at the churchyard gate
Stopped short,—and thence, at leisure, limb by limb
Perused him with a gay complacency.
Ay, thought the Vicar, smiling to himself,
'Tis one of those who needs must leave the path
Of the world's business to go wild alone :
His arms have a perpetual holiday ;
The happy man will creep about the fields,
Following his fancies by the hour, to bring
Tears down his cheek, or solitary smiles
Into his face, until the setting sun
Write Fool upon his forehead.   Planted thus
Beneath a shed that over-arched the gate
Of this rude churchyard, till the stars appeared
The good Man might have communed with himself,
But that the Stranger, who had left the grave,
Approached ; he recognised the Priest at once,
And, after greetings interchanged, and given
By Leonard to the Vicar as to one
Unknown to him, this dialogue ensued.

                    LEONARD.

You live, Sir, in these dales, a quiet life :
Your years make up one peaceful family ;

And who would grieve and fret, if, welcome come
And welcome gone, they are so like each other,
They cannot be remembered? Scarce a funeral
Comes to this churchyard once in eighteen months;
And yet, some changes must take place among you:
And you, who dwell here, even among these rocks,
Can trace the finger of mortality,
And see, that with our threescore years and ten
We are not all that perish.——I remember,
(For many years ago I passed this road)
There was a foot-way all along the fields
By the brook-side—'tis gone—and that dark cleft!
To me it does not seem to wear the face
Which then it had.

PRIEST.

                    Nay, Sir, for aught I know,
That chasm is much the same—

LEONARD.

                    But, surely, yonder—

PRIEST.

Ay, there, indeed, your memory is a friend
That does not play you false.—On that tall pike
(It is the loneliest place of all these hills)
There were two Springs which bubbled side by side,
As if they had been made that they might be
Companions for each other: the huge crag
Was rent with lightning—one hath disappeared;
The other, left behind, is flowing still.[1]
For accidents and changes such as these,

1 This actually took place upon Kidstow Pike at the head of
Haweswater.

We want not store of them ;—a water-spout
Will bring down half a mountain ; what a feast
For folks that wander up and down like you,
To see an acre's breadth of that wide cliff
One roaring cataract !—a sharp May-storm
Will come with loads of January snow,
And in one night send twenty score of sheep
To feed the ravens ; or a Shepherd dies
By some untoward death among the rocks :
The ice breaks up and sweeps away a bridge—
A wood is felled :—and then for our own homes !
A Child is born or christened, a Field ploughed,
A Daughter sent to service, a Web spun,
The old House-clock is decked with a new face ;
And hence, so far from wanting facts or dates
To chronicle the time, we all have here
A pair of diaries,—one serving, Sir,
For the whole dale, and one for each fireside—
Yours was a stranger's judgment : for historians,
Commend me to these valleys !

LEONARD.

                    Yet your Churchyard
Seems, if such freedom may be used with you,
To say that you are heedless of the past :
An orphan could not find his mother's grave :
Here's neither head nor foot stone, plate of brass,
Cross-bones nor skull,—type of our earthly state
Nor emblem of our hopes : the dead man's home
Is but a fellow to that pasture-field.

PRIEST.

Why, there, Sir, is a thought that's new to me !
The Stone-cutters, 'tis true, might beg their bread

If every English Churchyard were like ours ;
Yet your conclusion wanders from the truth :
We have no need of names and epitaphs ;
We talk about the dead by our firesides.
And then, for our immortal part ! *we* want
No symbols, Sir, to tell us that plain tale :
The thought of death sits easy on the man
Who has been born and dies among the mountains.

LEONARD.

Your Dalesmen, then, do in each other's thoughts
Possess a kind of second life : no doubt
You, Sir, could help me to the history
Of half these graves ?

PRIEST.

              For eight-score winters past,
With what I've witnessed, and with what I've heard,
Perhaps I might ; and, on a winter-evening,
If you were seated at my chimney's nook,
By turning o'er these hillocks one by one,
We two could travel, Sir, through a strange round ;
Yet all in the broad highway of the world.
Now there's a grave—your foot is half upon it,—
It looks just like the rest ; and yet that Man
Died broken-hearted.

LEONARD.

           'Tis a common case.
We'll take another : who is he that lies
Beneath yon ridge, the last of those three graves ?
It touches on that piece of native rock
Left in the churchyard wall.

PRIEST.

That's Walter Ewbank.
He had as white a head and fresh a cheek
As ever were produced by youth and age
Engendering in the blood of hale fourscore.
Through five long generations had the heart
Of Walter's forefathers o'erflowed the bounds
Of their inheritance, that single cottage—
You see it yonder!—and those few green fields.
They toiled and wrought, and still, from sire to son,
Each struggled, and each yielded as before
A little—yet a little—and old Walter,
They left to him the family heart, and land
With other burthens than the crop it bore.
Year after year the old man still kept up
A cheerful mind,—and buffeted with bond,
Interest, and mortgages; at last he sank,
And went into his grave before his time.
Poor Walter! whether it was care that spurred him
God only knows, but to the very last
He had the lightest foot in Ennerdale:
His pace was never that of an old man:
I almost see him tripping down the path
With his two Grandsons after him:—but You,
Unless our Landlord be your host to-night,
Have far to travel,—and on these rough paths
Even in the longest day of midsummer—

LEONARD.

But those two Orphans!

PRIEST.

Orphans!—Such they were—
Yet not while Walter lived:—for, though their parents

Lay buried side by side as now they lie,
The old Man was a father to the boys,
Two fathers in one father : and if tears,
Shed when he talked of them where they were not,
And hauntings from the infirmity of love,
Are aught of what makes up a mother's heart,
This old Man, in the day of his old age,
Was half a mother to them.—If you weep, Sir,
To hear a stranger talking about strangers,
Heaven bless you when you are among your kindred !
Ay—you may turn that way—it is a grave
Which will bear looking at.

LEONARD.

                              These Boys—I hope
They loved this good old Man ?

PRIEST.

                              They did—and truly :
But that was what we almost overlooked,
They were such darlings of each other.   For,
Though from their cradles they had lived with Walter,
The only kinsman near them, and though he
Inclined to them by reason of his age,
With a more fond, familiar tenderness,
They, notwithstanding, had much love to spare,
And it all went into each other's hearts.
Leonard, the elder by just eighteen months,
Was two years taller : 'twas a joy to see,
To hear, to meet them !—From their house the School
Is distant three short miles—and in the time
Of storm and thaw, when every water-course
And unbridged stream, such as you may have noticed
Crossing our roads at every hundred steps,

D 2

Was swoln into a noisy rivulet,
Would Leonard then, when elder boys perhaps
Remained at home, go staggering through the fords,
Bearing his Brother on his back.   I have seen him,
On windy days, in one of those stray brooks,
Ay, more than once I have seen him, mid-leg deep,
Their two books lying both on a dry stone,
Upon the hither side : and once I said,
As I remember, looking round these rocks
And hills on which we all of us were born,
That God who made the great book of the world
Would bless such piety—

LEONARD.

It may be then—

PRIEST.

Never did worthier lads break English bread ;
The finest Sunday that the Autumn saw
With all its mealy clusters of ripe nuts,
Could never keep these boys away from church,
Or tempt them to an hour of Sabbath breach.
Leonard and James ! I warrant, every corner
Among these rocks, and every hollow place
Where foot could come, to one or both of them
Was known as well as to the flowers that grow there.
Like Roe-bucks they went bounding o'er the hills ;
They played like two young Ravens on the crags :
Then they would write, ay and speak too, as well
As many of their betters—and for Leonard !
The very night before he went away,
In my own house I put into his hand
A Bible, and I'd wager house and field
That, if he is alive, he has it yet.

LEONARD.

It seems, these Brothers have not lived to be
A comfort to each other—

PRIEST.

That they might
Live to such end, is what both old and young
In this our valley all of us have wished,
And what, for my part, I have often prayed:
But Leonard—

LEONARD.

Then James still is left among you?

PRIEST.

'Tis of the elder Brother I am speaking:
They had an Uncle;—he was at that time
A thriving man, and trafficked on the seas:
And, but for that same Uncle, to this hour
Leonard had never handled rope or shroud:
For the Boy loved the life which we lead here;
And though of unripe years, a stripling only,
His soul was knit to this his native soil.
But, as I said, old Walter was too weak
To strive with such a torrent; when he died,
The Estate and House were sold; and all their Sheep,
A pretty flock, and which, for aught I know,
Had clothed the Ewbanks for a thousand years:—
Well—all was gone, and they were destitute.
And Leonard, chiefly for his Brother's sake,
Resolved to try his fortune on the seas.
Twelve years are past since we had tidings from him.
If there were one among us who had heard
That Leonard Ewbank was come home again,

From the great Gavel,[1] down by Leeza's Banks,
And down the Enna, far as Egremont,
The day would be a very festival ;
And those two bells of ours, which there you see—
Hanging in the open air—but, O good Sir !
This is sad talk—they'll never sound for him—
Living or dead.—When last we heard of him,
He was in slavery among the Moors
Upon the Barbary Coast.—'Twas not a little
That would bring down his spirit ; and no doubt,
Before it ended in his death, the Youth
Was sadly crossed—Poor Leonard ! when we parted,
He took me by the hand, and said to me,
If e'er he should grow rich, he would return,
To live in peace upon his father's land,
And lay his bones among us.

LEONARD.

                        If that day
Should come, 't would needs be a glad day for him ;
He would himself, no doubt, be happy then
As any that should meet him—

PRIEST.

                        Happy ! Sir—

LEONARD.

You said his kindred all were in their graves,
And that he had one Brother—

---

1 The Great Gavel, so called, I imagine, from its resemblance to
the Gable end of a house, is one of the highest of the Cumberland
mountains.   It stands at the head of the several vales of Ennerdale,
Wastdale, and Borrowdale.

The Leeza is a river which flows into the Lake of Ennerdale : on
issuing from the Lake, it changes its name, and is called the End,
Eyne, or Enna.   It falls into the sea a little below Egremont.

PRIEST.
That is but
A fellow tale of sorrow.   From his youth
James, though not sickly, yet was delicate ;
And Leonard being always by his side
Had done so many offices about him,
That, though he was not of a timid nature,
Yet still the spirit of a Mountain Boy
In him was somewhat checked ; and, when his Brother
Was gone to sea, and he was left alone,
The little colour that he had was soon
Stolen from his cheek ; he drooped, and pined, and pined—

LEONARD.

But these are all the graves of full-grown men !

PRIEST.

Ay, Sir, that passed away : we took him to us ;
He was the Child of all the dale—he lived
Three months with one, and six months with another ;
And wanted neither food, nor clothes, nor love :
And many, many happy days were his.
But, whether blithe or sad, 'tis my belief
His absent Brother still was at his heart.
And, when he dwelt beneath our roof, we found
(A practice till this time unknown to him)
That often, rising from his bed at night,
He in his sleep would walk about, and sleeping
He sought his Brother Leonard.—You are moved !
Forgive me, Sir : before I spoke to you,
I judged you most unkindly.

LEONARD.
But this Youth,

How did he die at last ?

PRIEST.

                    One sweet May morning,
(It will be twelve years since when Spring returns)
He had gone forth among the new-dropped lambs,
With two or three companions, whom their course
Of occupation led from height to height
Under a cloudless sun, till he, at length,
Through weariness, or, haply, to indulge
The humour of the moment, lagged behind.
You see yon precipice ;—it wears the shape
Of a vast building made of many crags ;
And in the midst is one particular rock
That rises like a column from the vale,
Whence by our shepherds it is called THE PILLAR.
Upon its aëry summit crowned with heath,
The Loiterer, not unnoticed by his comrades,
Lay stretched at ease ; but, passing by the place
On their return, they found that he was gone.
No ill was feared ; but one of them by chance
Entering, when evening was far spent, the house
Which at that time was James's home, there learned
That nobody had seen him all that day :
The morning came, and still he was unheard of :
The neighbours were alarmed, and to the brook
Some hastened, some towards the lake : ere noon
They found him at the foot of that same rock
Dead, and with mangled limbs.   The third day after
I buried him, poor Youth, and there he lies !

LEONARD.

And that then *is* his grave !—Before his death
You say that he saw many happy years?

PRIEST.

Ay, that ne did—

LEONARD.

And all went well with him ?—

PRIEST.

If he had one, the youth had twenty homes.

LEONARD.

And you believe, then, that his mind was easy ?—

PRIEST.

Yes, long before he died, he found that time
Is a true friend to sorrow ; and unless
His thoughts were turned on Leonard's luckless fortune,
He talked about him with a cheerful love.

LEONARD.

He could not come to an unhallowed end !

PRIEST.

Nay, God forbid !—You recollect I mentioned
A habit which disquietude and grief
Had brought upon him ; and we all conjectured
That, as the day was warm, he had lain down
Upon the grass,—and waiting for his comrades,
He there had fallen asleep ; that in his sleep
He to the margin of the precipice
Had walked, and from the summit had fallen headlong.
And so, no doubt, he perished : at the time,
We guess, that in his hand he must have held
His Shepherd's staff ; for midway in the cliff
It had been caught ; and there for many years
It hung—and mouldered there.

                              The Priest here ended—
The Stranger would have thanked him, but he felt

A gushing from his heart, that took away
The power of speech.   Both left the spot in silence ;
And Leonard, when they reached the churchyard gate,
As the Priest lifted up the latch turned round,—
And, looking at the grave, he said, "My Brother !"
The Vicar did not hear the words : and now,
Pointing towards the Cottage, he entreated
That Leonard would partake his homely fare :
The Other thanked him with a fervent voice ;
But added, that, the evening being calm,
He would pursue his journey.   So they parted.
It was not long ere Leonard reached a grove
That overhung the road ; he there stopped short,
And, sitting down beneath the trees, reviewed
All that the Priest had said : his early years
Were with him in his heart : his cherished hopes,
And thoughts which had been his an hour before,
All pressed on him with such a weight, that now,
This vale, where he had been so happy, seemed
A place in which he could not bear to live :
So he relinquished all his purposes.
He travelled on to Egremont : and thence,
That night, he wrote a letter to the Priest,
Reminding him of what had passed between them ;
And adding, with a hope to be forgiven,
That it was from the weakness of his heart
He had not dared to tell him who he was.

This done, he went on shipboard, and is now
A Seaman, a gray-headed Mariner.

MICHAEL.

A PASTORAL POEM.

IF from the public way you turn your steps
Up the tumultuous brook of Green-head Ghyll,
You will suppose that with an upright path
Your feet must struggle ; in such bold ascent
The pastoral mountains front you, face to face.
But, courage ! for around that boisterous Brook
The mountains have all opened out themselves,
And made a hidden valley of their own.
No habitation can be seen ; but they
Who journey hither find themselves alone
With a few sheep, with rocks and stones, and kites
That overhead are sailing in the sky.
It is in truth an utter solitude ;
Nor should I have made mention of this Dell
But for one object which you might pass by,
Might see and notice not.   Beside the brook
Appears a straggling heap of unhewn stones !
And to that place a story appertains,
Which, though it be ungarnished with events,
Is not unfit, I deem, for the fireside,
Or for the summer shade.   It was the first
Of those domestic tales that spake to me
Of Shepherds, dwellers in the valleys, men
Whom I already loved ;—not verily
For their own sakes, but for the fields and hills
Where was their occupation and abode.
And hence this tale, while I was yet a Boy
Careless of books, yet having felt the power
Of Nature, by the gentle agency
Of natural objects led me on to feel

For passions that were not my own, and think
(At random and imperfectly indeed)
On man, the heart of man, and human life.
Therefore, although it be a history
Homely and rude, I will relate the same
For the delight of a few natural hearts;
And, with yet fonder feeling, for the sake
Of youthful Poets, who among these Hills
Will be my second self when I am gone.

Upon the Forest-side in Grasmere Vale
There dwelt a Shepherd, Michael was his name;
An old man, stout of heart, and strong of limb.
His bodily frame had been from youth to age
Of an unusual strength: his mind was keen,
Intense, and frugal, apt for all affairs,
And in his Shepherd's calling he was prompt
And watchful more than ordinary men.
Hence had he learned the meaning of all winds,
Of blasts of every tone; and, oftentimes,
When others heeded not, He heard the South
Make subterraneous music, like the noise
Of Bagpipers on distant Highland hills.
The Shepherd, at such warning, of his flock
Bethought him, and he to himself would say,
"The winds are now devising work for me!"
And, truly, at all times, the storm—that drives
The traveller to a shelter—summoned him
Up to the mountains: he had been alone
Amid the heart of many thousand mists,
That came to him and left him on the heights.
So lived he till his eightieth year was past.
And grossly that man errs, who should suppose
That the green Valleys, and the Streams and Rocks,
Were things indifferent to the Shepherd's thoughts.

Fields, where with cheerful spirits he had breathed
The common air; the hills, which he so oft
Had climbed with vigorous steps; which had impressed
So many incidents upon his mind
Of hardship, skill or courage, joy or fear;
Which, like a book, preserved the memory
Of the dumb animals, whom he had saved,
Had fed or sheltered, linking to such acts,
The certainty of honourable gain,
Those fields, those hills—what could they less? had laid
Strong hold on his affections, were to him
A pleasurable feeling of blind love,
The pleasure which there is in life itself.

His days had not been passed in singleness.
His Helpmate was a comely Matron, old—
Though younger than himself full twenty years.
She was a woman of a stirring life,
Whose heart was in her house: two wheels she had
Of antique form, this large for spinning wool,
That small for flax; and if one wheel had rest,
It was because the other was at work.
The Pair had but one inmate in their house,
An only Child, who had been born to them
When Michael, telling o'er his years, began
To deem that he was old,—in Shepherd's phrase,
With one foot in the grave. This only Son
With two brave Sheep-dogs tried in many a storm,
The one of an inestimable worth,
Made all their household. I may truly say,
That they were as a proverb in the vale
For endless industry. When day was gone,
And from their occupations out of doors
The Son and Father were come home, even then
Their labour did not cease; unless when all

Turned to their cleanly supper-board, and there,
Each with a mess of pottage and skimmed milk,
Sat round their basket piled with oaten cakes,
And their plain home-made cheese. Yet when their meal
Was ended, LUKE (for so the Son was named)
And his old Father both betook themselves
To such convenient work as might employ
Their hands by the fireside ; perhaps to card
Wool for the Housewife's spindle, or repair
Some injury done to sickle, flail, or scythe,
Or other implement of house or field.

Down from the ceiling, by the chimney's edge,
That in our ancient uncouth country style
Did with a huge projection overbrow
Large space beneath, as duly as the light
Of day grew dim the Housewife hung a Lamp ;
An aged utensil, which had performed
Service beyond all others of its kind.
Early at evening did it burn and late,
Surviving comrade of uncounted Hours,
Which, going by from year to year, had found,
And left the couple neither gay perhaps
Nor cheerful, yet with objects and with hopes,
Living a life of eager industry.
And now, when LUKE had reached his eighteenth year
There by the light of this old lamp they sat,
Father and Son, while late into the night
The Housewife plied her own peculiar work,
Making the cottage through the silent hours
Murmur as with the sound of summer flies.
This Light was famous in its neighbourhood,
And was a public symbol of the life
That thrifty Pair had lived. For, as it chanced,
Their Cottage on a plot of rising ground

Stood single, with large prospect, North and South,
High into Easedale, up to Dunmail-Raise,
And westward to the village near the Lake ;
And from this constant light, so regular
And so far seen, the House itself, by all
Who dwelt within the limits of the vale,
Both old and young, was named THE EVENING STAR.

Thus living on through such a length of years,
The Shepherd, if he loved himself, must needs
Have loved his Helpmate ; but to Michael's heart
This Son of his old age was yet more dear—
Less from instinctive tenderness, the same
Blind spirit, which is in the blood of all—
Than that a child more than all other gifts,
Brings hope with it, and forward-looking thoughts,
And stirrings of inquietude, when they
By tendency of nature needs must fail.
Exceeding was the love he bare to him,
His Heart and his Heart's joy ! For oftentimes
Old Michael, while he was a babe in arms,
Had done him female service, not alone
For pastime and delight, as is the use
Of fathers, but with patient mind enforced
To acts of tenderness ; and he had rocked
His cradle with a woman's gentle hand.

And, in a later time, ere yet the Boy
Had put on boy's attire, did Michael love,
Albeit of a stern unbending mind,
To have the Young-one in his sight, when he
Had work by his own door, or when he sat
With sheep before him on his Shepherd's stool,
Beneath that large old Oak, which near their door
Stood,—and, from its enormous breadth of shade

Chosen for the shearer's covert from the sun,
Thence in our rustic dialect was called
The CLIPPING TREE,[1] a name which yet it bears.
There, while they two were sitting in the shade,
With others round them, earnest all and blithe,
Would Michael exercise his heart with looks
Of fond correction and reproof bestowed
Upon the Child, if he disturbed the sheep
By catching at their legs, or with his shouts
Scared them, while they lay still beneath the shears.

And when by Heaven's good grace the Boy grew up
A healthy lad, and carried in his cheek
Two steady roses that were five years old,
Then Michael from a winter coppice cut
With his own hand a sapling, which he hooped
With iron, making it throughout in all
Due requisites a perfect Shepherd's Staff,
And gave it to the Boy; wherewith equipt
He as a watchman oftentimes was placed
At gate or gap, to stem or turn the flock;
And, to his office prematurely called,
There stood the Urchin, as you will divine,
Something between a hinderance and a help;
And for this cause not always, I believe,
Receiving from his Father hire of praise;
Though nought was left undone which staff, or voice,
Or looks, or threatening gestures, could perform.

But soon as Luke, full ten years old, could stand
Against the mountain blasts; and to the heights,
Not fearing toil, nor length of weary ways,
He with his Father daily went, and they
Were as companions, why should I relate

---

[1] Clipping is the word used in the North of England for shearing.

That objects which the Shepherd loved before
Were dearer now? that from the Boy there came
Feelings and emanations—things which were
Light to the sun and music to the wind;
And that the Old Man's heart seemed born again?

Thus in his Father's sight the boy grew up:
And now, when he had reached his eighteenth year,
He was his comfort and his daily hope.

WHILE in this sort the simple Household lived
From day to day, to Michael's ear there came
Distressful tidings.   Long before the time
Of which I speak, the Shepherd had been bound
In surety for his Brother's Son, a man
Of an industrious life, and ample means,—
But unforeseen misfortunes suddenly
Had prest upon him,—and old Michael now
Was summoned to discharge the forfeiture,
A grievous penalty, but little less
Than half his substance.   This unlooked for claim,
At the first hearing, for a moment took
More hope out of his life than he supposed
That any old man ever could have lost.
As soon as he had gathered so much strength
That he could look his trouble in the face,
It seemed that his sole refuge was to sell
A portion of his patrimonial fields.
Such was his first resolve; he thought again,
And his heart failed him.   "Isabel," said he,
Two evenings after he had heard the news,
" I have been toiling more than seventy years,
And in the open sunshine of God's love
Have we all lived; yet if these fields of ours
Should pass into a stranger's hand, I think

That I could not lie quiet in my grave.
Our lot is a hard lot; the sun himself
Has scarcely been more diligent than I;
And I have lived to be a fool at last
To my own family. An evil Man
That was, and made an evil choice, if he
Were false to us; and if he were not false,
There are ten thousand to whom loss like this
Had been no sorrow. I forgive him—but
'Twere better to be dumb than to talk thus.
When I began, my purpose was to speak
Of remedies, and of a cheerful hope.
Our Luke shall leave us, Isabel; the land
Shall not go from us, and it shall be free;
He shall possess it, free as is the wind
That passes over it. We have, thou know'st,
Another Kinsman—he will be our friend
In this distress. He is a prosperous man,
'Thriving in trade—and Luke to him shall go,
And with his Kinsman's help and his own thrift
He quickly will repair this loss, and then
May come again to us. If here he stay,
What can be done? Where every one is poor,
What can be gained?" At this the Old Man paused,
And Isabel sat silent, for her mind
Was busy, looking back into past times.
There's Richard Bateman, thought she to herself,
He was a Parish-boy—at the Church-door
They made a gathering for him, shillings, pence,
And halfpennies, wherewith the neighbours bought
A basket, which they filled with pedlar's wares;
And, with this basket on his arm, the Lad
Went up to London, found a Master there,
Who, out of many, chose the trusty Boy
To go and overlook his merchandise

Beyond the seas : where he grew wondrous rich,
And left estates and monies to the poor,
And, at his birth-place, built a Chapel floored
With marble, which he sent from foreign lands.
These thoughts, and many others of like sort,
Passed quickly through the mind of Isabel,
And her face brightened. The Old Man was glad,
And thus resumed :—" Well, Isabel ! this scheme,
These two days, has been meat and drink to me.
Far more than we have lost is left us yet.
We have enough—I wish indeed that I
Were younger, but this hope is a good hope.
—Make ready Luke's best garments, of the best
Buy for him more, and let us send him forth
To-morrow, or the next day, or to-night :
—If he *could* go, the Boy should go to-night."
Here Michael ceased, and to the fields went forth
With a light heart. The Housewife for five days
Was restless morn and night, and all day long
Wrought on with her best fingers to prepare
Things needful for the journey of her son.
But Isabel was glad when Sunday came
To stop her in her work : for when she lay
By Michael's side, she through the two last nights
Heard him, how he was troubled in his sleep :
And when they rose at morning she could see
That all his hopes were gone. That day at noon
She said to Luke, while they two by themselves
Were sitting at the door, "Thou must not go :
We have no other Child but thee to lose,
None to remember—do not go away,
For if thou leave thy Father he will die."
The Youth made answer with a jocund voice ;
And Isabel, when she had told her fears,
Recovered heart. That evening her best fare

Did she bring forth, and all together sat
Like happy people round a Christmas fire.

With daylight Isabel resumed her work;
And all the ensuing week the house appeared
As cheerful as a grove in Spring: at length
The expected letter from their Kinsman came,
With kind assurances that he would do
His utmost for the welfare of the Boy;
To which, requests were added, that forthwith
He might be sent to him.   Ten times or more
The letter was read over; Isabel
Went forth to show it to the neighbours round;
Nor was there at that time on English land
A prouder heart than Luke's.   When Isabel
Had to her house returned, the Old Man said,
He shall depart to-morrow."   To this word
The Housewife answered, talking much of things
Which, if at such short notice he should go,
Would surely be forgotten.   But at length
She gave consent, and Michael was at ease.

Near the tumultuous brook of Green-head Ghyll,
In that deep Valley, Michael had designed
To build a Sheep-fold; and, before he heard
The tidings of his melancholy loss,
For this same purpose he had gathered up
A heap of stones, which by the Streamlet's edge
Lay thrown together, ready for the work.
With Luke that evening thitherward he walked;
And soon as they had reached the place he stopped
And thus the Old Man spake to him:—"My Son,
To-morrow thou wilt leave me: with full heart
I look upon thee, for thou art the same
That wert a promise to me ere thy birth,

And all thy life hast been my daily joy.
I will relate to thee some little part
Of our two histories ; 'twill do thee good
When thou art from me, even if I should speak
Of things thou canst not know of.——After thou
First camest into the world—as oft befalls
To new-born infants—thou didst sleep away
Two days, and blessings from thy Father's tongue
Then fell upon thee. Day by day passed on,
And still I loved thee with increasing love.
Never to living ear came sweeter sounds
Than when I heard thee by our own fireside
First uttering, without words, a natural tune ;
When thou, a feeding babe, didst in thy joy
Sing at thy Mother's breast. Month followed month,
And in the open fields my life was passed
And on the mountains ; else I think that thou
Hadst been brought up upon thy Father's knees.
But we were playmates, Luke : among these hills,
As well thou knowest, in us the old and young
Have played together, nor with me didst thou
Lack any pleasure which a boy can know."
Luke had a manly heart ; but at these words
He sobbed aloud. The Old Man grasped his hand,
And said, " Nay, do not take it so—I see
That these are things of which I need not speak.
—Even to the utmost I have been to thee
A kind and a good Father : and herein
I but repay a gift which I myself
Received at others' hands ; for, though now old
Beyond the common life of man, I still
Remember them who loved me in my youth.
Both of them sleep together : here they lived,
As all their Forefathers had done ; and when
At length their time was come, they were not loth

To give their bodies to the family mould.
I wished that thou shouldst live the life they lived.
But, 'tis a long time to look back, my Son,
And see so little gain from threescore years.
These fields were burthened when they came to me ;
Till I was forty years of age, not more
Than half of my inheritance was mine.
I toiled and toiled ; God blessed me in my work,
And till these three weeks past the land was free.
—It looks as if it never could endure
Another Master.   Heaven forgive me, Luke,
If I judge ill for thee, but it seems good
That thou shouldst go."   At this the Old Man paused ;
Then, pointing to the Stones near which they stood,
Thus, after a short silence, he resumed :
' This was a work for us ; and now, my Son,
It is a work for me.   But, lay one stone—
Here, lay it for me, Luke, with thine own hands,
Nay, Boy, be of good hope ;—we both may live
To see a better day.   At eighty-four
I still am strong and hale ;—do thou thy part ;
I will do mine.—I will begin again
With many tasks that were resigned to thee :
Up to the heights, and in among the storms,
Will I without thee go again, and do
All works which I was wont to do alone,
Before I knew thy face.—Heaven bless thee, Boy !
Thy heart these two weeks has been beating fast
With many hopes.—It should be so—Yes—yes—
I knew that thou couldst never have a wish
To leave me, Luke ; thou hast been bound to me
Only by links of love : when thou art gone
What will be left to us !—But, I forget
My purposes.   Lay now the corner-stone,
As I requested ; and hereafter, Luke,

When thou art gone away, should evil men
Be thy companions, think of me, my Son,
And of this moment ; hither turn thy thoughts,
And God will strengthen thee : amid all fear
And all temptation, Luke, I pray that thou
Mayst bear in mind the life thy Fathers lived,
Who, being innocent, did for that cause
Bestir them in good deeds.   Now, fare thee well—
When thou returnest, thou in this place wilt see
A work which is not here : a covenant
'Twill be between us——But, whatever fate
Befall thee, I shall love thee to the last,
And bear thy memory with me to the grave."

    The Shepherd ended here ; and Luke stooped down,
And, as his Father had requested, laid
The first stone of the Sheep-fold.   At the sight
The Old Man's grief broke from him ; to his heart
He pressèd his son, he kissèd him and wept ;
And to the house together they returned.
—Hushed was that House in peace, or seeming peace,
Ere the night fell :—with morrow's dawn the Boy
Began his journey, and when he had reached
The public way, he put on a bold face ;
And all the neighbours, as he passed their doors,
Came forth with wishes and with farewell prayers,
That followed him till he was out of sight.

    A good report did from their Kinsman come,
Of Luke and his well-doing : and the Boy
Wrote loving letters, full of wondrous news,
Which, as the Housewife phrased it, were throughout
" The prettiest letters that were ever seen."
Both parents read them with rejoicing hearts.
So, many months passed on : and once again

The Shepherd went about his daily work
With confident and cheerful thoughts ; and now
Sometimes when he could find a leisure hour
He to that valley took his way, and there
Wrought at the Sheep-fold.   Meantime Luke began
To slacken in his duty ; and, at length
He in the dissolute city gave himself
To evil courses : ignominy and shame
Fell on him; so that he was driven at last
To seek a hiding-place beyond the seas.

There is a comfort in the strength of love ;
'Twill make a thing endurable, which else
Would overset the brain, or break the heart :
I have conversed with more than one who well
Remember the Old Man, and what he was
Years after he had heard this heavy news.
His bodily frame had been from youth to age
Of an unusual strength.   Among the rocks
He went, and still looked up towards the sun,
And listened to the wind ; and, as before,
Performed all kinds of labour for his Sheep,
And for the land his small inheritance.
And to that hollow Dell from time to time
Did he repair, to build the Fold of which
His flock had need.   'Tis not forgotten yet
The pity which was then in every heart
For the Old Man—and 'tis believed by all
That many and many a day he thither went,
And never lifted up a single stone.

There, by the Sheep-fold, sometimes was he seen
Sitting alone, with that his faithful Dog,
Then old, beside him, lying at his feet.
The length of full seven years, from time to time,

He at the building of this sheep-fold wrought,
And left the work unfinished when he died.
Three years, or little more, did Isabel
Survive her Husband : at her death the estate
Was sold, and went into a stranger's hand.
The Cottage which was named the EVENING STAR
Is gone—the ploughshare has been through the ground
On which it stood ; great changes have been wrought
In all the neighbourhood :—yet the Oak is left
That grew beside their door ; and the remains
Of the unfinished Sheep-fold may be seen
Beside the boisterous brook of Green-head Ghyll.

MARGARET.

'TWAS summer, and the sun had mounted high :
Southward the landscape indistinctly glared
Through a pale steam ; but all the northern downs,
In clearest air ascending, showed far off
A surface dappled o'er with shadows flung
From brooding clouds ; shadows that lay in spots
Determined and unmoved, with steady beams
Of bright and pleasant sunshine interposed ;
Pleasant to him who on the soft cool moss
Extends his careless limbs along the front
Of some huge cave, whose rocky ceiling casts
A twilight of its own, an ample shade,
Where the Wren warbles ; while the dreaming Man
Half conscious of the soothing melody,
With side-long eye looks out upon the scene,
By power of that impending covert thrown
To finer distance.   Other lot was mine ;
Yet with good hope that soon I should obtain
As grateful resting-place, and livelier joy.
Across a bare wide common I was toiling
With languid steps that by the slippery ground
Were baffled ; nor could my weak arm disperse
The host of insects gathering round my face,
And ever with me as I paced along.

Upon that open level stood a Grove,
The wished-for port to which my course was bound.
Thither I came, and there, amid the gloom
Spread by a brotherhood of lofty elms,
Appeared a roofless Hut ; four naked walls

That stared upon each other! I looked round,
And to my wish and to my hope espied
Him whom I sought; a Man of reverend age,
But stout and hale, for travel unimpaired.
There was he seen upon the Cottage bench,
Recumbent in the shade, as if asleep;
An iron-pointed staff lay at his side.

Unnoticed did I stand, some minutes' space.
At length I hailed him, seeing that his hat
Was moist with water-drops, as if the brim
Had newly scooped a running stream. He rose,
And ere our lively greeting into peace
Had settled "'Tis," said I, "a burning day:
My lips are parched with thirst, but you, it seems,
Have somewhere found relief." He, at the word,
Pointing towards a sweet-brier, bade me climb
The fence where that aspiring shrub looked out
Upon the public way. It was a plot
Of garden ground run wild, its matted weeds
Marked with the steps of those, whom, as they passed,
The gooseberry trees that shot in long lank slips,
Or currants, hanging from their leafless stems
In scanty strings, had tempted to o'erleap
The broken wall. I looked around, and there,
Where two tall hedge-rows of thick alder boughs
Joined in a cold damp nook, espied a Well
Shrouded with willow-flowers and plumy fern.
My thirst I slaked, and from the cheerless spot
Withdrawing, straightway to the shade returned
Where sate the Old Man on the Cottage bench;
And, while, beside him, with uncovered head,
I yet was standing, freely to respire,
And cool my temples in the fanning air,
Thus did he speak. "I see around me here

E

Things which you cannot see : we die, my Friend,
Nor we alone, but that which each man loved
And prized in his peculiar nook of earth
Dies with him, or is changed ; and very soon
Even of the good is no memorial left.
—The Poets, in their elegies and songs
Lamenting the departed, call the groves,
They call upon the hills and streams to mourn,
And senseless rocks ; nor idly ; for they speak,
In these their invocations, with a voice
Obedient to the strong creative power
Of human passion.   Sympathies there are
More tranquil, yet perhaps of kindred birth,
That steal upon the meditative mind,
And grow with thought.   Beside yon Spring I stood,
And eyed its waters till we seemed to feel
One sadness, they and I.   For them a bond
Of brotherhood is broken : time has been
When, every day, the touch of human hand
Dislodged the natural sleep that binds them up
In mortal stillness ; and they ministered
To human comfort.   Stooping down to drink,
Upon the slimy foot-stone I espied
The useless fragment of a wooden bowl,
Green with the moss of years, and subject only
To the soft handling of the Elements :
There let the relic lie—fond thought—vain words !
Forgive them ;—never—never did my steps
Approach this door but she who dwelt within
A daughter's welcome gave me, and I loved her
As my own child.   Oh, Sir ! the good die first,
And they whose hearts are dry as summer dust
Burn to the socket.   Many a passenger
Hath blessed poor Margaret for her gentle looks,
When she upheld the cool refreshment drawn

From that forsaken Spring : and no one came
But he was welcome ; no one went away
But that it seemed she loved him.   She is dead,
The light extinguished of her lonely Hut,
The Hut itself abandoned to decay,
And She forgotten in the quiet grave !

"I speak," continued he, "of One whose stock
Of virtues bloomed beneath this lowly roof.
She was a woman of a steady mind,
Tender and deep in her excess of love,
Not speaking much, pleased rather with the joy
Of her own thoughts : by some especial care
Her temper had been framed, as if to make
A being—who by adding love to peace
Might live on earth a life of happiness.
Her wedded Partner lacked not on his side
The humble worth that satisfied her heart :
Frugal, affectionate, sober, and withal
Keenly industrious.   She with pride would tell
That he was often seated at his loom,
In summer, ere the mower was abroad
Among the dewy grass,—in early spring,
Ere the last star had vanished.—They who passed
At evening, from behind the garden fence
Might hear his busy spade, which he would ply,
After his daily work, until the light
Had failed, and every leaf and flower were lost
In the dark hedges.   So their days were spent
In peace and comfort ; and a pretty Boy
Was their best hope,—next to the God in Heaven.

"Not twenty years ago, but you I think
Can scarcely bear it now in mind, there came
Two blighting seasons, when the fields were left

With half a harvest.   It pleased Heaven to add
A worse affliction in the plague of war;
This happy land was stricken to the heart !
A Wanderer then among the Cottages
I, with my freight of winter raiment, saw
The hardships of that season ; many rich
Sank down, as in a dream, among the poor ;
And of the poor did many cease to be,
And their place knew them not.   Meanwhile, abridged
Of daily comforts, gladly reconciled
To numerous self-denials, Margaret
Went struggling on through those calamitous years
With cheerful hope, until the second autumn,
When her life's Helpmate on a sick-bed lay,
Smitten with perilous fever.   In disease
He lingered long ; and when his strength returned,
He found the little he had stored, to meet
The hour of accident or crippling age,
Was all consumed.   A second Infant now
Was added to the troubles of a time
Laden, for them and all of their degree,
With care and sorrow ; shoals of artisans
From ill-requited labour turned adrift
Sought daily bread from public charity,
They, and their wives and children—happier far
Could they have lived as do the little birds
That peck along the hedge-rows, or the kite
That makes her dwelling on the mountain rocks .

   " A sad reverse it was for him who long
Had filled with plenty, and possessed in peace,
This lonely Cottage.   At his door he stood,
And whistled many a snatch of merry tunes
That had no mirth in them ; or with his knife
Carved uncouth figures on the heads of sticks—

Then, not less idly, sought, through every nook
In house or garden, any casual work
Of use or ornament ; and with a strange,
Amusing, yet uneasy novelty,
He blended, where he might, the various tasks
Of summer, autumn, winter, and of spring.
But this endured not ; his good humour soon
Became a weight in which no pleasure was :
And poverty brought on a petted mood
And a sore temper : day by day he drooped,
And he would leave his work—and to the Town,
Without an errand, would direct his steps,
Or wander here and there among the fields.
One while he would speak lightly of his Babes,
And with a cruel tongue : at other times
He tossed them with a false unnatural joy :
And 'twas a rueful thing to see the looks
Of the poor innocent children.   ' Every smile,'
Said Margaret to me, here beneath these trees,
' Made my heart bleed.'"

              At this the Wanderer paused ;
And, looking up to those enormous Elms,
He said, "'Tis now the hour of deepest noon.—
At this still season of repose and peace,
This hour when all things which are not at rest
Are cheerful ; while this multitude of flies
Is filling all the air with melody ;
Why should a tear be in an Old Man's eye ?
Why should we thus, with an untoward mind,
And in the weakness of humanity,
From natural wisdom turn our hearts away,
To natural comfort shut our eyes and ears,
And, feeding on disquiet, thus disturb
The calm of nature with our restless thoughts ?"

HE spake with somewhat of a solemn tone :
But, when he ended, there was in his face
Such easy cheerfulness, a look so mild,
That for a little time it stole away
All recollection, and that simple Tale
Passed from my mind like a forgotten sound.
A while on trivial things we held discourse,
To me soon tasteless.   In my own despite,
I thought of that poor Woman as of one
Whom I had known and loved.   He had rehearsed
Her homely tale with such familiar power,
With such an active countenance, an eye
So busy, that the things of which he spake
Seemed present ; and, attention now relaxed,
A heart-felt chillness crept along my veins.
I rose ; and, having left the breezy shade,
Stood drinking comfort from the warmer sun,
That had not cheered me long—ere, looking round
Upon that tranquil Ruin, I returned,
And begged of the Old Man that, for my sake,
He would resume his story.—
                              He replied,
" It were a wantonness, and would demand
Severe reproof, if we were men whose hearts
Could hold vain dalliance with the misery
Even of the dead ; contented thence to draw
A momentary pleasure, never marked
By reason, barren of all future good.
But we have known that there is often found
In mournful thoughts, and always might be found,
A power to virtue friendly ; were 't not so,
I am a dreamer among men, indeed
An idle dreamer ! 'Tis a common tale,
An ordinary sorrow of Man's life,
A tale of silent suffering, hardly clothed

In bodily form.—But without further bidding
I will proceed.

        " While thus it fared with them,
To whom this Cottage, till those hapless years,
Had been a blessed home, it was my chance
To travel in a country far remote ;
And when these lofty Elms once more appeared,
What pleasant expectations lured me on
O'er the flat Common !—With quick step I reached
The threshold, lifted with light hand the latch ;
But, when I entered, Margaret looked at me
A little while ; then turned her head away
Speechless,—and, sitting down upon a chair,
Wept bitterly.   I wist not what to do,
Nor how to speak to her.   Poor Wretch ! at last
She rose from off her seat, and then,—O Sir !
I cannot *tell* how she pronounced my name :—
With fervent love, and with a face of grief
Unutterably helpless, and a look
That seemed to cling upon me, she enquired
If I had seen her Husband.   As she spake
A strange surprise and fear came to my heart,
Nor had I power to answer ere she told
That he had disappeared—not two months gone.
He left his house : two wretched days had past,
And on the third, as wistfully she raised
Her head from off her pillow, to look forth,
Like one in trouble, for returning light,
Within her chamber-casement she espied
A folded paper, lying as if placed
To meet her waking eyes.   This tremblingly
She opened—found no writing, but beheld
Pieces of money carefully enclosed,
Silver and gold.—' I shuddered at the sight,'
Said Margaret, 'for I knew it was his hand

Which placed it there : and ere that day was ended,
That long and anxious day ! I learned from one
Sent hither by my Husband to impart
The heavy news,—that he had joined a Troop
Of Soldiers, going to a distant land.
—He left me thus—he could not gather heart
To take a farewell of me ; for he feared
That I should follow with my Babes, and sink
Beneath the misery of that wandering life.'

"This tale did Margaret tell with many tears :
And, when she ended, I had little power
To give her comfort, and was glad to take
Such words of hope from her own mouth as served
To cheer us both :—but long we had not talked
Ere we built up a pile of better thoughts,
And with a brighter eye she looked around
As if she had been shedding tears of joy.
We parted.—'Twas the time of early spring ;
I left her busy with her garden tools ;
And well remember, o'er that fence she look'd,
And, while I paced along the foot-way path,
Called out, and sent a blessing after me,
With tender cheerfulness ; and with a voice
That seemed the very sound of happy thoughts.

"I roved o'er many a hill and many a dale,
With my accustomed load ; in heat and cold,
Through many a wood, and many an open ground,
In sunshine and in shade, in wet and fair,
Drooping or blithe of heart, as might befal ;
My best companions now the driving winds,
And now the ' trotting brooks ' and whispering trees,
And now the music of my own sad steps,
With many a short-lived thought that passed between,

And disappeared.—I journeyed back this way,
When, in the warmth of Midsummer, the wheat
Was yellow ; and the soft and bladed grass,
Springing afresh, had o'er the hay-field spread
Its tender verdure. At the door arrived,
I found that she was absent. In the shade,
Where now we sit, I waited her return.
Her Cottage, then a cheerful object, wore
Its customary look,—only, it seemed,
The honeysuckle, crowding round the porch,
Hung down in heavier tufts : and that bright weed,
The yellow stone-crop, suffered to take root
Along the window's edge, profusely grew,
Blinding the lower panes. I turned aside,
And strolled into her garden. It appeared
To lag behind the season, and had lost
Its pride of neatness. Daisy-flowers and thrift
Had broken their trim lines, and straggled o'er
The paths they used to deck :—Carnations, once
Prized for surpassing beauty, and no less
For the peculiar pains they had required,
Declined their languid heads, wanting support.
The cumbrous bind-weed, with its wreaths and bells,
Had twined about her two small rows of pease,
And dragged them to the earth.—Ere this an hour
Was wasted.—Back I turned my restless steps ;
A stranger passed ; and, guessing whom I sought,
He said that she was used to ramble far.—
The sun was sinking in the west ; and now
I sate with sad impatience. From within
Her solitary Infant cried aloud ;
Then, like a blast that dies away self-stilled,
The voice was silent. From the bench I rose ;
But neither could divert nor soothe my thoughts.
The spot, though fair, was very desolate—

The longer I remained more desolate :
And, looking round me, now I first observed
The corner stones, on either side the porch,
With dull red stains discoloured, and stuck o'er
With tufts and hairs of wool, as if the sheep,
That fed upon the common, thither came
Familiarly : and found a couching-place
Even at her threshold.   Deeper shadows fell
From these tall elms ;—the Cottage-clock struck eight ;—
I turned, and saw her distant a few steps.
Her face was pale and thin—her figure, too,
Was changed.   As she unlocked the door, she said,
'It grieves me you have waited here so long,
But, in good truth, I've wandered much of late,
And, sometimes—to my shame I speak—have need
Of my best prayers to bring me back again.'
While on the board she spread our evening meal,
She told me—interrupting not the work
Which gave employment to her listless hands—
That she had parted with her elder Child ;
To a kind master on a distant farm
Now happily apprenticed.—'I perceive
You look at me, and you have cause ; to-day
I have been travelling far ; and many days
About the fields I wander, knowing this
Only, that what I seek I cannot find ;
And so I waste my time : for I am changed ;
And to myself,' said she, 'have done much wrong
And to this helpless Infant.   I have slept
Weeping, and weeping have I waked ; my tears
Have flowed as if my body were not such
As others are ; and I could never die.
But I am now in mind and in my heart
More easy ; and I hope,' said she, 'that God
Will give me patience to endure the things

Which I behold at home.'   It would have grieved
Your very soul to see her ; Sir, I feel
The story linger in my heart ; I fear
'Tis long and tedious : but my spirit clings
To that poor Woman : so familiarly
Do I perceive her manner, and her look,
And presence, and so deeply do I feel
Her goodness, that, not seldom, in my walks
A momentary trance comes over me ;
And to myself I seem to muse on One
By sorrow laid asleep ;—or borne away,
A human being destined to awake
To human life, or something very near
To human life, when he shall come again
For whom she suffered.   Yes, it would have grieved
Your very soul to see her : evermore
Her eyelids drooped, her eyes were downward cast ;
And, when she at her table gave me food,
She did not look at me.   Her voice was low,
Her body was subdued.   In every act
Pertaining to her house affairs, appeared
The careless stillness of a thinking mind
Self-occupied ; to which all outward things
Are like an idle matter.   Still she sighed,
But yet no motion of the breast was seen,
No heaving of the heart.   While by the fire
We sate together, sighs came on my ear,
I knew not how, and hardly whence they came.

" Ere my departure, to her care I gave,
For her son's use, some tokens of regard,
Which with a look of welcome she received ;
And I exhorted her to place her trust
In God's good love, and seek his help by prayer.
I took my staff, and when I kissed her babe

The tears stood in her eyes. I left her then
With the best hope and comfort I could give;
She thanked me for my wish;—but for my hope
Methought she did not thank me.

                              " I returned,
And took my rounds along this road again
Ere on its sunny bank the primrose flower
Peeped forth, to give an earnest of the Spring.
I found her sad and drooping; she had learned
No tidings of her Husband; if he lived,
She knew not that he lived; if he were dead,
She knew not he was dead.   She seemed the same
In person and appearance; but her house
Bespake a sleepy hand of negligence;
The floor was neither dry nor neat, the hearth
Was comfortless, and her small lot of books,
Which, in the Cottage window, heretofore
Had been piled up against the corner panes
In seemly order, now, with straggling leaves
Lay scattered here and there, open or shut,
As they had chanced to fall.   Her infant Babe
Had from its Mother caught the trick of grief,
And sighed among its playthings.   Once again
I turned towards the garden gate, and saw,
More plainly still, that poverty and grief
Were now come nearer to her: weeds defaced
The hardened soil, and knots of withered grass:
No ridges there appeared of clear black mould,
No winter greenness; of her herbs and flowers,
It seemed the better part were gnawed away
Or trampled into earth; a chain of straw,
Which had been twined about the slender stem
Of a young apple-tree, lay at its root,
The bark was nibbled round by truant sheep.
—Margaret stood near, her Infant in her arms,

And, noting that my eye was on the tree,
She said, 'I fear it will be dead and gone
Ere Robert come again.'   Towards the house
Together we returned ; and she enquired
If I had any hope :—but for her Babe
And for her little orphan Boy, she said,
She had no wish to live, that she must die
Of sorrow.   Yet I saw the idle loom
Still in its place ; his Sunday garments hung
Upon the self-same nail ; his very staff
Stood undisturbed behind the door.   And when,
In bleak December, I retraced this way,
She told me that her little Babe was dead,
And she was left alone.   She now, released
From her maternal cares, had taken up
The employment common through these wilds, and gained.
By spinning hemp, a pittance for herself :
And for this end had hired a neighbour's boy
To give her needful help.   That very time
Most willingly she put her work aside,
And walked with me along the miry road,
Heedless how far ; and in such piteous sort
That any heart had ached to hear her, begged
That, whereso'er I went, I still would ask
For him whom she had lost.   We parted then—
Our final parting ; for from that time forth
Did many seasons pass ere I returned
Into this tract again.

     " Nine tedious years ;
From their first separation, nine long years,
She lingered in unquiet widowhood ;
A Wife and Widow.   Needs must it have been
A sore heart-wasting !   I have heard, my Friend,
That in yon arbour oftentimes she sate
Alone, through half the vacant Sabbath day ;

And, if a dog passed by, she still would quit
The shade, and look abroad.   On this old bench
For hours she sate ; and evermore her eye
Was busy in the distance, shaping things
That made her heart beat quick.   You see that path,
Now faint,—the grass has crept o'er its grey line ;
There, to and fro, she paced through many a day
Of the warm summer, from a belt of hemp
That girt her waist, spinning the long drawn thread
With backward steps.   Yet ever as there passed
A man whose garments showed the soldier's red,
Or crippled mendicant in sailor's garb,
The little Child who sate to turn the wheel
Ceased from his task ; and she with faltering voice
Made many a fond enquiry ; and when they,
Whose presence gave no comfort, were gone by,
Her heart was still more sad.   And by yon gate,
That bars the traveller's road, she often stood,
And when a stranger Horseman came, the latch
Would lift, and in his face look wistfully :
Most happy, if, from ought discovered there
Of tender feeling, she might dare repeat
The same sad question.   Meanwhile her poor Hut
Sank to decay : for he was gone, whose hand,
At the first nipping of October frost,
Closed up each chink, and with fresh bands of straw
Chequered the green-grown thatch.   And so she lived
Through the long winter, reckless and alone ;
Until her house by frost, and thaw, and rain,
Was sapped ; and while she slept, the nightly damps
Did chill her breast ; and in the stormy day
Her tattered clothes were ruffled by the wind ;
Even at the side of her own fire.   Yet still
She loved this wretched spot, nor would for worlds
Have parted hence ; and still that length of road,

And this rude bench, one torturing hope endeared,
Fast rooted at her heart : and here, my Friend,
In sickness she remained ; and here she died,
Last human tenant of these ruined walls."
   The Old Man ceased : he saw that I was moved ;
From that low bench, rising instinctively
I turned aside in weakness, nor had power
To thank him for the tale which he had told.
I stood, and leaning o'er the garden wall,
Reviewed that Woman's sufferings ; and it seemed
To comfort me while with a brother's love
I blessed her—in the impotence of grief.
At length towards the Cottage I returned
Fondly,—and traced, with interest more mild,
That secret spirit of humanity
Which, mid the calm oblivious tendencies
Of nature, mid her plants, and weeds, and flowers,
And silent overgrowings still survived.
The Old Man, noting this, resumed, and said,
"My Friend ! enough to sorrow you have given,
The purposes of wisdom ask no more ;
Be wise and cheerful ; and no longer read
The forms of things with an unworthy eye.
She sleeps in the calm earth, and peace is here.
I well remember that those very plumes,
Those weeds, and the high spear-grass on that wall,
By mist and silent rain-drops silvered o'er,
As once I passed, did to my heart convey
So still an image of tranquillity,
So calm and still, and looked so beautiful
Amid the uneasy thoughts which filled my mind,
That what we feel of sorrow and despair
From ruin and from change, and all the grief
The passing shows of Being leave behind,
Appeared an idle dream, that could not live

Where meditation was. I turned away,
And walked along my road in happiness."

He ceased. Ere long the sun declining shot
A slant and mellow radiance, which began
To fall upon us, while, beneath the trees,
We sate on that low bench : and now we felt,
Admonished thus, the sweet hour coming on.
A linnet warbled from those lofty elms,
A thrush sang loud, and other melodies,
At distance heard, peopled the milder air.
The Old Man rose, and, with a sprightly mien
Of hopeful preparation, grasped his staff :
Together casting then a farewell look
Upon those silent walls, we left the shade ;
And, ere the stars were visible, had reached
A village Inn,—our evening resting-place.

LYRICAL POEMS

"MY HEART LEAPS UP."

My heart leaps up when I behold
    A Rainbow in the sky:
So was it when my life began;
So is it now I am a Man;
So be it when I shall grow old,
    Or let me die!
The Child is Father of the Man;
And I could wish my days to be
Bound each to each by natural piety.

TO A BUTTERFLY.

Stay near me—do not take thy flight!
A little longer stay in sight!
Much converse do I find in Thee,
Historian of my Infancy!
Float near me; do not yet depart!
Dead times revive in thee:
Thou bring'st, gay Creature as thou art!
A solemn image to my heart,
My Father's Family!

Oh! pleasant, pleasant were the days,
The time, when, in our childish plays,
My Sister Emmeline and I
Together chased the Butterfly!
A very hunter did I rush
Upon the prey :—with leaps and springs
I followed on from brake to bush ;
But she, God love her! feared to brush
The dust from off its wings.

THE SPARROW'S NEST.

BEHOLD, within the leafy shade,
Those bright blue eggs together laid !
On me the chance-discovered sight
Gleamed like a vision of delight.
I started—seeming to espy
The home and sheltered bed,
The Sparrow's dwelling, which, hard by
My Father's house, in wet or dry
My Sister Emmeline and I
    Together visited.
She looked at it as if she feared it ;
Still wishing, dreading, to be near it :
Such heart was in her, being then
A little Prattler among men.
The Blessing of my later years
Was with me when a Boy :
She gave me eyes, she gave me ears ;
And humble cares, and delicate fears ;
A heart, the fountain of sweet tears ;
    And love, and thought, and joy.

TO A BUTTERFLY.

I'VE watched you now a full half-hour,
Self-poised upon that yellow flower;
And, little Butterfly! indeed
I know not if you sleep or feed.
How motionless!—not frozen seas
More motionless! and then
What joy awaits you, when the breeze
Hath found you out among the trees,
And calls you forth again!

This plot of Orchard-ground is ours;
My trees they are, my Sister's flowers;
Here rest your wings when they are weary;
Here lodge as in a sanctuary!
Come often to us, fear no wrong;
Sit near us on the bough!
We'll talk of sunshine and of song;
And summer days, when we were young;
Sweet childish days, that were as long
As twenty days are now.

THE REDBREAST AND BUTTERFLY.

ART thou the Bird whom Man loves best,
The pious Bird with the scarlet breast,
          Our little English Robin;
The Bird that comes about our doors
When Autumn winds are sobbing?
Art thou the Peter of Norway boors?
          Their Thomas in Finland,
          And Russia far inland?
The Bird, who by some name or other
All men who know thee call their Brother,
The Darling of children and men?
Could Father Adam[1] open his eyes
And see this sight beneath the skies,
He'd wish to close them again.

If the Butterfly knew but his friend,
Hither his flight he would bend;
And find his way to me,
Under the branches of the tree:
In and out, he darts about;
Can this be the Bird, to man so good,
That, after their bewildering,
Covered with leaves the little children,
          So painfully in the wood?

---

[1] See Paradise Lost, Book XI., where Adam points out to Eve
the ominous sign of the Eagle chasing "two Birds of gayest plume,"
and the gentle Hart and Hind pursued by their enemy.

What ailed thee, Robin, that thou could'st pursue
     A beautiful Creature,
That is gentle by nature?
Beneath the summer sky
From flower to flower let him fly;
'Tis all that he wishes to do.
The cheerer Thou of our in-door sadness,
He is the friend of our summer gladness:
What hinders, then, that ye should be
Playmates in the sunny weather,
And fly about in the air together!
His beautiful bosom is drest,
In crimson as bright as thine own:
If thou would'st be happy in thy nest,
O pious Bird! whom man loves best,
Love him or leave him alone!

WRITTEN IN MARCH,

WHILE RESTING ON THE BRIDGE AT THE FOOT OF BROTHER'S WATER.

THE cock is crowing,
The stream is flowing,
The small birds twitter,
The lake doth glitter,
The green field sleeps in the sun;
The oldest and youngest
Are at work with the strongest;
The cattle are grazing,
Their heads never raising;
There are forty feeding like one!

Like an army defeated
The Snow hath retreated,
And now doth fare ill
On the top of the bare hill ;
The Ploughboy is whooping—anon—anon :
There's joy in the mountains ;
There's life in the fountains ;
Small clouds are sailing,
Blue sky prevailing ;
The rain is over and gone !

TO THE DAISY.

In youth from rock to rock I went.
From hill to hill in discontent
Of pleasure high and turbulent,
    Most pleased when most uneasy :
But now my own delights I make,—
My thirst at every rill can slake,
And gladly Nature's love partake
    Of thee, sweet Daisy !

Thee Winter in the garland wears
That thinly decks his few grey hairs ;
Spring parts the clouds with softest airs,
    That she may sun thee ;
Whole summer-fields are thine by right ;
And Autumn, melancholy wight !
Doth in thy crimson head delight
    When rains are on thee.

In shoals and bands, a morrice train.
Thou greet'st the traveller in the lane,
Pleased at his greeting thee again;
    Yet nothing daunted,
Nor grieved, if thou be set at nought :
And oft alone in nooks remote
We meet thee, like a pleasant thought,
    When such are wanted.

Be violets in their secret mews
The flowers the wanton Zephyrs choose;
Proud be the rose, with rains and dews
    Her head impearling.
Thou liv'st with less ambitious aim,
Yet hast not gone without thy fame;
Thou art indeed by many a claim
    The Poet's darling.

If to a rock from rains he fly,
Or, some bright day of April sky,
Imprisoned by hot sunshine lie
    Near the green holly,
And wearily at length should fare ;
He needs but look about, and there
Thou art !—a friend at hand, to scare
    His melancholy.

A hundred times, by rock or bower,
Ere thus I have lain crouched an hour,
Have I derived from thy sweet power
    Some apprehension ;

Some steady love ; some brief delight ;
Some memory that had taken flight ;
Some chime of fancy wrong or right ;
  Or stray invention.

If stately passions in me burn,
And one chance look to Thee should turn,
I drink out of an humbler urn
  A lowlier pleasure ;
The homely sympathy that heeds
The common life our nature breeds :
A wisdom fitted to the needs
  Of hearts at leisure.

Fresh smitten by the morning ray,
When thou art up, alert and gay,
Then, cheerful Flower ! my spirits play
  With kindred gladness :
And when, at dusk, by dews opprest
Thou sink'st, the image of thy rest
Hath often eased my pensive breast
  Of careful sadness.

And all day long I number yet,
All seasons through, another debt,
Which I, wherever thou art met,
  To thee am owing ;
An instinct call it, a blind sense ;
A happy, genial influence,
Coming one knows not how, nor whence,
  Nor whither going.

Child of the Year! that round dost run
Thy course, bold lover of the sun,
And cheerful when the day's begun
    As lark or leveret,
Thy long-lost praise[1] thou shalt regain;
Nor be less dear to future men
Than in old time;—thou not in vain
    Art Nature's favourite.

TO THE SAME.

BRIGHT flower, whose home is everywhere!
A Pilgrim bold in Nature's care,
And oft, the long year through, the heir
    Of joy or sorrow;
Methinks that there abides in thee
Some concord with humanity,
Given to no other flower I see
    The forest through!

And wherefore? Man is soon deprest;
A thoughtless Thing! who, once unblest,
Does little on his memory rest,
    Or on his reason;
But Thou would'st teach him how to find
A shelter under every wind,
A hope for times that are unkind
    And every season.

[1] See, in Chaucer and the elder Poets, the honours formerly paid
to this flower.

TO THE SMALL CELANDINE.[1]

PANSIES, Lilies, Kingcups, Daisies,
Let them live upon their praises ;
Long as there's a sun that sets,
Primroses will have their glory ;
Long as there are Violets,
They will have a place in story :
There's a flower that shall be mine,
'Tis the little Celandine.

Eyes of some men travel far
For the finding of a star ;
Up and down the heavens they go,
Men that keep a mighty rout !
I'm as great as they, I trow,
Since the day I found thee out,
Little flower !—I'll make a stir,
Like a great astronomer.

Modest, yet withal an Elf
Bold, and lavish of thyself ;
Since we needs must first have met
I have seen thee, high and low,
Thirty years or more, and yet
'Twas a face I did not know ;
Thou hast now, go where I may,
Fifty greetings in a day.

1 Common Pilewort.

Ere a leaf is on a bush,
In the time before the Thrush
Has a thought about her nest,
Thou wilt come with half a call,
Spreading out thy glossy breast
Like a careless prodigal ;
Telling tales about the sun,
When we've little warmth, or none.

Poets, vain men in their mood !
Travel with the multitude :
Never heed them ; I aver
That they all are wanton wooers ;
But the thrifty Cottager,
Who stirs little out of doors,
Joys to spy thee near her home ;
Spring is coming, Thou art come !

Comfort have thou of thy merit,
Kindly, unassuming Spirit !
Careless of thy neighbourhood,
Thou dost show thy pleasant face
On the moor, and in the wood,
In the lane—there's not a place,
Howsoever mean it be,
But 'tis good enough for thee.

Ill befall the yellow Flowers,
Children of the flaring hours !
Buttercups, that will be seen,
Whether we will see or no ;
Others, too, of lofty mien ;
They have done as worldlings do,
Taken praise that should be thine,
Little, humble Celandine !

Prophet of delight and mirth,
Scorned and slighted upon earth;
Herald of a mighty band,
Of a joyous train ensuing,
Singing at my heart's command,
In the lanes my thoughts pursuing,
I will sing, as doth behove,
Hymns in praise of what I love!

TO THE SAME FLOWER.

PLEASURES newly found are sweet
When they lie about our feet:
February last, my heart
First at sight of thee was glad;
All unheard of as thou art,
Thou must needs, I think, have had,
Celandine! and long ago,
Praise of which I nothing know.

I have not a doubt but he,
Whosoe'er the man might be,
Who the first with pointed rays
(Workman worthy to be sainted)
Set the Sign-board in a blaze,
When the risen sun he painted,
Took the fancy from a glance
At thy glittering countenance.

Soon as gentle breezes bring
News of winter's vanishing,
And the children build their bowers,
Sticking 'kerchief-plots of mould
All about with full-blown flowers,
Thick as sheep in shepherd's fold !
With the proudest thou art there,
Mantling in the tiny square.

Often have I sighed to measure
By myself a lonely pleasure,
Sighed to think, I read a book
Only read, perhaps, by me ;
Yet I long could overlook
Thy bright coronet and Thee,
And thy arch and wily ways,
And thy store of other praise.

Blithe of heart, from week to week
Thou dost play at hide-and-seek ;
While the patient Primrose sits
Like a beggar in the cold,
Thou, a Flower of wiser wits,
Slipp'st into thy sheltering hold ;
Bright as any of the train
When ye all are out again.

Thou art not beyond the moon,
But a thing " beneath our shoon ;"
Let the bold Adventurer thrid
In his bark the polar sea ;
Rear who will a pyramid ;
Praise it is enough for me,
If there be but three or four
Who will love my little Flower.

" I WANDERED LONELY AS A CLOUD. "

I WANDERED lonely as a Cloud
That floats on high o'er vales and hills,
When all at once I saw a crowd,
A host of golden Daffodils ;
Beside the Lake, beneath the trees,
Fluttering and dancing in the breeze.

Continuous as the stars that shine
And twinkle on the milky way,
They stretched in never-ending line
Along the margin of a bay :
Ten thousand saw I at a glance,
Tossing their heads in sprightly dance.

The waves beside them danced, but they
Out-did the sparkling waves in glee :—
A poet could not but be gay,
In such a jocund company ;
I gazed—and gazed—but little thought
What wealth the show to me had brought :

For oft, when on my couch I lie
In vacant or in pensive mood,
They flash upon that inward eye
Which is the bliss of solitude,
And then my heart with pleasure fills,
And dances with the Daffodils.

THE GREEN LINNET.

BENEATH these fruit-tree boughs that shed
Their snow-white blossoms on my head,
With brightest sunshine round me spread
    Of spring's unclouded weather,
In this sequestered nook how sweet
To sit upon my orchard-seat !
And birds and flowers once more to greet,
    My last year's friends together.

One have I marked, the happiest guest
In all this covert of the blest :
Hail to Thee, far above the rest
    In joy of voice and pinion !
Thou, Linnet ! in thy green array,
Presiding Spirit here to-day,
Dost lead the revels of the May ;
    And this is thy dominion.

While birds, and butterflies, and flowers,
Make all one band of paramours,
Thou, ranging up and down the bowers,
    Art sole in thy employment :
A Life, a Presence like the Air,
Scattering thy gladness without care
Too blest with any one to pair ;
    Thyself thy own enjoyment.

F

Amid yon tuft of hazel trees
That twinkle to the gusty breeze,
Behold him perched in ecstasies,
 Yet seeming still to hover;
There! where the flutter of his wings
Upon his back and body flings
Shadows and sunny glimmerings,
 That cover him all over.

My dazzled sight he oft deceives,
A brother of the dancing leaves;
Then flits, and from the cottage-eaves
 Pours forth his song in gushes;
As if by that exulting strain
He mocked and treated with disdain
The voiceless Form he chose to feign,
 While fluttering in the bushes.

TO A SKY-LARK.

Up with me! up with me into the clouds!
 For thy song, Lark, is strong;
Up with me, up with me into the clouds!
 Singing, singing,
With clouds and sky about thee ringing,
 Lift me, guide me till I find
That spot which seems so to thy mind!

I have walked through wildernesses dreary,
And to-day my heart is weary;
Had I now the wings of a Faery,
Up to thee would I fly.
There's madness about thee, and joy divine
In that song of thine;
Lift me, guide me high and high
To thy banqueting-place in the sky.

Joyous as morning,
Thou art laughing and scorning;
Thou hast a nest for thy love and thy rest,
And, though little troubled with sloth,
Drunken Lark! thou would'st be loth
To be such a traveller as I.
Happy, happy Liver,
With a soul as strong as a mountain River
Pouring out praise to the Almighty Giver,
        Joy and jollity be with us both!

Alas! my journey, rugged and uneven,
Through prickly moors or dusty ways must wind
But hearing thee, or others of thy kind,
As full of gladness and as free of heaven,
I, with my fate contented, will plod on,
And hope for higher raptures, when Life's day is done.

STRAY PLEASURES.

"—Pleasure is spread through the earth
In stray gifts to be claimed by whoever shall find."

By their floating Mill,
That lies dead and still,
Behold yon Prisoners three,
The Miller with two Dames, on the breast of the Thames !
The Platform is small, but gives room for them all ;
And they're dancing merrily.

From the shore come the notes
To their Mill where it floats,
To their House and their Mill tethered fast ;
To the small wooden Isle where, their work to beguile,
They from morning to even take whatever is given ;—
And many a blithe day they have past.

In sight of the Spires,
All alive with the fires
Of the Sun going down to his rest,
In the broad open eye of the solitary sky,
They dance,—there are three, as jocund as free,
While they dance on the calm river's breast.

Man and Maidens wheel,
They themselves make the Reel,
And their Music's a prey which they seize ;
It plays not for them,—what matter ? 'tis theirs ;
And if they had care, it has scattered their cares,
While they dance, crying, " Long as ye please ! "

They dance not for me,
    Yet mine is their glee !
Thus pleasure is spread through the earth
In stray gifts to be claimed by whoever shall find ;
Thus a rich loving-kindness, redundantly kind,
Moves all nature to gladness and mirth.

The Showers of the Spring
    Rouse the Birds, and they sing ;
If the Wind do but stir for his proper delight,
Each Leaf, that and this, his neighbour will kiss ;
Each Wave, one and t'other, speeds after his brother ;
They are happy, for that is their right !

TO MY SISTER.

WRITTEN AT A SMALL DISTANCE FROM MY HOUSE, AND
SENT BY MY LITTLE BOY.

It is the first mild day of March :
Each minute sweeter than before,
The Redbreast sings from the tall Larch
That stands beside our door.

There is a blessing in the air,
Which seems a sense of joy to yield
To the bare trees, and mountains bare,
And grass in the green field.

My Sister ! ('tis a wish of mine)
Now that our morning meal is done,
Make haste, your morning task resign ;
Come forth and feel the sun.

Edward will come with you ;—and, pray,
Put on with speed your woodland dress ;
And bring no book : for this one day
We'll give to idleness.

No joyless forms shall regulate
Our living Calendar :
We from to-day, my Friend, will date
The opening of the year.

Love, now an universal birth,
From heart to heart is stealing,
From earth to man, from man to earth :
– ·It is the hour of feeling.

One moment now may give us more
Than fifty years of reason :
Our minds shall drink at every pore
The spirit of the season.

Some silent laws our hearts will make,
Which they shall long obey :
We for the year to come may take
Our temper from to-day.

And from the blessed power that rolls
About, below, above,
We'll frame the measure of our souls :
They shall be tuned to love.

Then come, my Sister ! come, I pray,
With speed put on your woodland dress ;
—And bring no book : for this one day
We'll give to idleness.

LINES

WRITTEN IN EARLY SPRING.

I HEARD a thousand blended notes,
While in a grove I sate reclined,
In that sweet mood when pleasant thoughts
Bring sad thoughts to the mind.

To her fair works did Nature link
The human soul that through me ran;
And much it grieved my heart to think
What man has made of man.

Through primrose tufts, in that sweet bower,
The periwinkle trailed its wreaths;
And 'tis my faith that every flower
Enjoys the air it breathes.

The birds around me hopped and played;
Their thoughts I cannot measure:—
But the least motion that they made,
It seemed a thrill of pleasure.

The budding twigs spread out their fan,
To catch the breezy air;
And I must think, do all I can,
That there was pleasure there.

From Heaven if this belief be sent,
If such be Nature's holy plan,
Have I not reason to lament
What man has made of man?

EXPOSTULATION AND REPLY.

" WHY, William, on that old grey stone,
    Thus for the length of half a day,
    Why, William, sit you thus alone,
    And dream your time away ?

" Where are your books ?—that light bequeathed
    To beings else forlorn and blind !
    Up ! up ! and drink the spirit breathed
    From dead men to their kind.

" You look round on your mother Earth,
    As if she for no purpose bore you ;
    As if you were her first-born birth,
    And none had lived before you !"

One morning thus, by Esthwaite lake,
    When life was sweet, I knew not why,
    To me my good friend Matthew spake,
    And thus I made reply :

" The eye—it cannot choose but see ;
    We cannot bid the ear be still ;
    Our bodies feel, where'er they be,
    Against, or with our will.

" Nor less I deem that there are Powers
    Which of themselves our minds impress ;
    That we can feed this mind of ours
    In a wise passiveness.

" Think you, 'mid all this mighty sum
    Of things for ever speaking,
That nothing of itself will come,
    But we must still be seeking?

" — Then ask not wherefore, here, alone,
    Conversing as I may,
I sit upon this old grey stone,
    And dream my time away."

THE TABLES TURNED;

AN EVENING SCENE ON THE SAME SUBJECT.

Up! up! my Friend, and quit your books;
    Or surely you'll grow double:
Up! up! my Friend, and clear your looks;
    Why all this toil and trouble?

The sun, above the mountain's head,
    A freshening lustre mellow
Through all the long green fields has spread,
    His first sweet evening yellow.

Books! 'tis a dull and endless strife:
    Come, hear the woodland Linnet,
How sweet his music! on my life,
    There's more of wisdom in it.

And hark ! how blithe the Throstle sings !
He, too, is no mean preacher :
Come forth into the light of things,
Let Nature be your teacher.

She has a world of ready wealth,
Our minds and hearts to bless—
Spontaneous wisdom breathed by health,
Truth breathed by cheerfulness.

One impulse from a vernal wood
May teach you more of man,
Of moral evil and of good,
Than all the sages can.

Sweet is the lore which Nature brings ;
Our meddling intellect
Mis-shapes the beauteous forms of things :
—We murder to dissect.

Enough of Science and of Art ;
Close up these barren leaves :
Come forth, and bring with you a heart
That watches and receives.

TO A YOUNG LADY,

WHO HAD BEEN REPROACHED FOR TAKING LONG WALKS IN THE COUNTRY.

DEAR Child of Nature, let them rail !
·—There is a nest in a green dale,
A harbour and a hold ;
Where thou, a Wife and Friend, shalt see
Thy own delightful days, and be
A light to young and old.

There, healthy as a Shepherd-boy,
And treading among flowers of joy
Which at no season fade,
Thou, while thy Babes around thee cling,
Shalt show us how divine a thing
A Woman may be made.

Thy thoughts and feelings shall not die,
Nor leave thee, when grey hairs are nigh,
A melancholy slave ;
But an old age serene and bright,
And lovely as a Lapland night,
Shall lead thee to thy grave.

To HARTLEY COLERIDGE,

SIX YEARS OLD.

O THOU ! whose fancies from afar are brought ;
Who of thy words dost make a mock apparel,
And fittest to unutterable thought
The breeze-like motion and the self-born carol ;
Thou faery Voyager ! that dost float
In such clear water, that thy boat
May rather seem
To brood on air than on an earthly stream ;
Suspended in a stream as clear as sky,
Where earth and heaven do make one imagery ;
O blessed Vision ! happy Child !
That art so exquisitely wild,
I think of thee with many fears
For what may be thy lot in future years.

I thought of times when Pain might be thy guest,
Lord of thy house and hospitality ;
And Grief, uneasy Lover ! never rest
But when she sate within the touch of thee.
O too industrious folly !
O vain and causeless melancholy !
Nature will either end thee quite ;
Or, lengthening out thy season of delight,
Preserve for thee, by individual right,
A young Lamb's heart among the full-grown flocks.
What hast Thou to do with sorrow,
Or the injuries of to-morrow ?

Thou art a Dew-drop, which the morn brings forth,
Ill fitted to sustain unkindly shocks ;
Or to be trailed along the soiling earth ;
A gem that glitters while it lives,
And no forewarning gives ;
But, at the touch of wrong, without a strife
Slips in a moment out of life.

"O NIGHTINGALE, THOU SURELY ART."

O NIGHTINGALE ! thou surely art
A Creature of a fiery heart ;—
These notes of thine—they pierce and pierce ;
Tumultuous harmony and fierce !
Thou sing'st as if the God of wine
Had helped thee to a Valentine ;
A song in mockery and despite
Of shades, and dews, and silent night ;
And steady bliss, and all the loves
Now sleeping in these peaceful groves.

I heard a Stock-dove sing or say
His homely tale, this very day ;
His voice was buried among trees,
Yet to be come at by the breeze :
He did not cease ; but cooed—and cooed ;
And somewhat pensively he wooed :
He sang of love, with quiet blending,
Slow to begin, and never ending ;
Of serious faith, and inward glee ;
That was the Song—the Song for me !

"STRANGE FITS OF PASSION HAVE I KNOWN."

STRANGE fits of passion have I known :
And I will dare to tell,
But in the Lover's ear alone,
What once to me befel.

When she I loved was strong and gay,
And like a rose in June,
I to her cottage bent my way,
Beneath the evening Moon.

Upon the Moon I fixed my eye,
All over the wide lea ;
My Horse trudged on—and we drew nigh
Those paths so dear to me.

And now we reached the orchard plot ;
And, as we climbed the hill,
Towards the roof of Lucy's cot
The Moon descended still.

In one of those sweet dreams I slept,
Kind Nature's gentlest boon !
And all the while my eyes I kept
On the descending Moon.

My Horse moved on ; hoof after hoof
He raised, and never stopped :
When down behind the cottage roof,
At once, the bright Moon dropped.

What fond and wayward thoughts will slide
Into a Lover's head !—
"O mercy !" to myself I cried,
"If Lucy should be dead !"

"THREE YEARS SHE GREW."

THREE years she grew in sun and shower,
Then Nature said, " A lovelier flower
On earth was never sown ;
This Child I to myself will take ;
She shall be mine, and I will make
A Lady of my own.

" Myself will to my darling be
Both law and impulse : and with me
The Girl, in rock and plain,
In earth and heaven, in glade and bower,
Shall feel an overseeing power
To kindle or restrain.

" She shall be sportive as the Fawn
That wild with glee across the lawn
Or up the mountain springs ;
And hers shall be the breathing balm,
And hers the silence and the calm
Of mute insensate things.

" The floating Clouds their state shall lend
To her ; for her the willow bend ;
Nor shall she fail to see
Even in the motions of the Storm
Grace that shall mould the Maiden's form
By silent sympathy.

" The Stars of midnight shall be dear
To her ; and she shall lean her ear
In many a secret place
Where Rivulets dance their wayward round,
And beauty born of murmuring sound
Shall pass into her face.

" And vital feelings of delight
    Shall rear her form to stately height,
        Her virgin bosom swell ;
    Such thoughts to Lucy I will give
    While she and I together live
        Here in this happy Dell."

Thus Nature spake—The work was done—
How soon my Lucy's race was run !
    She died, and left to me
This heath, this calm and quiet scene ;
    The memory of what has been,
    And never more will be.

"SHE DWELT AMONG THE UNTRODDEN WAYS."

SHE dwelt among the untrodden ways
    Beside the springs of Dove,
A Maid whom there were none to praise
    And very few to love :

A Violet by a mossy stone
    Half hidden from the eye !
—Fair as a star, when only one
    Is shining in the sky.

She lived unknown, and few could know
    When Lucy ceased to be ;
But she is in her grave, and, oh,
    The difference to me !

"A SLUMBER DID MY SPIRIT SEAL."

A SLUMBER did my spirit seal ;
    I had no human fears :
She seemed a thing that could not feel
    The touch of earthly years.

No motion has she now, no force ;
    She neither hears nor sees,
Rolled round in earth's diurnal course,
    With rocks, and stones, and trees.

"I TRAVELLED AMONG UNKNOWN MEN."

I TRAVELLED among unknown men,
    In lands beyond the sea ;
Nor, England ! did I know till then
    What love I bore to thee.

'Tis past, that melancholy dream !
    Nor will I quit thy shore
A second time ; for still I seem
    To love thee more and more.

Among thy mountains did I feel
    The joy of my desire ;
And she I cherished turned her wheel
    Beside an English fire.

Thy mornings showed, thy nights concealed
    The bowers where Lucy played ;
And thine is too the last green field
    That Lucy's eyes surveyed.

TO THE CUCKOO.

O BLITHE New-comer! I have heard,
I hear thee and rejoice.
O Cuckoo! shall I call thee Bird,
Or but a wandering Voice?

While I am lying on the grass
Thy twofold shout I hear;
From hill to hill it seems to pass,
At once far off and near.

Though babbling only, to the Vale,
Of sunshine and of flowers,
Thou bringest unto me a tale
Of visionary hours.

Thrice welcome, darling of the Spring!
Even yet thou art to me
No Bird: but an invisible Thing,
A voice, a mystery;

The same whom in my School-boy days
I listened to; that Cry
Which made me look a thousand ways
In bush, and tree, and sky.

To seek thee did I often rove
Through woods and on the green;
And thou wert still a hope, a love;
Still longed for, never seen.

And I can listen to thee yet ;
Can lie upon the plain
And listen, till I do beget
That golden time again.

O blessed Bird ! the earth we pace
Again appears to be
An unsubstantial, faery place ;
That is fit home for Thee !

THE CUCKOO AGAIN.

Yes, it was the mountain Echo,
Solitary, clear, profound,
Answering to the shouting Cuckoo,
Giving to her sound for sound !

Unsolicited reply
To a babbling wanderer sent ;
Like her ordinary cry,
Like—but oh, how different !

Hears not also mortal life ?
Hear not we, unthinking creatures !
Slaves of folly, love, or strife—
Voices of two different natures ?

Have not *we* too ?—yes, we have
Answers, and we know not whence ;
Echoes from beyond the grave,
Recognised intelligence !

Often as thy inward ear
Catches such rebounds, beware !—
Listen, ponder, hold them dear ;
For of God,—of God they are.

TO A SKYLARK.

ETHEREAL Minstrel ! Pilgrim of the sky !
Dost thou despise the earth where cares abound ?
Or, while the wings aspire, are heart and eye
Both with thy nest upon the dewy ground ?
Thy nest which thou canst drop into at will,
Those quivering wings composed, that music still !

To the last point of vision, and beyond,
Mount, daring Warbler ! that love-prompted strain,
('Twixt thee and thine a never-failing bond)
Thrills not the less the bosom of the plain :
Yet might'st thou seem, proud privilege ! to sing
All independent of the leafy spring.

Leave to the Nightingale her shady wood ;
A privacy of glorious light is thine ;
Whence thou dost pour upon the world a flood
Of harmony, with instinct more divine ;
Type of the wise who soar, but never roam ;
True to the kindred points of Heaven and Home !

"SHE WAS A PHANTOM OF DELIGHT.

SHE was a Phantom of delight
When first she gleamed upon my sight ;
A lovely Apparition, sent
To be a moment's ornament ;
Her eyes as stars of Twilight fair ;
Like Twilight's, too, her dusky hair ;
But all things else about her drawn
From May-time and the cheerful Dawn ;
A dancing Shape, an Image gay,
To haunt, to startle, and waylay.

I saw her upon nearer view,
A Spirit, yet a Woman too !
Her household motions light and free,
And steps of virgin liberty ;
A countenance in which did meet
Sweet records, promises as sweet ;
A Creature not too bright or good
For human nature's daily food ;
For transient sorrows, simple wiles,
Praise, blame, love, kisses, tears, and smiles.

And now I see with eye serene
The very pulse of the machine ;
A Being breathing thoughtful breath,
A Traveller between life and death ;
The reason firm, the temperate will,
Endurance, foresight, strength, and skill ;
A perfect Woman, nobly planned,
To warn, to comfort, and command ;
And yet a Spirit still, and bright
With something of an angel light.

TO A HIGHLAND GIRL.

(AT INVERSNEYDE, UPON LOCH LOMOND.)

SWEET Highland Girl, a very shower
Of beauty is thy earthly dower !
Twice seven consenting years have shed
Their utmost bounty on thy head :
And these grey Rocks ; this household Lawn ·
These Trees, a veil just half withdrawn ;
This fall of water, that doth make
A murmur near the silent Lake ;
This little Bay, a quiet road
That holds in shelter thy abode ;

In truth together do ye seem
Like something fashioned in a dream ;
Such forms as from their covert peep
When earthly cares are laid asleep !
Yet, dream and vision as thou art,
I bless thee with a human heart :
God shield thee to thy latest years !
Thee neither know I nor thy peers ;
And yet my eyes are filled with tears

With earnest feeling I shall pray
For thee when I am far away :
For never saw I mien, or face,
In which more plainly I could trace
Benignity and home-bred sense
Ripening in perfect innocence.
Here scattered like a random seed,
Remote from men, Thou dost not need

The embarrassed look of shy distress,
And maidenly shamefacedness :
Thou wear'st upon thy forehead clear
The freedom of a Mountaineer :
A face with gladness overspread !
Soft smiles, by human kindness bred !
And seemliness complete, that sways
Thy courtesies, about thee plays ;
With no restraint, but such as springs
From quick and eager visitings
Of thoughts that lie beyond the reach
Of thy few words of English speech :
A bondage sweetly brooked, a strife
That gives thy gestures grace and life !
So have I, not unmoved in mind,
Seen birds of tempest-loving kind,
Thus beating up against the wind.

What hand but would a garland cull
For thee who art so beautiful ?
O happy pleasure ! here to dwell
Beside thee in some heathy dell ;
Adopt your homely ways, and dress,
A Shepherd, thou a Shepherdess !
But I could frame a wish for thee
More like a grave reality :
Thou art to me but as a wave
Of the wild sea : and I would have
Some claim upon thee, if I could,
Though but of common neighbourhood.
What joy to hear thee, and to see !
Thy elder Brother I would be,
Thy Father, any thing to thee !

Now thanks to Heaven ! that of its grace
Hath led me to this lonely place.
Joy have I had ; and going hence
I bear away my recompence.
In spots like these it is we prize
Our Memory, feel that she hath eyes :
Then, why should I be loth to stir ?
I feel this place was made for her ;
To give new pleasure like the past,
Continued long as life shall last.
Nor am I loth, though pleased at heart,
Sweet Highland Girl ! from Thee to part ;
For I, methinks, till I grow old,
As fair before me shall behold,
As I do now, the Cabin small,
The Lake, the Bay, the Waterfall ;
And Thee, the Spirit of them all !

STEPPING WESTWARD.

While my Fellow-traveller and I were walking by the side of Loch
    Katrine, one fine evening after sunset, in our road to a Hut
    where in the course of our Tour we had been hospitably enter-
    tained some weeks before, we met, in one of the loneliest parts
    of that solitary region, two well-dressed Women, one of whom
    said to us, by way of greeting, "What, you are stepping west-
    ward?"

" *What, you are stepping westward?*"—" *Yea.*"
    —'Twould be a *wildish* destiny,
    If we, who thus together roam
    In a strange land, and far from home,
    Were in this place the guests of Chance :
    Yet who would stop, or fear to advance,
    Though home or shelter he had none,
    With such a Sky to lead him on ?

The dewy ground was dark and cold ;
    Behind, all gloomy to behold ;
    And stepping westward seemed to be
    A kind of *heavenly* destiny :
    I liked the greeting ; 'twas a sound
    Of something without place or bound ;
    And seemed to give me spiritual right
    To travel through that region bright.

The voice was soft, and she who spake
    Was walking by her native Lake :
    The salutation had to me
    The very sound of courtesy :
    Its power was felt ; and while my eye
    Was fixed upon the glowing sky,
    The echo of the voice enwrought
    A human sweetness with the thought
    Of travelling through the world that lay
    Before me in my endless way.

THE SOLITARY REAPER.

BEHOLD her, single in the field,
Yon solitary Highland Lass !
Reaping and singing by herself;
Stop here, or gently pass !
Alone she cuts, and binds the grain,
And sings a melancholy strain ;
O listen ! for the Vale profound
Is overflowing with the sound.

No Nightingale did ever chant
So sweetly to reposing bands
Of Travellers in some shady haunt,
Among Arabian sands :
A voice so thrilling ne'er was heard
In spring-time from the Cuckoo-bird,
Breaking the silence of the seas
Among the farthest Hebrides.

Will no one tell me what she sings ?
Perhaps the plaintive numbers flow
For old, unhappy, far-off things,
And battles long ago :
Or is it some more humble lay,
Familiar matter of to-day ?
Some natural sorrow, loss, or pain,
That has been, and may be again !

Whate'er the theme, the Maiden sang
As if her song could have no ending ;
I saw her singing at her work,
And o'er the sickle bending ;—
I listened till I had my fill,
And when I mounted up the hill,
The music in my heart I bore,
Long after it was heard no more.

AT THE GRAVE OF BURNS,

1803.

SEVEN YEARS AFTER HIS DEATH.

I SHIVER, Spirit fierce and bold,
At thought of what I now behold :
As vapours breathed from dungeons cold
  Strike pleasure dead,
So sadness comes from out the mould
  Where Burns is laid.

And have I then thy bones so near,
And thou forbidden to appear ?
As if it were thyself that's here
  I shrink with pain ;
And both my wishes and my fear
  Alike are vain.

Off weight—nor press on weight !—away
Dark thoughts !—they came, but not to stay ;
With chastened feelings would I pay
  The tribute due
To him, and aught that hides his clay
  From mortal view.

Fresh as the flower, whose modest worth
He sang, his genius "glinted" forth,
Rose like a star that touching earth,
  For so it seems,
Doth glorify its humble birth
  With matchless beams.

The piercing eye, the thoughtful brow,
The struggling heart, where be they now?--
Full soon the Aspirant of the plough,
    The prompt, the brave,
Slept, with the obscurest, in the low
    And silent grave.

'Well might I mourn that He was gone,
Whose light I hail'd when first it shone
When, breaking forth as nature's own,
    It showed my youth
How Verse may build a princely throne
    On humble truth.

Alas! where'er the current tends,
Regret pursues and with it blends,--
Huge Criffel's hoary top ascends
    By Skiddaw seen,--
Neighbours we were, and loving friends
    We might have been:

True friends though diversely inclined;
But heart with heart and mind with mind,
Where the main fibres are entwined,
    Through Nature's skill,
May even by contraries be joined
    More closely still.

The tear will start, and let it flow;
Thou "poor Inhabitant below,"
At this dread moment—even so—
    Might we together
Have sate and talked where gowans blow,
    Or on wild heather.

What treasures would have then been placed
Within my reach ; of knowledge graced
By fancy what a rich repast !
        But why go on ?—
Oh ! spare to sweep, thou mournful blast,
        His grave grass-grown.

There, too, a Son, his joy and pride,
(Not three weeks past the Stripling died,)
Lies gathered to his Father's side,
        Soul-moving sight !
Yet one to which is not denied
        Some sad delight.

For *he* is safe, a quiet bed
Hath early found among the dead,
Harboured where none can be misled,
        Wronged, or distrest ;
And surely here it may be said
        That such are blest.

And oh for Thee, by pitying grace
Checked oft-times in a devious race,
May He, who halloweth the place
        Where Man is laid,
Receive thy Spirit in the embrace
        For which it prayed !

Sighing I turned away ; but ere
Night fell, I heard, or seemed to hear,
Music that sorrow comes not near,
        A ritual hymn,
Chaunted in love that casts out fear
        By Seraphim.

THOUGHTS

SUGGESTED THE DAY FOLLOWING, ON THE BANKS OF
NITH, NEAR THE POET'S RESIDENCE.

Too frail to keep the lofty vow
That must have followed when his brow
Was wreathed—"The Vision" tells us how—
    With holly spray,
He faultered, drifted to and fro,
    And passed away.

Well might such thoughts, dear Sister, throng
Our minds when, lingering all too long,
Over the grave of Burns we hung
    In social grief—
Indulged as if it were a wrong
    To seek relief.

But, leaving each unquiet theme
Where gentlest judgments may misdeem,
And prompt to welcome every gleam
    Of good and fair,
Let us beside this limpid Stream
    Breathe hopeful air.

Enough of sorrow, wreck, and blight :
Think rather of those moments bright
When to the consciousness of right
    His course was true,
When wisdom prospered in his sight
    And virtue grew.

Yes, freely let our hearts expand,
Freely as in youth's season bland,
When side by side, his Book in hand,
    We wont to stray,
Our pleasure varying at command
    Of each sweet Lay.

How oft inspired must he have trode
These pathways, yon far-stretching road!
There lurks his home; in that Abode,
    With mirth elate,
Or in his nobly-pensive mood,
    The Rustic sate.

Proud thoughts that Image overawes.
Before it humbly let us pause,
And ask of Nature, from what cause
    And by what rules
She trained her Burns to win applause
    That shames the Schools.

Through busiest street and loneliest glen
Are felt the flashes of his pen:
He rules mid winter snows, and when
    Bees fill their hives:
Deep in the general heart of men
    His power survives.

What need of fields in some far clime
Where Heroes, Sages, Bards sublime,
And all that fetched the flowing rhyme
    From genuine springs,
Shall dwell together till old Time
    Folds up his wings?

Sweet Mercy ! to the gates of Heaven
This Minstrel lead, his sins forgiven ;
The rueful conflict, the heart riven
    With vain endeavour,
And memory of Earth's bitter leaven
    Effaced for ever.

But why to Him confine the prayer,
When kindred thoughts and yearnings bear
On the frail heart the purest share
    With all that live ?—
The best of what we do and are,
    Just God, forgive !

YARROW UNVISITED.

(See the various Poems the Scene of which is laid upon the Banks
  of the Yarrow ; in particular, the exquisite Ballad of Hamilton,
  beginning

     " Busk ye, busk ye, my bonny, bonny Bride,
      Busk ye, busk ye, my winsome Marrow !"—)

    FROM Stirling Castle we had seen
    The mazy Forth unravelled ;
    Had trod the banks of Clyde, and Tay,
    And with the Tweed had travelled ;
    And when we came to Clovenford,
    Then said my "*winsome Marrow*,"
    " Whate'er betide, we'll turn aside,
    And see the Braes of Yarrow."

'' Let Yarrow Folk, *frae* Selkirk Town,
Who have been buying, selling,
Go back to Yarrow, 'tis their own ;
Each Maiden to her Dwelling !
On Yarrow's banks let herons feed,
Hares couch, and rabbits burrow !
But we will downward with the Tweed,
Nor turn aside to Yarrow.

" There's Galla Water, Leader Haughs,
Both lying right before us ;
And Dryborough, where with chiming Tweed
The Lintwhites sing in chorus ;
There's pleasant Tiviot-dale, a land
Made blithe with plough and harrow .
Why throw away a needful day
To go in search of Yarrow ?

" What's Yarrow but a River bare,
That glides the dark hills under ?
There are a thousand such elsewhere
As worthy of your wonder."
—Strange words they seemed of slight and scorn ;
My True-love sighed for sorrow ;
And looked me in the face, to think
I thus could speak of Yarrow !

"Oh ! green," said I, "are Yarrow's Holms,
And sweet is Yarrow's flowing !
Fair hangs the apple frae the rock,[1]
But we will leave it growing.
O'er hilly path, and open Strath,
We'll wander Scotland thorough ;
But, though so near, we will not turn
Into the Dale of Yarrow.

[1] See Hamilton's Ballad as above

" Let beeves and home-bred kine partake
    The sweets of Burn-mill meadow ;
The swan on still St. Mary's Lake
    Float double, swan and shadow !
We will not see them ; will not go,
    To-day, nor yet to-morrow ;
Enough if in our hearts we know
    There's such a place as Yarrow.

" Be Yarrow Stream unseen, unknown !
    It must, or we shall rue it :
We have a vision of our own ;
    Ah ! why should we undo it ?
The treasured dreams of times long past,
    We'll keep them, winsome Marrow !
For when we're there, although 'tis fair,
    'Twill be another Yarrow.

" If Care with freezing years should come,
    And wandering seem but folly,—
Should we be loth to stir from home,
    And yet be melancholy ;
Should life be dull, and spirits low,
    'Twill soothe us in our sorrow,
That earth has something yet to show,
    The bonny Holms of Yarrow !"

G

YARROW VISITED,

SEPTEMBER, 1814.

AND is this—Yarrow?—*This* the Stream
Of which my fancy cherished,
So faithfully, a waking dream?
An image that hath perished!
O that some Minstrel's harp were near,
To utter notes of gladness,
And chase this silence from the air,
That fills my heart with sadness!

Yet why?—a silvery current flows
With uncontrolled meanderings;
Nor have these eyes by greener hills
Been soothed, in all my wanderings.
And, through her depths, Saint Mary's Lake
Is visibly delighted;
For not a feature of those hills
Is in the mirror slighted.

A blue sky bends o'er Yarrow vale,
Save where that pearly whiteness
Is round the rising sun diffused,
A tender hazy brightness;
Mild dawn of promise! that excludes
All profitless dejection;
Though not unwilling here to admit
A pensive recollection.

Where was it that the famous Flower
Of Yarrow Vale lay bleeding?
His bed perchance was yon smooth mound
On which the herd is feeding:
And haply from this crystal pool,
Now peaceful as the morning,
The Water-wraith ascended thrice—
And gave his doleful warning.

Delicious is the Lay that sings
The haunts of happy Lovers,
The path that leads them to the grove,
The leafy grove that covers:
And Pity sanctifies the verse
That paints, by strength of sorrow,
The unconquerable strength of love;
Bear witness, rueful Yarrow!

But thou, that didst appear so fair
To fond imagination,
Dost rival in the light of day
Her delicate creation:
Meek loveliness is round thee spread,
A softness still and holy;
The grace of forest charms decayed,
And pastoral melancholy.

That Region left, the Vale unfolds
Rich groves of lofty stature,
With Yarrow winding through the pomp
Of cultivated nature;
And, rising from those lofty groves,
Behold a Ruin hoary!
The shattered front of Newark's Towers,
Renowned in Border story.

Fair scenes for childhood's opening bloom,
For sportive youth to stray in ;
For manhood to enjoy his strength ;
And age to wear away in !
Yon Cottage seems a bower of bliss,
A covert for protection
Of tender thoughts that nestle there,
The brood of chaste affection.

How sweet, on this autumnal day,
The wild-wood fruits to gather,
And on my True-love's forehead plant
A crest of blooming heather !
And what if I enwreathed my own !
Twere no offence to reason ;
The sober Hills thus deck their brows
To meet the wintry season.

I see—but not by sight alone,
Loved Yarrow, have I won thee ;
A ray of Fancy still survives—
Her sunshine plays upon thee !
Thy ever-youthful waters keep
A course of lively pleasure ;
And gladsome notes my lips can breathe,
Accordant to the measure.

The vapours linger around the Heights,
They melt—and soon must vanish ;
One hour is theirs, nor more is mine—
Sad thought, which I would banish,
But that I know, where'er I go,
Thy genuine image, Yarrow !
Will dwell with me—to heighten joy,
And cheer my mind in sorrow.

YARROW REVISITED.

[The following Stanzas are a memorial of a day passed with Sir Walter Scott, and other Friends visiting the Banks of the Yarrow under his guidance, immediately before his departure from Abbotsford for Naples.]

THE gallant Youth, who may have gained,
　　Or seeks, a " winsome Marrow,"
Was but an infant in the lap
　　When first I looked on Yarrow ;
Once more, by Newark's Castle-gate
　　Long left without a warder,
I stood, looked, listened, and with Thee,
　　Great Minstrel of the Border !

Grave thoughts ruled wide on that sweet day,
　　Their dignity installing
In gentle bosoms, while sere leaves
　　Were on the bough, or falling ;
But breezes played, and sunshine gleamed—
　　The forest to embolden ;
Reddened the fiery hues, and shot
　　Transparence through the golden.

For busy thoughts the Stream flowed on
　　In foamy agitation ;
And slept in many a crystal pool
　　For quiet contemplation :
No public and no private care
　　The freeborn mind enthralling,
We made a day of happy hours,
　　Our happy days recalling.

Brisk Youth appeared, the Morn of youth.
  With freaks of graceful folly—
Life's temperate Noon, her sober Eve,
  Her Night not melancholy;
Past, present, future, all appeared
  In harmony united,
Like guests that meet, and some from far,
  By cordial love invited.

And if, as Yarrow, through the woods
  And down the meadow ranging,
Did meet us with unaltered face,
  Though we were changed and changing :
If, *then*, some natural shadows spread
  Our inward prospect over,
The soul's deep valley was not slow
  Its brightness to recover.

Eternal blessings on the Muse,
  And her divine employment !
The blameless Muse, who trains her Sons
  For hope and calm enjoyment ;
Albeit sickness, lingering yet,
  Has o'er their pillow brooded ;
And Care waylays their steps—a Sprite
  Not easily eluded.

For thee, O SCOTT ! compelled to change
  Green Eildon-hill and Cheviot
For warm Vesuvio's vine-clad slopes,
  And leave thy Tweed and Teviot
For mild Sorrento's breezy waves ;
  May classic Fancy, linking
With native Fancy her fresh aid,
  Preserve thy heart from sinking !

O ! while they minister to thee,
   Each vying with the other,
May Health return to mellow Age
   With Strength her venturous brother ;
And Tiber, and each brook and rill
   Renowned in song and story,
With unimagined beauty shine,
   Nor lose one ray of glory !

For Thou, upon a hundred streams,
   By tales of love and sorrow,
Of faithful love, undaunted truth,
   Hast shed the power of Yarrow ;
And streams unknown, hills yet unseen,
   Wherever they invite Thee,
At parent Nature's grateful call,
   With gladness must requite Thee.

A gracious welcome shall be thine,
   Such looks of love and honour
As thy own Yarrow gave to me
   When first I gazed upon her ;
Beheld what I had feared to see,
   Unwilling to surrender
Dreams treasured up from early days,
   The holy and the tender.

And what, for this frail world, were all
   That mortals do or suffer,
Did no responsive harp, no pen,
   Memorial tribute offer ?
Yea, what were mighty Nature's self ?
   Her features, could they win us,
Unhelped by the poetic voice
   That hourly speaks within us ?

Nor deem that localised Romance
  Plays false with our affections;
Unsanctifies our tears—made sport
  For fanciful dejections:
Oh, no! the visions of the past
  Sustain the heart in feeling
Life as she is—our changeful Life,
  With friends and kindred dealing.

Bear witness, Ye, whose thoughts that day
  In Yarrow's groves were centred;
Who through the silent portal arch
  Of mouldering Newark enter'd;
And clomb the winding stair that once
  Too timidly was mounted
By the "last Minstrel," (not the last!)
  Ere he his Tale recounted.

Flow on for ever, Yarrow Stream!
  Fulfil thy pensive duty,
Well pleased that future Bards should chant
  For simple hearts thy beauty;
To dream-light dear while yet unseen,
  Dear to the common sunshine,
And dearer still, as now I feel,
  To memory's shadowy moonshine!

TO MAY.

THOUGH many suns have risen and set
   Since thou, blithe May, wert born,
And Bards, who hailed thee, may forget
   Thy gifts, thy beauty scorn;
There are who to a birthday strain
   Confine not harp and voice,
But evermore throughout thy reign
   Are grateful and rejoice!

Delicious odours! music sweet,
   Too sweet to pass away!
Oh for a deathless song to meet
   The soul's desire—a lay
That, when a thousand years are told,
   Should praise thee, genial Power!
Through summer heat, autumnal cold,
   And winter's dreariest hour.

Earth, Sea, thy presence feel—nor less,
   If yon ethereal blue
With its soft smile the truth express,
   The Heavens have felt it too.
The inmost heart of man if glad
   Partakes a livelier cheer;
And eyes that cannot but be sad
   Let fall a brightened tear.

Since thy return, through days and weeks
   Of hope that grew by stealth,
How many wan and faded cheeks
   Have kindled into health!
The old, by thee revived, have said,
   " Another year is ours:"
And wayworn wanderers, poorly fed,
   Have smiled upon thy flowers.

G 2

Who tripping lisps a merry song
    Amid his playful peers?
The tender Infant who was long
    A prisoner of fond fears;
But now, when every sharp-edged blast
    Is quiet in its sheath,
His Mother leaves him free to taste
    Earth's sweetness in thy breath.

Thy help is with the weed that creeps
    Along the humblest ground;
No cliff so bare but on its steeps
    Thy favours may be found;
But most on some peculiar nook
    That our own hands have drest,
Thou and thy train are proud to look,
    And seem to love it best.

And yet how pleased we wander forth
    When May is whispering, "Come!"
Choose from the bowers of virgin earth
    The happiest for your home;
Heaven's bounteous love through me is spread
    From sunshine, clouds, winds, waves,
Drops on the mouldering turret's head,
    And on your turf-clad graves!"

Such greeting heard, away with sighs
    For lilies that must fade,
Or "the rathe primrose as it dies
    Forsaken" in the shade!
Vernal fruitions and desires
    Are linked in endless chase:
While, as one kindly growth retires,
    Another takes its place.

And what if thou, sweet May, hast known
   Mishap by worm and blight ;
If expectations newly blown
   Have perished in thy sight ;
If loves and joys, while up they sprung,
   Were caught as in a snare ;
Such is the lot of all the young,
   However bright and fair.

Lo ! streams that April could not check
   Are patient of thy rule ;
Gurgling in foamy water-break,
   Loitering in glassy pool :
By thee, thee only, could be sent
   Such gentle mists as glide,
Curling with unconfirmed intent,
   On that green mountain's side.

How delicate the leafy veil
   Through which yon House of God
Gleams 'mid the peace of this deep dale
   By few but shepherds trod !
And lowly huts near beaten ways,
   No sooner stand attired
In thy fresh wreaths, than they for praise
   Peep forth, and are admired.

Season of fancy and of hope,
   Permit not for one hour
A blossom from thy crown to drop,
   Nor add to it a flower !
Keep, lovely May, as if by touch
   Of self-restraining art,
This modest charm of not too much,
   Part seen, imagined part !

THE PRIMROSE OF THE ROCK.

A ROCK there is whose homely front
  The passing traveller slights ;
Yet there the glow-worms hang their lamps,
  Like stars, at various heights ;
And one coy Primrose to that Rock
  The vernal breeze invites.

What hideous warfare hath been waged,
  What kingdoms overthrown,
Since first I spied that Primrose-tuft
  And marked it for my own ;
A lasting link in Nature's chain
  From highest heaven let down !

The flowers, still faithful to the stems,
  Their fellowship renew ;
The stems are faithful to the root,
  That worketh out of view ;
And to the rock the root adheres
  In every fibre true.

Close clings to earth the living rock,
  Though threatening still to fall ;
The earth is constant to her sphere ;
  And God upholds them all :
So blooms this lonely Plant, nor dreads
  Her annual funeral.

Here closed the meditative strain ;
    But air breathed soft that day,
The hoary mountain-heights were cheered,
    The sunny vale looked gay ;
And to the Primrose of the Rock
    I gave this after-lay.

I sang—Let myriads of bright flowers,
    Like Thee, in field and grove
Revive unenvied ;—mightier far
    Than tremblings that reprove
Our vernal tendencies to hope
    Is God's redeeming love ;

That love which changed—for wan disease,
    For sorrow that had bent
O'er hopeless dust, for withered age—
    Their moral element,
And turned the thistles of a curse
    To types beneficent.

Sin-blighted though we are, we too,
    The reasoning Sons of Men,
From one oblivious winter called
    Shall rise, and breathe again ;
And in eternal summer lose
    Our threescore years and ten.

To humbleness of heart descends
    This prescience from on high,
The faith that elevates the just,
    Before and when they die ;
And makes each soul a separate heaven,
    A court for Deity.

POEMS

AKIN TO THE ANTIQUE

AND

ODES

LAODAMEIA.

" WITH sacrifice, before the rising morn
  Performed, my slaughtered Lord have I required ;
  And in thick darkness, amid shades forlorn,
  Him of the infernal Gods have I desired :
  Celestial pity I again implore :—
  Restore him to my sight—great Jove, restore ! "

So speaking, and by fervent love endowed
With faith, the Suppliant heavenward lifts her hands;
While, like the sun emerging from a cloud,
Her countenance brightens—and her eye expands ;
Her bosom heaves and spreads, her stature grows ;
And she expects the issue in repose.

O terror ! what hath she perceived ?—O joy !
What doth she look on ?—whom doth she behold ?
Her Hero slain upon the beach of Troy ?
His vital presence ? his corporeal mould ?
It is—if sense deceive her not—'tis He !
And a God leads him, wingèd Mercury !

Mild Hermes spake—and touched her with his wand
That calms all fear : " Such grace hath crowned thy
      prayer,
Laodameia ! that at Jove's command
Thy husband walks the paths of upper air :
He comes to tarry with thee three hours' space :
Accept the gift, behold him face to face ! "

Forth sprang the impassioned Queen her Lord to clasp:
Again that consummation she essayed:
But unsubstantial form eludes her grasp
As often as that eager grasp was made.
The Phantom parts—but parts to re-unite,
And re-assume his place before her sight.

" Protesilaos, lo! thy guide is gone!
Confirm, I pray, the vision with thy voice:
This is our palace,—yonder is thy throne;
Speak, and the floor thou tread'st on will rejoice.
Not to appal me have the Gods bestowed
This precious boon; and blest a sad abode."

" Great Jove, Laodameia! doth not leave
His gifts imperfect:—Spectre though I be,
I am not sent to scare thee or deceive;
But in reward of thy fidelity.
And something also did my worth obtain;
For fearless virtue bringeth boundless gain.

" Thou knowest, the Delphic oracle foretold
That the first Greek who touched the Trojan strand
Should die; but me the threat could not withhold:
A generous cause a victim did demand;
And forth I leapt upon the sandy plain;
A self-devoted chief—by Hector slain."

" Supreme of heroes—bravest, noblest, best!
Thy matchless courage I bewail no more,
Which then, when tens of thousands were deprest
By doubt, propelled thee to the fatal shore;
Thou found'st—and I forgive thee—here thou art—
A nobler counsellor than my poor heart.

" But thou, though capable of sternest deed,
  Wert kind as resolute, and good as brave ;
And he, whose power restores thee, hath decreed
  That thou should'st cheat the malice of the grave :
Redundant are thy locks, thy lips as fair
As when their breath enriched Thessalian air.

" No Spectre greets me—no vain Shadow this ;
  Come, blooming Hero, place thee by my side !
Give, on this well-known couch, one nuptial kiss
  To me, this day, a second time thy bride ! "
Jove frowned in heaven ; the conscious Parcæ threw
Upon those roseate lips a Stygian hue.

" This visage tells thee that my doom is past :
  Know, virtue were not virtue, if the joys
Of sense were able to return as fast
  And surely as they vanish.—Earth destroys
Those raptures duly—Erebus disdains :
Calm pleasures there abide—majestic pains.

" Be taught, O faithful consort, to control
  Rebellious passion : for the Gods approve
The depth, and not the tumult, of the soul ;
  A fervent, not ungovernable, love.
Thy transports moderate ; and meekly mourn
When I depart, for brief is my sojourn——"

" Ah, wherefore ?—Did not Hercules by force
  Wrest from the guardian Monster of the tomb
Alcestis, a reanimated corse,
  Given back to dwell on earth in vernal bloom ?
Medea's spells dispersed the weight of years,
And Æson stood a youth 'mid youthful peers.

" The Gods to us are merciful—and they
    Yet further may relent : for mightier far
Than strength of nerve and sinew, or the sway
    Of magic potent over sun and star,
Is love, though oft to agony distrest,
And though his favourite seat be feeble woman's breast.

" But if thou goest, I follow——" " Peace !" he said.—
    She looked upon him and was calmed and cheered ;
The ghastly colour from his lips had fled ;
    In his deportment, shape, and mien, appeared
Elysian beauty, melancholy grace,
Brought from a pensive though a happy place.

He spake of love, such love as spirits feel
    In worlds whose course is equable and pure ;
No fears to beat away—no strife to heal—
    The past unsigh'd for, and the future sure ;
Spake of heroic arts in graver mood
Revived, with finer harmony pursued ;

Of all that is most beauteous—imaged there
    In happier beauty : more pellucid streams,
An ampler ether, a diviner air,
    And fields invested with purpureal gleams ;
Climes which the sun, who sheds the brightest day
Earth knows, is all unworthy to survey.

Yet there the Soul shall enter which hath earned
    That privilege by virtue.—" Ill," said he,
" The end of man's existence I discerned,
    Who from ignoble games and revelry
Could draw, when we had parted, vain delight,
While tears were thy best pastime, day and night :

" And while my youthful peers before my eyes
  (Each hero following his peculiar bent)
Prepared themselves for glorious enterprise
  By martial sports,—or, seated in the tent,
Chieftains and kings in counsel were detained ;
What time the fleet at Aulis lay enchained.

" The wished-for wind was given :—I then revolved
  The oracle, upon the silent sea ;
And, if no worthier led the way, resolved
  That, of a thousand vessels, mine should be
The foremost prow in pressing to the strand,—
Mine the first blood that tinged the Trojan sand.

" Yet bitter, oft-times bitter, was the pang
  When of thy loss I thought, beloved Wife !
On thee too fondly did my memory hang,
  And on the joys we shared in mortal life,
The paths which we have trod—these fountains, flowers;
My new-planned cities, and unfinished towers.

" But should suspense permit the foe to cry,
  ' Behold they tremble !—haughty their array
Yet of their number no one dares to die' ?
  In soul I swept the indignity away :
Old frailties then recurred :—but lofty thought,
In act embodied, my deliverance wrought.

" And thou, though strong in love, art all too weak ;
  In reason, in self-government too slow ;
I counsel thee by fortitude to seek
  Our blest re-union in the shades below.
The invisible world with thee hath sympathised ;
Be thy affections raised and solemnised.

Learn, by a mortal yearning, to ascend—
Towards a higher object.—Love was given,
Encouraged, sanctioned, chiefly for that end ;
For this the passion to excess was driven—
That self might be annulled : her bondage prove
The fetters of a dream, opposed to love."——

Aloud she shrieked ! for Hermes re-appears !
Round the dear Shade she would have clung—'tis vain
The hours are past—too brief had they been years—
And him no mortal effort can detain :
Swift, toward the realms that know not earthly day,
He through the portal takes his silent way,
And on the palace-floor a lifeless corse she lay.

Ah, judge her gently who so deeply loved !
Her, who in reason's spite, yet without crime,
Was in a trance of passion thus removed ;
Delivered from the galling yoke of time
And these frail elements—to gather flowers
Of blissful quiet 'mid unfading bowers.

—Yet tears to human suffering are due ;
And mortal hopes defeated and o'erthrown
Are mourned by man, and not by man alone,
As fondly he believes.—Upon the side
Of Hellespont (such faith was entertained)
A knot of spiry trees for ages grew
From out the tomb of him for whom she died ;
And ever, when such stature they had gained
That Ilium's walls were subject to their view,
The trees' tall summits withered at the sight :
A constant interchange of growth and blight !

DION.

(SEE PLUTARCH.)

I.

FAIR is the swan, whose majesty, prevailing
O'er breezeless water, on Locarno's lake,
Bears him on while proudly sailing
He leaves behind a moon-illumined wake :
Behold ! the mantling spirit of reserve
Fashions his neck into a goodly curve ;
An arch thrown back between luxuriant wings
Of whitest garniture, like fir-tree boughs
To which, on some unruffled morning, clings
A flaky weight of winter's purest snows !
—Behold !—as with a gushing impulse heaves
That downy prow, and softly cleaves
The mirror of the crystal flood,
Vanish inverted hill, and shadowy wood,
And pendent rocks, where'er, in gliding state,
Winds the mute Creature without visible mate
Or rival, save the Queen of night
Showering down a silver light,
From heaven, upon her chosen favourite !

II.

So pure, so bright, so fitted to embrace,
Where'er he turned, a natural grace
Of haughtiness without pretence,
And to unfold a still magnificence,
Was princely Dion, in the power
And beauty of his happier hour.

Nor less the homage that was seen to wait
On Dion's virtues, when the lunar beam
Of Plato's genius, from its lofty sphere,
Fell round him in the grove of Academe,
Softening their inbred dignity austere ;
 That he, not too elate
 With self-sufficing solitude,
But with majestic lowliness endued,
 Might in the universal bosom reign,
And from affectionate observance gain
Help, under every change of adverse fate.

III.

Five thousand warriors—O the rapturous day !
Each crowned with flowers, and armed with spear and
  shield,
Or ruder weapon which their course might yield,
To Syracuse advance in bright array.
Who leads them on ?—The anxious people see
Long-exiled Dion marching at their head,
He also crowned with flowers of Sicily,
And in a white, far-beaming corslet clad !
Pure transport undisturbed by doubt or fear
The gazers feel ; and, rushing to the plain,
Salute those strangers as a holy train
Or blest procession (to the Immortals dear)
That brought their precious liberty again.
Lo ! when the gates are entered, on each hand,
Down the long street, rich goblets filled with wine
   In seemly order stand,
On tables set, as if for rites divine ;—
And, as the great Deliverer marches by,
 He looks on festal ground with fruits bestrown :
And flowers are on his person thrown
 In boundless prodigality ;

Nor doth the general voice abstain from prayer,
Invoking Dion's tutelary care,
As if a very Deity he were!

IV.

Mourn, hills and groves of Attica! and mourn
Ilissus, bending o'er thy classic urn!
Mourn, and lament for him whose spirit dreads
Your once sweet memory, studious walks and shades!
For him who to divinity aspired,
Not on the breath of popular applause,
But through dependence on the sacred laws
Framed in the schools where Wisdom dwelt retired,
Intent to trace the ideal path of right
(More fair than heaven's broad causeway paved with stars)
Which Dion learned to measure with delight;
But he hath overleaped the eternal bars;
And, following guides whose craft holds no consent
With aught that breathes the ethereal element,
Hath stained the robes of civil power with blood,
Unjustly shed, though for the public good.
Whence doubts that came too late, and wishes vain,
Hollow excuses, and triumphant pain;
And oft his cogitations sink as low
As, through the abysses of a joyless heart,
The heaviest plummet of despair can go.
But whence that sudden check? that fearful start!
   He hears an uncouth sound—
    Anon his lifted eyes
Saw at a long-drawn gallery's dusky bound,
A Shape of more than mortal size
And hideous aspect, stalking round and round!
   A woman's garb the Phantom wore,
   And fiercely swept the marble floor,—

> Like Auster whirling to and fro,
>   His force on Caspian foam to try;
> Or Boreas when he scours the snow
> That skins the plains of Thessaly,
> Or when aloft on Mænalus he stops
> His flight, 'mid eddying pine-tree tops!

v.

So, but from toil less sign of profit reaping,
The sullen Spectre to her purpose bowed,
        Sweeping—vehemently sweeping—
No pause admitted, no design avowed!
"Avaunt, inexplicable Guest!—avaunt,"
Exclaimed the Chieftain—"Let me rather see
The coronal that coiling vipers make;
The torch that flames with many a lurid flake,
And the long train of doleful pageantry
Which they behold, whom vengeful Furies haunt;
Who, while they struggle from the scourge to flee,
Move where the blasted soil is not unworn,
And, in their anguish, bear what other minds have borne!"

vi.

But Shapes that come not at an earthly call,
Will not depart when mortal voices bid;
Lords of the visionary eye whose lid,
Once raised, remains aghast, and will not fall!
Ye Gods, thought He, that servile implement
Obeys a mystical intent!
Your Minister would brush away
The spots that to my soul adhere;
But should she labour night and day,
They will not, cannot disappear;
Whence angry perturbations,—and that look
Which no philosophy can brook!

VII.

Ill-fated Chief ! there are whose hopes are built
Upon the ruins of thy glorious name ;
Who, through the portal of one moment's guilt,
Pursue thee with their deadly aim !
O matchless perfidy ! portentous lust
Of monstrous crime !—that horror-striking blade,
Drawn in defiance of the Gods, hath laid
The noble Syracusan low in dust !
Shudder'd the walls—the marble city wept—
And sylvan places heaved a pensive sigh ;
But in calm peace the appointed Victim slept,
As he had fallen in magnanimity :
Of spirit too capacious to require
That Destiny her course should change ; too just
To his own native greatness to desire
That wretched boon, days lengthened by mistrust.
So were the hopeless troubles, that involved
The soul of Dion, instantly dissolved.
Released from life and cares of princely state,
He left this moral grafted on his Fate :
" Him only pleasure leads, and peace attends,
  Him, only him, the shield of Jove defends,
  Whose means are fair and spotless as his ends."

CHARACTER OF THE HAPPY WARRIOR.

WHO is the happy Warrior ?   Who is he
That every man in arms should wish to be ?
——It is the generous Spirit, who, when brought
Among the tasks of real life, hath wrought
Upon the plan that pleased his childish thought :
Whose high endeavours are an inward light
That makes the path before him always bright :
Who, with a natural instinct to discern
What knowledge can perform, is diligent to learn
Abides by this resolve, and stops not there,
But makes his moral being his prime care ;
Who, doomed to go in company with Pain,
And Fear, and Bloodshed, miserable train !
Turns his necessity to glorious gain ;
In face of these doth exercise a power
Which is our human nature's highest dower ;
Controls them and subdues, transmutes, bereaves
Of their bad influence, and their good receives :
By objects, which might force the soul to abate
Her feeling, rendered more compassionate ;
Is placable—because occasions rise
So often that demand such sacrifice ;
More skilful in self-knowledge, even more pure,
As tempted more ; more able to endure,
As more exposed to suffering and distress ;
Thence, also, more alive to tenderness.
—'Tis he whose law is reason ; who depends
Upon that law as on the best of friends ;

Whence, in a state where men are tempted still
To evil for a guard against worse ill,
And what in quality or act is best
Doth seldom on a right foundation rest,
He fixes good on good alone, and owes
To virtue every triumph that he knows :
—Who, if he rise to station of command,
Rises by open means ; and there will stand
On honourable terms, or else retire,
And in himself possess his own desire ;
Who comprehends his trust, and to the same
Keeps faithful with a singleness of aim ;
And therefore does not stoop, nor lie in wait
For wealth, or honours, or for worldly state ;
Whom they must follow ; on whose head must fall,
Like showers of manna, if they come at all :
Whose powers shed round him in the common strife,
Or mild concerns of ordinary life,
A constant influence, a peculiar grace ;
But who, if he be called upon to face
Some awful moment to which Heaven has joined
Great issues, good or bad for human kind,
Is happy as a lover ; and attired
With sudden brightness, like a man inspired ;
And, through the heat of conflict, keeps the law
In calmness made, and sees what he foresaw ;
Or if an unexpected call succeed,
Come when it will, is equal to the need :
—He who though thus endued as with a sense
And faculty for storm and turbulence,
Is yet a Soul whose master-bias leans
To homefelt pleasures and to gentle scenes ;
Sweet images ! which, wheresoe'er he be,
Are at his heart ; and such fidelity
It is his darling passion to approve ;

More brave for this, that he hath much to love :—
'Tis, finally, the man, who, lifted high,
Conspicuous object in a Nation's eye,
Or left unthought-of in obscurity,—
Who, with a toward or untoward lot,
Prosperous or adverse, to his wish or not,
Plays, in the many games of life, that one
Where what he most doth value must be won :
Whom neither shape of danger can dismay,
Nor thought of tender happiness betray ;
Who, not content that former worth stand fast,
Looks forward, persevering to the last,
From well to better, daily self-surpast :
Who, whether praise of him must walk the earth
For ever, and to noble deeds give birth,
Or he must go to dust without his fame,
And leave a dead unprofitable name,
Finds comfort in himself and in his cause ;
And, while the mortal mist is gathering, draws
His breath in confidence of Heaven's applause :
This is the happy Warrior ; this is he
Whom every man in arms should wish to be.

LINES ON THE EXPECTED INVASION.

1803.

COME ye—who, if (which Heaven avert!) the Land
Were with herself at strife, would take your stand,
Like gallant Falkland, by the Monarch's side,
And, like Montrose, make Loyalty your pride—
Come ye—who, not less zealous, might display
Banners at enmity with regal sway,
And, like the Pyms and Miltons of that day,
Think that a State would live in sounder health
If Kingship bowed its head to Commonwealth—
Ye too—whom no discreditable fear
Would keep, perhaps with many a fruitless tear,
Uncertain what to choose and how to steer—
And ye—who might mistake for sober sense
And wise reserve the plea of indolence—
Come ye—whate'er your creed—O waken all,
Whate'er your temper, at your Country's call;
Resolving (this a free-born Nation can)
To have one soul, and perish to a man,
Or save this honoured Land from every lord
But British reason and the British sword.

THE PILLAR OF TRAJAN.

[I had observed in the newspaper that the Pillar of Trajan was given as a subject for a prize-poem in English verse. I had a wish that my son, who was then an undergraduate at Oxford, should try his fortune, and I told him so; but he, not having been accustomed to write verse, wisely declined to enter on the task; whereupon I showed him these lines as a proof of what might be, without difficulty, done on that subject.]

WHERE towers are crushed, and unforbidden weeds
O'er mutilated arches shed their seeds;
And temples, doomed to milder change, unfold
A new magnificence that vies with old;
Firm in its pristine majesty hath stood
A votive Column, spared by fire and flood :—
And, though the passions of man's fretful race
Have never ceased to eddy round its base,
Not injured more by touch of meddling hands
Than a lone obelisk, 'mid Nubian sands,
Or aught in Syrian deserts left to save
From death the memory of the good and brave.
Historic figures round the shaft embost
Ascend, with lineaments in air not lost :
Still as he turns, the charmed spectator sees
Group winding after group with dream-like ease,
Triumphs in sunbright gratitude displayed,
Or softly stealing into modest shade.
—So, pleased with purple clusters to entwine
Some lofty elm-tree, mounts the daring vine;
The woodbine so, with spiral grace, and breathes
Wide-spreading odours from her flowery wreaths.

Borne by the Muse from rills in shepherds' ears
Murmuring but one smooth story for all years,
I gladly commune with the mind and heart
Of him who thus survives by classic art,
His actions witness, venerate his mien,
And study Trajan as by Pliny seen ;
Behold how fought the Chief whose conquering sword
Stretched far as earth might own a single lord ;
In the delight of moral prudence schooled,
How feelingly at home the Sovereign ruled ;
Best of the good—in pagan faith allied
To more than Man, by virtue deified.

Memorial Pillar ! 'mid the wrecks of Time
Preserve thy charge with confidence sublime—
The exultations, pomps, and cares of Rome,
Whence half the breathing world received its doom ;
Things that recoil from language ; that, if shown
By apter pencil, from the light had flown.
A Pontiff, Trajan *here* the Gods implores,
There greets an embassy from Indian shores :
Lo ! he harangues his cohorts —*there* the storm
Of battle meets him in authentic form !
Unharnessed, naked, troops of Moorish horse
Sweep to the charge ; more high, the Dacian force,
To hoof and finger mailed ;—yet, high or low,
None bleed, and none lie prostrate but the foe :
In every Roman, through all turns of fate,
Is Roman dignity inviolate ;
Spirit in him pre-eminent, who guides,
Supports, adorns, and over all presides ;
Distinguished only by inherent state
From honoured instruments that round him wait ;
Rise as he may, his grandeur scorns the test
Of outward symbol, nor will deign to rest
On aught by which another is deprest.

H

—Alas ! that one thus disciplined could toil
To enslave whole nations on their native soil ;
So emulous of Macedonian fame,
That, when his age was measured with his aim,
He drooped, 'mid else unclouded victories,
And turned his eagles back with deep-drawn sighs ;
O weakness of the great ! O folly of the wise !

Where now the haughty Empire that was spread
With such fond hope ? her very speech is dead ;
Yet glorious Art the power of Time defies,
And Trajan still, through various enterprise,
Mounts, in this fine illusion, toward the skies :
Still are we present with the imperial Chief,
Nor cease to gaze upon the bold relief
Till Rome, to silent marble unconfined,
Becomes with all her years a vision of the mind.

SEPTEMBER 1819.

DEPARTING Summer hath assumed
An aspect tenderly illumed,
The gentlest look of Spring ;
That calls from yonder leafy shade
Unfaded, yet prepared to fade,
A timely carolling.

No faint and hesitating trill—
Such tribute as to Winter chill
The lonely Redbreast pays !
Clear, loud, and lively is the din,
From social warblers gathering in
Their harvest of sweet lays.

Nor doth the example fail to cheer
Me, conscious that my leaf is sere,
And yellow on the bough :—
Fall, rosy garlands, from my head !
Ye myrtle wreaths, your fragrance shed
Around a younger brow !

Yet will I temperately rejoice ;
Wide is the range, and free the choice
Of undiscordant themes ;
Which, haply, kindred souls may prize
Not less than vernal ecstasies,
And passion's feverish dreams.

For deathless powers to verse belong,
And they like Demigods are strong
On whom the Muses smile ;
But some their function have disclaimed.
Best pleased with what is aptliest framed
To enervate and defile.

Not such the initiatory strains
Committed to the silent plains
In Britain's earliest dawn :
Trembled the groves, the stars grew pale,
While all-too-daringly the veil
Of nature was withdrawn !

Nor such the spirit-stirring note
When the live chords Alcæus smote,
Inflamed by sense of wrong ;
Woe ! woe to Tyrants ! from the lyre
Broke threateningly, in sparkles dire
Of fierce vindictive song.

And not unhallowed was the page
By wingèd Love inscribed, to assuage
The pangs of vain pursuit ;
Love listening while the Lesbian Maid
With finest touch of passion swayed
Her own Æolian lute.

O ye, who patiently explore
The wreck of Herculanean lore,
What rapture ! could ye seize
Some Theban fragment, or unroll
One precious, tender-hearted scroll
Of pure Simonides.

That were, indeed, a genuine birth
Of poesy ; a bursting forth
Of genius from the dust !
What Horace gloried to behold,
What Maro loved, shall we unfold ?
Can haughty Time be just ?

ODE TO LYCORIS.

MAY 1817.

I.

AN age hath been when Earth was proud
Of lustre too intense
To be sustained ; and mortals bowed
The front in self-defence.
Who *then*, if Dian's crescent gleamed,
Or Cupid's sparkling arrow streamed
While on the wing the urchin played,
Could fearlessly approach the shade ?
—Enough for one soft vernal day,
If I, a bard of ebbing time,
And nurtured in a fickle clime,
May haunt this hornèd bay ;
Whose amorous water multiplies
The flitting halcyon's vivid dyes ;
And smooths her liquid breast—to show
These swan-like specks of mountain snow,
White as the pair that slid along the plains
Of Heaven, when Venus held the reins !

II.

In youth we love the darksome lawn
Brushed by the owlet's wing ;
Then, Twilight is preferred to Dawn,
And Autumn to the Spring.

Sad fancies do we then affect,
In luxury of disrespect
To our own prodigal excess
Of too familiar happiness.
Lycoris (if such name befit
Thee, thee my life's celestial sign !)
When Nature marks the year's decline,
Be ours to welcome it ;
Pleased with the harvest hope that runs
Before the path of milder suns ;
Pleased while the sylvan world displays
Its ripeness to the feeding gaze ;
Pleased when the sullen winds resound the knell
Of the resplendent miracle.

III.

But something whispers to my heart
That, as we downward tend,
Lycoris ! life requires an *art*
To which our souls must bend ;
A skill—to balance and supply ;
And, ere the flowing fount be dry,
As soon it must, a sense to sip,
Or drink, with no fastidious lip.
Then welcome, above all, the Guest
Whose smiles, diffused o'er land and sea,
Seem to recall the Deity
Of youth into the breast :
May pensive Autumn ne'er present
A claim to her disparagement !
While blossoms and the budding spray
Inspire us in our own decay ;
Still, as we nearer draw to life's dark goal,
Be hopeful Spring the favourite of the soul !

ODE TO DUTY.

"Jam non consilio bonus, sed more eò perductus, ut non tantum
    rectè facere possim, sed nisi rectè facere non possim."

Stern Daughter of the Voice of God!
O Duty! if that name thou love
Who art a light to guide, a rod
To check the erring, and reprove;
Thou, who art victory and law
When empty terrors overawe;
From vain temptations dost set free;
And calm'st the weary strife of frail humanity!

There are who ask not if thine eye
Be on them; who, in love and truth,
Where no misgiving is, rely
Upon the genial sense of youth:
Glad Hearts! without reproach or blot;
Who do thy work, and know it not:
Long may the kindly impulse last!
But Thou, if they should totter, teach them to
        stand fast!

Serene will be our days and bright,
And happy will our nature be,
When love is an unerring light,
And joy its own security.
And they a blissful course may hold
Even now, who, not unwisely bold,
Live in the spirit of this creed;
Yet seek thy firm support, according to their
        need.

I, loving freedom, and untried ;
No sport of every random gust,
Yet being to myself a guide,
Too blindly have reposed my trust ;
And oft, when in my heart was heard
Thy timely mandate, I deferred
The task, in smoother walks to stray ;
But thee I now would serve more strictly, if I may.

Through no disturbance of my soul,
Or strong compunction in me wrought,
I supplicate for thy control ;
But in the quietness of thought :
Me this unchartered freedom tires ;
I feel the weight of chance-desires :
My hopes no more must change their name,
I long for a repose that ever is the same.

Stern Lawgiver ! yet thou dost wear
The Godhead's most benignant grace ;
Nor know we anything so fair
As is the smile upon thy face :
Flowers laugh before thee on their beds
And fragrance in thy footing treads ;
Thou dost preserve the Stars from wrong ;
And the most ancient Heavens, through Thee, are
fresh and strong.

To humbler functions, awful Power !
I call thee : I myself commend
Unto thy guidance from this hour ;
Oh, let my weakness have an end !
Give unto me, made lowly wise,
The spirit of self-sacrifice ;
The confidence of reason give ;
And in the light of truth thy bondman let me live !

ODE ON INTIMATIONS OF
IMMORTALITY

FROM RECOLLECTIONS OF EARLY CHILDHOOD.

I.

THERE was a time when meadow, grove, and stream
The earth, and every common sight,
    To me did seem
    Apparelled in celestial light,
The glory and the freshness of a dream.
It is not now as it hath been of yore ;—
    Turn wheresoe'er I may,
      By night or day,
The things which I have seen I now can see no more.

II.

    The Rainbow comes and goes,
    And lovely is the Rose ;
    The Moon doth with delight
Look round her when the heavens are bare ;
    Waters on a starry night
    Are beautiful and fair ;
The sunshine is a glorious birth ;
But yet I know, where'er I go,
That there hath past away a glory from the earth.

III.

Now, while the Birds thus sing a joyous song,
    And while the young Lambs bound
      As to the tabor's sound,
To me alone there came a thought of grief :
A timely utterance gave that thought relief,
      And I again am strong :
The Cataracts blow their trumpets from the steep ;
No more shall grief of mine the season wrong ;
I hear the Echoes through the mountains throng,
The Winds come to me from the fields of sleep,
      And all the earth is gay ;
        Land and sea
    Give themselves up to jollity,
      And with the heart of May
    Doth every beast keep holiday ;—
        Thou child of joy,
Shout round me, let me hear thy shouts, thou happy
    Shepherd-boy !

IV.

Ye blessed Creatures, I have heard the call
    Ye to each other make ; I see
The heavens laugh with you in your jubilee ;
    My heart is at your festival,
      My head hath its coronal,
The fulness of your bliss, I feel—I feel it all.
    O evil day ! if I were sullen
    While the Earth herself is adorning
      This sweet May-morning,
    And the children are pulling

On every side,
In a thousand valleys far and wide,
Fresh flowers ; while the sun shines warm,
And the babe leaps up on his mother's arm :—
I hear, I hear, with joy I hear !
—But there's a Tree, of many one,
A single Field which I have looked upon,
Both of them speak of something that is gone ;
The Pansy at my feet
Doth the same tale repeat :
Whither is fled the visionary gleam ?
Where is it now, the glory and the dream ?

v.

Our birth is but a sleep and a forgetting :
The Soul that rises with us, our life's Star,
Hath had elsewhere its setting,
And cometh from afar :
Not in entire forgetfulness,
And not in utter nakedness,
But trailing clouds of glory do we come
From God, who is our home :
Heaven lies about us in our infancy !
Shades of the prison-house begin to close
Upon the growing Boy,
But He beholds the light, and whence it flows
He sees it in his joy ;
The Youth, who daily farther from the East
Must travel, still is Nature's Priest,
And by the vision splendid
Is on his way attended ;
At length the Man perceives it die away,
And fade into the light of common day.

VI.

Earth fills her lap with pleasures of her own ;
Yearnings she hath in her own natural kind,
And even with something of a mother's mind,
      And no unworthy aim,
      The homely Nurse doth all she can
To make her foster-child, her inmate Man,
      Forget the glories he hath known,
And that imperial palace whence he came.

VII.

Behold the Child among his new-born blisses,
A six years' darling of a pigmy size !
See, where 'mid work of his own hand he lies,
Fretted by sallies of his Mother's kisses,
With light upon him from his Father's eyes !
See, at his feet, some little plan or chart,
Some fragment from his dream of human life,
Shaped by himself with newly-learnèd art ;
      A wedding or a festival,
      A mourning or a funeral,
        And this hath now his heart,
      And unto this he frames his song :
        Then will he fit his tongue
To dialogues of business, love, or strife ;
      But it will not be long
      Ere this be thrown aside,
      And with new joy and pride
The little Actor cons another part ;
Filling from time to time his " humorous stage "
With all the persons, down to palsied age,
That Life brings with her in her equipage ;
      As if his whole vocation
      Were endless imitation.

VIII.

Thou, whose exterior semblance doth belie
      Thy soul's immensity ;
Thou best Philosopher, who yet dost keep
Thy heritage, thou Eye among the blind,
That, deaf and silent, read'st the eternal deep,
Haunted for ever by the eternal mind,—
      Mighty Prophet ! Seer blest !
      On whom those truths do rest,
Which we are toiling all our lives to find,
In darkness lost, the darkness of the grave ;
Thou, over whom thy immortality
Broods like the day, a master o'er a slave,
A presence which is not to be put by ;
Thou little Child, yet glorious in the might
Of heaven-born freedom on thy being's height,
Why with such earnest pains dost thou provoke
The years to bring the inevitable yoke,
Thus blindly with thy blessedness at strife ?
Full soon thy soul shall have her earthly freight,
And custom lie upon thee with a weight,
Heavy as frost, and deep almost as life !

IX.

      O joy ! that in our embers
      Is something that doth live,
      That nature yet remembers
      What was so fugitive !
The thought of our past years in me doth breed
Perpetual benediction : not indeed
For that which is most worthy to be blest ;

Delight and liberty, the simple creed
Of childhood, whether busy or at rest,
With new-fledged hope still fluttering in his breast :—
   Not for these I raise
   The song of thanks and praise ;
   But for those obstinate questionings
   Of sense and outward things,
   Fallings from us, vanishings ;
   Blank misgivings of a Creature
Moving about in worlds not realised,
High instincts before which our mortal Nature
Did tremble like a guilty thing surprised :
   But for those first affections,
   Those shadowy recollections,
   Which, be they what they may,
Are yet the fountain light of all our day,
Are yet a master light of all our seeing ;
  Uphold us, cherish, and have power to make
Our noisy years seem moments in the being
Of the eternal Silence : truths that wake,
   To perish never ;
Which neither listlessness, nor mad endeavour.
  Nor Man nor Boy,
Nor all that is at enmity with joy,
Can utterly abolish or destroy !
   Hence, in a season of calm weather,
   Though inland far we be,
Our souls have sight of that immortal sea
   Which brought us hither,
   Can in a moment travel thither,
And see the children sport upon the shore.
And hear the mighty waters rolling evermore.

X.

Then sing, ye Birds, sing, sing a joyous song !
    And let the young Lambs bound
    As to the tabor's sound !
We in thought will join your throng,
    Ye that pipe and ye that play,
    Ye that through your hearts to-day
    Feel the gladness of the May !
What though the radiance which was once so bright
Be now for ever taken from my sight,
    Though nothing can bring back the hour
Of splendour in the grass, of glory in the flower ;
    We will grieve not, rather find
    Strength in what remains behind ;
    In the primal sympathy
    Which having been must ever be,
    In the soothing thoughts that spring
    Out of human suffering,
    In the faith that looks through death,
In years that bring the philosophic mind.

XI.

And O, ye Fountains, Meadows, Hills, and Groves,
Think not of any severing of our loves !
Yet in my heart of hearts I feel your might ;
I only have relinquished one delight
To live beneath your more habitual sway.
I love the Brooks which down their channels fret,
Even more than when I tripped lightly as they ;
The innocent brightness of a new-born Day
    Is lovely yet ;
The Clouds that gather round the setting sun
Do take a sober colouring from an eye

That hath kept watch o'er man's mortality;
Another race hath been, and other palms are won
Thanks to the human heart by which we live,
Thanks to its tenderness, its joys, and fears,
To me the meanest flower that blows can give
Thoughts that do often lie too deep for tears

SONNETS

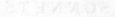

I.—COMPOSED BY THE SEA-SIDE, NEAR CALAIS.
AUGUST 1802.

FAIR Star of Evening, Splendour of the West,
Star of my country!—on the horizon's brink
Thou hangest, stooping, as might seem, to sink
On England's bosom; yet well pleased to rest,
Meanwhile, and be to her a glorious crest
Conspicuous to the Nations. Thou, I think,
Should'st be my Country's emblem; and should'st wink,
Bright Star! with laughter on her banners, drest
In thy fresh beauty. There! that dusky spot
Beneath thee, it is England; there it lies.
Blessings be on you both! one hope, one lot,
One life, one glory! I with many a fear
For my dear Country, many heartfelt sighs,
Among Men who do not love her, linger here.

II.—CALAIS, AUGUST 1802.

Is it a Reed that's shaken by the wind,
Or what is it that ye go forth to see?
Lords, Lawyers, Statesmen, Squires of low degree,
Men known, and men unknown, sick, lame, and blind,
Post forward all, like creatures of one kind,
With first-fruit offerings crowd to bend the knee
In France, before the new-born Majesty.
'Tis ever thus. Ye Men of prostrate mind!
A seemly reverence may be paid to power;
But that's a loyal virtue, never sown
In haste, nor springing with a transient shower:
When truth, when sense, when liberty were flown,
What hardship had it been to wait an hour?
Shame on you, feeble Heads, to slavery prone!

III.—On the Extinction of the Venetian Republic.

ONCE did She hold the gorgeous East in fee ;
And was the safeguard of the West : the worth
Of Venice did not fall below her birth,
Venice, the eldest Child of Liberty.
She was a Maiden City, bright and free ;
No guile seduced, no force could violate ;
And, when She took unto herself a Mate,
She must espouse the everlasting Sea.
And what if she had seen those glories fade,
Those titles vanish, and that strength decay :
Yet shall some tribute of regret be paid
When her long life hath reached its final day :
Men are we, and must grieve when even the Shade
Of that which once was great, is passed away.

IV.—To Toussaint l'Ouverture.

TOUSSAINT, the most unhappy Man of Men !
Whether the whistling Rustic tend his plough
Within thy hearing, or thy head be now
Pillowed in some deep dungeon's earless den ;—
O miserable Chieftain ! where and when
Wilt thou find patience ?   Yet die not ; do thou
Wear rather in thy bonds a cheerful brow :
Though fallen Thyself, never to rise again,
Live, and take comfort.   Thou hast left behind
Powers that will work for thee ; air, earth, and skies ;
There's not a breathing of the common wind
That will forget thee ; thou hast great allies ;
Thy friends are exultations, agonies,
And love, and Man's unconquerable mind

V.—SEPTEMBER 1802.

INLAND, within a hollow Vale, I stood ;
And saw, while sea was calm and air was clear,
The Coast of France, the Coast of France how near !
Drawn almost into frightful neighbourhood,
I shrunk, for verily the barrier flood
Was like a Lake, or River bright and fair,
A span of waters ; yet what power is there !
What mightiness for evil and for good !
Even so doth God protect us if we be
Virtuous and wise.   Winds blow, and Waters roll,
Strength to the brave, and Power, and Deity,
Yet in themselves are nothing !   One decree
Spake laws to *them*, and said that, by the Soul
Only, the Nations shall be great and free.

VI.—THOUGHT OF A BRITON ON THE SUBJUGATION OF SWITZERLAND.

TWO Voices are there ; one is of the Sea,
One of the Mountains ; each a mighty Voice :
In both from age to age Thou didst rejoice,
They were thy chosen Music, Liberty !
There came a Tyrant, and with holy glee
Thou fought'st against Him ; but hast vainly striven :
Thou from the Alpine holds at length art driven,
Where not a torrent murmurs heard by thee.
Of one deep bliss thine ear hath been bereft :
Then cleave, O cleave to that which still is left ;
For, high-souled Maid, what sorrow would it be
That mountain Floods should thunder as before,
And Ocean bellow from his rocky shore,
And neither awful Voice be heard by thee !

VII.—Written in London, September 1802.

O Friend! I know not which way I must look
For comfort, being, as I am, opprest,
To think that now our Life is only drest
For show; mean handy-work of craftsman, cook,
Or groom!—We must run glittering like a Brook
In the open sunshine, or we are unblest:
The wealthiest man among us is the best:
No grandeur now in nature or in book
Delights us. Rapine, avarice, expense,
This is idolatry; and these we adore:
Plain living and high thinking are no more:
The homely beauty of the good old cause
Is gone; our peace, our fearful innocence,
And pure religion breathing household laws.

VIII.

The world is too much with us; late and soon,
Getting and spending, we lay waste our powers:
Little we see in Nature that is ours;
We have given our hearts away, a sordid boon!
This Sea that bares her bosom to the moon;
The winds that will be howling at all hours,
And are up-gathered now like sleeping flowers;
For this, for every thing, we are out of tune;
It moves us not.—Great God! I'd rather be
A Pagan suckled in a creed outworn;
So might I, standing on this pleasant lea,
Have glimpses that would make me less forlorn;
Have sight of Proteus rising from the sea;
Or hear old Triton blow his wreathèd horn.

IX.—LONDON, 1802.

MILTON! thou shouldst be living at this hour:
England hath need of thee: she is a fen
Of stagnant waters: altar, sword, and pen,
Fireside, the heroic wealth of hall and bower,
Have forfeited their ancient English dower
Of inward happiness.   We are selfish men;
Oh! raise us up, return to us again;
And give us manners, virtue, freedom, power.
Thy soul was like a Star, and dwelt apart:
Thou hadst a voice whose sound was like the sea:
Pure as the naked heavens, majestic, free,
So didst thou travel on life's common way,
In cheerful godliness; and yet thy heart
The lowliest duties on herself did lay.

X.

IT is not to be thought of that the Flood
Of British freedom, which to the open Sea
Of the world's praise from dark antiquity
Hath flowed, "with pomp of waters, unwithstood,"
Roused though it be full often to a mood
Which spurns the check of salutary bands,
That this most famous Stream in Bogs and Sands
Should perish; and to evil and to good
Be lost for ever.   In our Halls is hung
Armoury of the invincible Knights of old:
We must be free or die, who speak the tongue
That Shakspeare spake; the faith and morals hold
Which Milton held.—In every thing we are sprung
Of Earth's first blood, have titles manifold.

XI.

WHEN I have borne in memory what has tamed
Great Nations, how ennobling thoughts depart
When men change Swords for Ledgers, and desert
The Student's bower for gold, some fears unnamed
I had, my Country !—am I to be blamed?
But when I think of Thee, and what Thou art.
Verily, in the bottom of my heart,
Of those unfilial fears I am ashamed.
But dearly must we prize thee ; we who find
In thee a bulwark for the cause of men ;
And I by my affection was beguiled :
What wonder if a Poet now and then,
Among the many movements of his mind,
Felt for thee as a Lover or a Child !

XII.—OCTOBER 1803.

THESE times touch monied Worldlings with dismay :
Even rich men, brave by nature, taint the air
With words of apprehension and despair :
While tens of thousands, thinking on the affray,
Men unto whom sufficient for the day
And minds not stinted or untilled are given,
Sound, healthy Children of the God of Heaven,
Are cheerful as the rising Sun in May.
What do we gather hence but firmer faith
That every gift of noble origin
Is breathed upon by Hope's perpetual breath ;
That virtue and the faculties within
Are vital,—and that riches are akin
To fear, to change, to cowardice, and death ?

XIII.—To the Men of Kent. October 1803.

Vanguard of Liberty, ye Men of Kent,
Ye children of a soil that doth advance
Her haughty brow against the coast of France,
Now is the time to prove your hardiment!
To France be words of invitation sent!
They from their fields can see the countenance
Of your fierce war, may ken the glittering lance,
And hear you shouting forth your brave intent.
Left single, in bold parley, Ye, of yore,
Did from the Norman win a gallant wreath;
Confirmed the charters that were yours before;—
No parleying now! In Britain is one breath;
We all are with you now from shore to shore:—
Ye Men of Kent, 'tis Victory or Death!

XIV.—In the Pass of Killicranky, an Invasion
being expected, October 1803.

Six thousand Veterans practised in War's game,
Tried men, at Killicranky were arrayed
Against an equal host that wore the plaid,
Shepherds and Herdsmen.—Like a whirlwind came
The Highlanders, the slaughter spread like flame;
And Garry, thundering down his mountain road,
Was stopped, and could not breathe beneath the load
Of the dead bodies.—'Twas a day of shame
For them whom precept and the pedantry
Of cold mechanic battle do enslave.
O for a single hour of that Dundee,
Who on that day the word of onset gave!
Like conquest would the Men of England see;
And her Foes find a like inglorious grave.

XV.

ENGLAND! the time is come when thou should'st wean
Thy heart from its emasculating food;
The truth should now be better understood;
Old things have been unsettled; we have seen
Fair seed-time, better harvest might have been
But for thy trespasses; and, at this day,
If for Greece, Egypt, India, Africa,
Aught good were destined, Thou would'st step between.
England! all nations in this charge agree:
But worse, more ignorant in love and hate,
Far, far more abject is thine Enemy:
Therefore the wise pray for thee, though the freight
Of thy offences be a heavy weight;
Oh grief, that Earth's best hopes rest all with Thee!

XVI.—NOVEMBER 1806.

ANOTHER year!—another deadly blow!
Another mighty Empire overthrown!
And We are left, or shall be left, alone;
The last that dare to struggle with the Foe.
'Tis well! from this day forward we shall know
That in ourselves our safety must be sought;
That by our own right hands it must be wrought,
That we must stand unpropped, or be laid low.
O Dastard whom such foretaste doth not cheer!
We shall exult, if they who rule the land
Be men who hold its many blessings dear,
Wise, upright, valiant; not a servile band,
Who are to judge of danger which they fear,
And honour which they do not understand.

XVII.—To Thomas Clarkson, on the Final Passing of the Bill for the Abolition of the Slave Trade, March 1807.

Clarkson ! it was an obstinate hill to climb :
How toilsome—nay, how dire it was, by Thee
Is known,—by none, perhaps, so feelingly ;
But Thou, who, starting in thy fervent prime,
Didst first lead forth this pilgrimage sublime,
Hast heard the constant Voice its charge repeat,
Which, out of thy young heart's oracular seat,
First roused thee.—O true yoke-fellow of Time,
Duty's intrepid liegeman, see, the palm
Is won, and by all Nations shall be worn !
The bloody Writing is for ever torn,
And Thou henceforth shalt have a good man's calm,
A great man's happiness ; thy zeal shall find
Repose at length, firm Friend of human kind !

XVIII.—1811.

Here pause : the poet claims at least this praise,
That virtuous Liberty hath been the scope
Of his pure song, which did not shrink from hope
In the worst moment of these evil days ;
From hope, the paramount *duty* that Heaven lays,
For its own honour, on man's suffering heart.
Never may from our souls one truth depart,
That an accursed thing it is to gaze
On prosperous Tyrants with a dazzled eye ;
Nor, touched with due abhorrence of their guilt
For whose dire ends tears flow, and blood is spilt
And justice labours in extremity,
Forget thy weakness, upon which is built,
O wretched Man, the throne of Tyranny !

XIX.

SCORN not the Sonnet; Critic, you have frowned,
Mindless of its just honours; with this key
Shakspeare unlocked his heart; the melody
Of this small lute gave ease to Petrarch's wound;
A thousand times this pipe did Tasso sound;
Camöens soothed with it an exile's grief;
The Sonnet glittered a gay myrtle leaf
Amid the cypress with which Dante crowned
His visionary brow: a glow-worm lamp,
It cheered mild Spenser, called from Faery-land
To struggle through dark ways; and, when a damp
Fell round the path of Milton, in his hand
The Thing became a trumpet, whence he blew
Soul-animating strains—alas, too few!

XX.

NUNS fret not at their convent's narrow room,
And Hermits are contented with their cells,
And Students with their pensive citadels;
Maids at the wheel, the Weaver at his loom,
Sit blithe and happy; Bees that soar for bloom,
High as the highest Peak of Furness Fells,
Will murmur by the hour in foxglove bells:
In truth, the prison, unto which we doom
Ourselves, no prison is: and hence to me,
In sundry moods, 'twas pastime to be bound
Within the Sonnet's scanty plot of ground:
Pleased if some Souls (for such there needs must be)
Who have felt the weight of too much liberty,
Should find brief solace there, as I have found.

XXI.—CATHERINE WORDSWORTH.
(DIED JUNE 4, 1812.)

SURPRISED by joy—impatient as the Wind
I turned to share the transport—Oh ! with whom
But Thee, deep buried in the silent tomb,
That spot which no vicissitude can find ?
Love, faithful love, recalled thee to my mind—
But how could I forget thee ?   Through what power,
Even for the least division of an hour,
Have I been so beguiled as to be blind
To my most grievous loss ?—That thought's return
Was the worst pang that sorrow ever bore,
Save one, one only, when I stood forlorn,
Knowing my heart's best treasure was no more ;
That neither present time, nor years unborn
Could to my sight that heavenly face restore.

XXII.—TO THE AUTHOR'S PORTRAIT.

[Painted at Rydal Mount, by W. Pickersgill, Esq., for St. John's
College, Cambridge.]

Go, faithful portrait ! and where long hath knelt
Margaret, the saintly Foundress, take thy place !
And, if Time spare the colours for the grace
Which to the work surpassing skill hath dealt,
Thou, on thy rock reclined, though kingdoms melt
And states be torn up by the roots, wilt seem
To breathe in rural peace, to hear the stream,
And think and feel as once the Poet felt.
Whate'er thy fate, those features have not grown
Unrecognised through many a household tear
More prompt, more glad to fall than drops of dew
By morning shed around a flower half-blown ;
Tears of delight, that testified how true
To life thou art, and, in thy truth, how dear !

XXIII.—PERSONAL TALK.

I AM not One who much or oft delight
To season my fireside with personal talk,—
Of friends, who live within an easy walk,
Or neighbours, daily, weekly, in my sight :
And, for my chance-acquaintance, ladies bright,
Sons, mothers, maidens withering on the stalk,
These all wear out of me, like forms with chalk
Painted on rich men's floors for one feast-night.
Better than such discourse doth silence long,
Long, barren silence, square with my desire ;
To sit without emotion, hope, or aim,
In the loved presence of my cottage-fire,
And listen to the flapping of the flame,
Or kettle whispering its faint undersong.

XXIV.—CONTINUED.

WINGS have we,—and as far as we can go
We may find pleasure : wilderness and wood,
Blank ocean and mere sky, support that mood
Which with the lofty sanctifies the low.
Dreams, books, are each a world ; and books, we know,
Are a substantial world, both pure and good :
Round these, with tendrils strong as flesh and blood,
Our pastime and our happiness will grow.
There find I personal themes, a plenteous store,
Matter wherein right voluble I am,
To which I listen with a ready ear ;
Two shall be named, pre-eminently dear,—
The gentle Lady married to the Moor ;
And heavenly Una with her milk-white Lamb.

XXV.—CONCLUDED.

Nor can I not believe but that hereby
Great gains are mine; for thus I live remote
From evil-speaking; rancour, never sought,
Comes to me not; malignant truth, or lie.
Hence have I genial seasons, hence have I
Smooth passions, smooth discourse, and joyous
    thought:
And thus from day to day my little boat
Rocks in its harbour, lodging peaceably.
Blessings be with them—and eternal praise,
Who gave us nobler loves, and nobler cares—
The Poets, who on earth have made us heirs
Of truth and pure delight by heavenly lays!
Oh! might my name be numbered among theirs,
Then gladly would I end my mortal days.

XXVI.—TO SLEEP.

A flock of sheep that leisurely pass by,
One after one; the sound of rain, and bees
Murmuring; the fall of rivers, winds and seas,
Smooth fields, white sheets of water, and pure sky.
By turns have all been thought of, yet I lie
Sleepless; and soon the small birds' melodies
Must hear, first uttered from my orchard trees;
And the first Cuckoo's melancholy cry.
Even thus last night, and two nights more, I lay,
And could not win thee, Sleep! by any stealth:
So do not let me wear to-night away:
Without Thee what is all the morning's wealth?
Come, blessed barrier between day and day,
Dear mother of fresh thoughts and joyous health!

XXVII.—COMPOSED UPON THE BEACH NEAR CALAIS, 1802.

IT is a beauteous Evening, calm and free ;
The holy time is quiet as a Nun
Breathless with adoration ; the broad sun
Is sinking down in its tranquillity ;
The gentleness of heaven is on the sea :
Listen ! the mighty Being is awake,
And doth with his eternal motion make
A sound like thunder—everlastingly.
Dear Child ! dear Girl ! that walkest with me here,
If thou appear'st untouched by solemn thought,
Thy nature is not therefore less divine :
Thou liest in Abraham's bosom all the year ;
And worshipp'st at the Temple's inner shrine,
God being with thee when we know it not.

XXVIII.

WHERE lies the Land to which yon Ship must go ?
Festively she puts forth in trim array ;
As vigorous as a Lark at break of day :
Is she for tropic suns, or polar snow ?
What boots the inquiry ?—Neither friend nor foe
She cares for ; let her travel where she may,
She finds familiar names, a beaten way
Ever before her, and a wind to blow.
Yet still I ask, what haven is her mark ?
And, almost as it was when ships were rare
(From time to time, like Pilgrims, here and there
Crossing the waters), doubt, and something dark,
Of the old Sea some reverential fear,
Is with me at thy farewell, joyous Bark !

XXIX.—Composed upon Westminster Bridge,
Sept. 3, 1803.

Earth has not anything to show more fair :
Dull would he be of soul who could pass by
A sight so touching in its majesty :
This City now doth like a garment wear
The beauty of the morning ; silent, bare,
Ships, towers, domes, theatres, and temples lie
Open unto the fields, and to the sky ;
All bright and glittering in the smokeless air.
Never did sun more beautifully steep
In his first splendour valley, rock, or hill ;
Ne'er saw I, never felt, a calm so deep !
The river glideth at his own sweet will :
Dear God ! the very houses seem asleep ;
And all that mighty heart is lying still !

XXX.—Scenery between Namur and Liege.

What lovelier home could gentle Fancy choose ?
Is this the Stream, whose cities, heights, and plains,
War's favourite playground, are with crimson stains
Familiar, as the Morn with pearly dews ?
The Morn, that now, along the silver Meuse,
Spreading her peaceful ensigns, calls the swains
To tend their silent boats and ringing wains,
Or strip the bough whose mellow fruit bestrews
The ripening corn beneath it.   As mine eyes
Turn from the fortified and threatening hill,
How sweet the prospect of yon watery glade,
With its grey rocks clustering in pensive shade,
That, shaped like old monastic turrets, rise
From the smooth meadow-ground, serene and still !

XXXI.—ADMONITION.

Intended more particularly for the Perusal of those who may have
happened to be enamoured of some beautiful Place of Retreat,
in the Country of the Lakes.

YES, there is holy pleasure in thine eye !
—The lovely Cottage in the guardian nook
Hath stirred thee deeply ; with its own dear brook,
Its own small pasture, almost its own sky !
But covet not the Abode ;—forbear to sigh,
As many do, repining while they look ;
Intruders—who would tear from Nature's book
This precious leaf, with harsh impiety.
Think what the Home must be if it were thine,
Even thine, though few thy wants !—Roof, window, door,
The very flowers are sacred to the Poor ;
The roses to the porch which they entwine.
Yea, all, that now enchants thee, from the day
On which it should be touched, would melt away.

XXXII.

I WATCH, and long have watched, with calm regret
Yon slowly-sinking star—immortal Sire
(So might he seem) of all the glittering quire !
Blue ether still surrounds him—yet—and yet ;
But now the horizon's rocky parapet
Is reached, where, forfeiting his bright attire,
He burns—transmuted to a sullen fire,
That droops and dwindles—and the appointed debt
To the flying moments paid, is seen no more.
Angels and gods ! *we* struggle with our fate,
While health, power, glory, pitiably decline,
Depressed and then extinguished : and our state
In this how different, lost star, from thine,
That no to-morrow shall our beams restore !

XXXIII.

SOLE listener, Duddon! to the breeze that played
With thy clear voice, I caught the fitful sound
Wafted o'er sullen moss and craggy mound,
Unfruitful solitudes, that seemed to upbraid
The sun in heaven!—but now, to form a shade
For Thee, green alders have together wound
Their foliage; ashes flung their arms around;
And birch-trees risen in silver colonnade.
And thou hast also tempted here to rise,
'Mid sheltering pines, this Cottage rude and grey;
Whose ruddy children, by the mother's eyes
Carelessly watched, sport through the summer day
Thy pleased associates:—light as endless May
On infant bosoms lonely Nature lies.

XXXIV.

WANSFELL![1] this Household has a favoured lot,
Living with liberty on thee to gaze,
To watch while Morn first crowns thee with her rays,
Or when along thy breast serenely float
Evening's angelic clouds. Yet ne'er a note
Hath sounded (shame upon the Bard!) thy praise
For all that thou, as if from heaven, hast brought
Of glory lavished on our quiet days.
Bountiful Son of Earth! when we are gone
From every object dear to mortal sight,
As soon we shall be, may these words attest
How oft, to elevate our spirits, shone
Thy visionary majesties of light,
How in thy pensive glooms our hearts found rest.

[1] The Hill that rises to the south-east, above Ambleside.

XXXV.

RETURN, Content! for fondly I pursued,
Even when a child, the Streams—unheard, unseen;
Through tangled woods, impending rocks between;
Or, free as air, with flying inquest viewed
The sullen reservoirs whence their bold brood,
Pure as the morning, fretful, boisterous, keen,
Green as the salt-sea billows, white and green,
Poured down the hills, a choral multitude?
Nor have I tracked their course for scanty gains;
They taught me random cares and truant joys,
That shield from mischief and preserve from stains
Vague minds, while men are growing out of boys;
Maturer Fancy owes to their rough noise
Impetuous thoughts that brook not servile reins.

XXXVI.—AFTER-THOUGHT.

I THOUGHT of Thee, my partner and my guide,
As being past away.—Vain sympathies!
For backward, Duddon! as I cast my eyes,
I see what was, and is, and will abide;
Still glides the Stream, and shall not cease to glide:
The Form remains, the Function never dies;
While we, the brave, the mighty, and the wise,
We Men, who in our morn of youth defied
The elements, must vanish;—be it so!
Enough, if something from our hands have power
To live, and act, and serve the future hour;
And if, as tow'rd the silent tomb we go,
Through love, through hope, and faith's transcendent
　　　dower,
We feel that we are greater than we know.

XXXVII.—SECLUSION.

LANCE, shield, and sword relinquished—at his side
A Bead-roll, in his hand a claspèd Book,
Or staff more harmless than a Shepherd's crook,
The war-worn Chieftain quits the world—to hide
His thin autumnal locks where Monks abide
In cloistered privacy.   But not to dwell
In soft repose he comes.   Within his cell,
Round the decaying trunk of human pride,
At morn, and eve, and midnight's silent hour,
Do penitential cogitations cling :
Like ivy round some ancient elm, they twine
In grisly folds and strictures serpentine ;
Yet, while they strangle without mercy, bring
For recompence their own perennial bower.

XXXVIII.—RUSH-BEARING.

CONTENT with calmer scenes around us spread
And humbler objects, give we to a day
Of annual joy one tributary lay ;
This day, when, forth by rustic music led,
The village Children, while the sky is red
With evening lights, advance in long array
Through the still Churchyard, each with garland gay,
That, carried sceptre-like, o'ertops the head
Of the proud Bearer.   To the wide Church-door,
Charged with these offerings which their Fathers bore
For decoration in the Papal time,
The innocent procession softly moves :—
The spirit of Laud is pleased in Heaven's pure clime,
And Hooker's voice the spectacle approves !

XXXIX.—INSIDE OF KING'S COLLEGE CHAPEL, CAMBRIDGE.

TAX not the royal Saint with vain expense,
With ill-matched aims the Architect who planned,
Albeit labouring for a scanty band
Of white robed Scholars only, this immense
And glorious work of fine intelligence !
Give all thou canst ; high Heaven rejects the lore
Of nicely-calculated less or more ;
So deemed the Man who fashioned for the sense
These lofty pillars, spread that branching roof
Self-poised, and scooped into ten thousand cells,
Where light and shade repose, where music dwells
Lingering—and wandering on as loth to die ;
Like thoughts whose very sweetness yieldeth proof
That they were born for immortality.

XL.—CONTINUED.

THEY dreamt not of a perishable home
Who thus could build.   Be mine, in hours of fear
Or grovelling thought, to seek a refuge here ;
Or through the aisles of Westminster to roam ;
Where bubbles burst, and folly's dancing foam
Melts, if it cross the threshold ; where the wreath
Of awe-struck wisdom droops :—or let my path
Lead to that younger Pile, whose sky-like dome
Hath typified by reach of daring art
Infinity's embrace ; whose guardian crest,
The silent Cross, among the stars shall spread
As now, when She hath also seen her breast
Filled with mementos, satiate with its part
Of grateful England's overflowing Dead.

XLI.—MARY, QUEEN OF SCOTS, LANDING AT THE MOUTH OF THE DERWENT, WORKINGTON.

DEAR to the Loves, and to the Graces vowed,
The Queen drew back the wimple that she wore ;
And to the throng, that on the Cumbrian shore
Her landing hailed, how touchingly she bowed !
And like a Star (that, from a heavy cloud
Of pine-tree foliage poised in air, forth darts
When a soft summer gale at evening parts
The gloom that did its loveliness enshroud)
She smiled : but Time, the old Saturnian seer,
Sighed on the wing as her foot pressed the strand,
With step prelusive to a long array
Of woes and degradations hand in hand—
Weeping captivity, and shuddering fear
Stilled by the ensanguined block of Fotheringay !

XLII.

MOST sweet is it with un-uplifted eyes
To pace the ground, if path be there or none,
While a fair region round the traveller lies
Which he forbears again to look upon ;
Pleased rather with some soft ideal scene,
The work of Fancy, or some happy tone
Of meditation, slipping in between
The beauty coming and the beauty gone.
If thought and Love desert us, from that day
Let us break off all commerce with the Muse
With Thought and Love companions of our way,
Whate'er the senses take or may refuse,
The Mind's internal heaven shall shed her dews
Of inspiration on the humblest lay.

XLIII.—On the Departure of Sir Walter Scott
  from Abbotsford, for Naples.

A TROUBLE, not of clouds, or weeping rain,
Nor of the setting sun's pathetic light
Engendered, hangs o'er Eildon's triple height :
Spirits of Power, assembled there, complain
For kindred Power departing from their sight ;
While Tweed, best pleased in chanting a blithe strain,
Saddens his voice again and yet again.
Lift up your hearts, ye Mourners ! for the might
Of the whole world's good wishes with him goes ;
Blessings and prayers, in nobler retinue
Than sceptred king or laurelled conqueror knows,
Follow this wondrous Potentate.   Be true,
Ye winds of ocean, and the midland sea,
Wafting your Charge to soft Parthenope !

XLIV.—To R. B. Haydon, Esq.

HIGH is our calling, Friend !—Creative Art
(Whether the instrument of words she use,
Or pencil pregnant with ethereal hues)
Demands the service of a mind and heart,
Though sensitive, yet, in their weakest part
Heroically fashioned—to infuse
Faith in the whispers of the lonely Muse,
While the whole world seems adverse to desert.
And, oh ! when Nature sinks, as oft she may,
Through long-lived pressure of obscure distress,
Still to be strenuous for the bright reward,
And in the soul admit of no decay,
Brook no continuance of weak-mindedness—
Great is the glory, for the strife is hard !

XLV.—MUTABILITY.

FROM low to high doth dissolution climb,
And sink from high to low, along a scale
Of awful notes, whose concord shall not fail :
A musical but melancholy chime,
Which they can hear who meddle not with crime,
Nor avarice, nor over-anxious care.
Truth fails not ; but her outward forms that bear
The longest date do melt like frosty rime,
That in the morning whitened hill and plain
And is no more ; drop like the tower sublime
Of yesterday, which royally did wear
His crown of weeds, but could not even sustain
Some casual shout that broke the silent air,
Or the unimaginable touch of Time.

XLVI.

THE pibroch's note, discountenanced or mute ;
The Roman kilt, degraded to a toy
Of quaint apparel for a half-spoilt boy ;
The target mouldering like ungathered fruit ;
The smoking steam-boat eager in pursuit,
As eagerly pursued ; the umbrella spread
To weather-fend the Celtic herdsman's head—
All speak of manners withering to the root,
And of old honours, too, and passions high :
Then may we ask, though pleased that thought should
        range
Among the conquests of civility,
Survives imagination—to the change
Superior ?   Help to virtue does she give ?
If not, O Mortals, better cease to live !

XLVII.

A Poet !—He hath put his heart to school,
Nor dares to move unpropped upon the staff
Which Art hath lodged within his hand—must laugh
By precept only, and shed tears by rule.
Thy Art be Nature ; the live current quaff,
And let the groveller sip his stagnant pool,
In fear that else, when Critics grave and cool
Have killed him, Scorn should write his epitaph.
How does the Meadow-flower its bloom unfold ?
Because the lovely little flower is free
Down to its root, and, in that freedom, bold ;
And so the grandeur of the Forest-tree
Comes not by casting in a formal mould
But from its *own* divine vitality.

XLVIII.—The Pine of Monte Mario at Rome.

I saw far off the dark top of a Pine
Look like a cloud—a slender stem the tie
That bound it to its native earth—poised high
'Mid evening hues, along the horizon line,
Striving in peace each other to outshine.
But when I learned the Tree was living there
Saved from the sordid axe by Beaumont's care,
Oh, what a gush of tenderness was mine !
The rescued Pine-tree, with its sky so bright
And cloud-like beauty, rich in thoughts of home,
Death-parted friends, and days too swift in flight,
Supplanted the whole majesty of Rome
(Then first apparent from the Pincian Height)
Crowned with St. Peter's everlasting Dome

XLIX.—To the Memory of Raisley Calvert.

CALVERT! it must not be unheard by them
Who may respect my name, that I to thee
Owed many years of early liberty.
This care was thine when sickness did condemn
Thy youth to hopeless wasting, root and stem—
That I, if frugal and severe, might stray
Where'er I liked; and finally array
My temples with the Muse's diadem.
Hence, if in freedom I have loved the truth;
If there be aught of pure, or good, or great,
In my past verse; or shall be, in the lays
Of higher mood which now I meditate;—
It gladdens me, O worthy, short-lived Youth!
To think how much of this will be thy praise.

L.—To Rotha Quillinan.

ROTHA, my Spiritual Child! this head was grey
When at the sacred font for thee I stood:
Pledged till thou reach the verge of womanhood,
And shalt become thy own sufficient stay:
Too late, I feel, sweet Orphan! was the day
For steadfast hope the contract to fulfil;
Yet shall my blessing hover o'er thee still,
Embodied in the music of this Lay,
Breathed forth beside the peaceful mountain Stream[1]
Whose murmur soothed thy languid Mother's ear
After her throes, this Stream of name more dear
Since thou dost bear it,—a memorial theme
For others; for thy future self, a spell
To summon fancies out of Time's dark cell.

[1] The river Rotha, that flows into Windermere from the Lakes of Grasmere and Rydal.

LI.—To Lady Fitzgerald, in her seventieth
year.

Such age how beautiful !   O Lady bright,
Whose mortal lineaments seem all refined
By favouring Nature and a saintly Mind
To something purer and more exquisite
Than flesh and blood ; whene'er thou meet'st my sight,
When I behold thy blanched unwithered cheek,
Thy temples fringed with locks of gleaming white,
And head that droops because the soul is meek,
Thee with the welcome Snowdrop I compare ;
That child of winter, prompting thoughts that climb
From desolation toward the genial prime ;
Or with the Moon conquering earth's misty air,
And filling more and more with crystal light
As pensive Evening deepens into night.

LII.—Composed on a May Morning, 1838.

Life with yon Lambs, like day, is just begun,
Yet Nature seems to them a heavenly guide.
Does joy approach ? they meet the coming tide,
And sullenness avoid, as now they shun
Pale twilight's lingering glooms and in the sun
Couch near their dams, with quiet satisfied ;
Or gambol—each with his shadow at his side,
Varying its shape wherever he may run.
As they from turf yet hoar with sleepy dew
All turn, and court the shining and the green,
Where herbs look up and opening flowers are seen,
Why to God's goodness cannot *we* be true ?
And so, His gifts and promises between,
Feed to the last on pleasures ever new ?

LIII.—HIGHLAND HUT.

SEE what gay wild flowers deck this earth-built Cot,
Whose smoke, forth-issuing whence and how it may,
Shines in the greeting of the sun's first ray
Like wreaths of vapour without stain or blot.
The limpid mountain rill avoids it not,
And why shouldst thou ?—If rightly trained and bred,
Humanity is humble, finds no spot
Which her Heaven-guided feet refuse to tread.
The walls are cracked, sunk is the flowery roof,
Undressed the pathway leading to the door.
But love, as Nature loves, the lonely Poor !
Search, for their worth, some gentle heart wrong-proof,
Meek, patient, kind,—and, were its trials fewer,
Belike less happy.—Stand no more aloof !

LIV.

" THERE !" said a Stripling, pointing with meet pride
Towards a low roof with green trees half concealed,
" Is Mosgiel Farm ; and that's the very field
Where Burns ploughed up the Daisy." Far and wide
A plain below stretched seaward, while, descried
Above sea-clouds, the Peaks of Arran rose ;
And, by that simple notice, the repose
Of earth, sky, sea, and air, was vivified.
Beneath "the random *bield* of clod or stone"
Myriads of daisies have shone forth in flower
Near the lark's nest, and in their natural hour
Have passed away ; less happy than the One
That, by the unwilling ploughshare, died to prove
The tender charm of poetry and love.

LV.—To a Painter

WHO HAD PAINTED MRS. WORDSWORTH'S PORTRAIT.

ALL praise the Likeness by thy skill pourtrayed ;
But 'tis a fruitless task to paint for me,
Who, yielding not to changes Time has made,
By the habitual light of memory see
Eyes unbedimmed, see bloom that cannot fade,
And smiles that from their birth-place ne'er shall flee
Into the land where ghosts and phantoms be ;
And, seeing this, own nothing in its stead.
Couldst thou go back into far distant years,
Or share with me, fond thought ! that inward eye,
Then, and then only, Painter ! could thy Art
The visual powers of Nature satisfy,
Which hold, whate'er to common sight appears,
Their sovereign empire in a faithful heart.

LVI.—On the same Subject.

THOUGH I beheld at first with blank surprise
This Work, I now have gazed on it so long
I see its truth with unreluctant eyes ;
O, my Belovèd ! I have done thee wrong,
Conscious of blessedness, but, whence it sprung,
Ever too heedless, as I now perceive :
Morn into noon did pass, noon into eve,
And the old day was welcome as the young,
As welcome, and as beautiful—in sooth
More beautiful, as being a thing more holy :
Thanks to thy virtues, to the eternal youth
Of all thy goodness, never melancholy ;
To thy large heart and humble mind, that cast
Into one vision. future, present, past.

LVII.—IN SIGHT OF THE TOWN OF COCKERMOUTH.

(Where the Author was born, and his Father's remains are laid.)

A POINT of life between my Parents' dust,
And yours, my buried Little-ones! am I;
And to those graves looking habitually
In kindred quiet I repose my trust.
Death to the innocent is more than just,
And, to the sinner, mercifully bent;
So may I hope, if truly I repent
And meekly bear the ills which bear I must:
And You, my Offspring! that do still remain,
Yet may outstrip me in the appointed race,
If e'er, through fault of mine, in mutual pain
We breathed together for a moment's space,
The wrong, by love provoked, let love arraign,
And only love keep in your hearts a place.

LVIII.

TRANQUILLITY! the sovereign aim wert thou
In heathen schools of philosophic lore;
Heart-stricken by stern destiny of yore
The Tragic Muse thee served with thoughtful vow;
And what of hope Elysium could allow
Was fondly seized by Sculpture, to restore
Peace to the Mourner. But when He, who wore
The crown of thorns around His bleeding brow,
Warmed our sad being with His glorious light,
Then Arts, which still had drawn a softening grace
From shadowy fountains of the Infinite,
Communed with that Idea face to face;
And move around it now, as planets run,
Each in its orbit, round the central Sun.

LIX.—DEATH.

METHOUGHT I saw the footsteps of a throne
Which mists and vapours from mine eyes did shroud—
Nor view of who might sit thereon allowed ;
But all the steps and ground about were strown
With sights the ruefullest that flesh and bone
Ever put on : a miserable crowd,
Sick, hale, old, young, who cried before that cloud,
" Thou art our king, O Death ! to thee we groan."
I seem'd to mount those steps ; the vapours gave
Smooth way : and I beheld the face of one
Sleeping alone within a mossy cave,
With her face up to heaven ; that seemed to have
Pleasing remembrance of a thought foregone ;
A lovely Beauty in a summer grave !

LX.—THE EVERLASTING TEMPLE.

IN my mind's eye a Temple, like a cloud
Slowly surmounting some invidious hill,
Rose out of darkness : the bright Work stood still,
And might of its own beauty have been proud,
But it was fashioned and to God was vowed
By Virtues that diffused, in every part,
Spirit divine through forms of human art :
Faith had her arch—her arch, when winds blow loud,
Into the consciousness of safety thrilled ;
And Love her towers of dread foundation laid
Under the grave of things ; Hope had her spire
Star-high, and pointing still to something higher.
Trembling I gazed, but heard a voice—it said :
" Hell-gates are powerless Phantoms when *we* build."

REFLECTIVE AND ELEGIAC
POEMS

"IF THOU INDEED."

IF Thou indeed derive thy light from Heaven,
Shine, Poet, in thy place, and be content!
The Star that from the zenith darts its beams,
Visible though it be to half the Earth,
Though half a sphere be conscious of its brightness,
Is yet of no diviner origin,
No purer essence, than the One that burns,
Like an untended watch-fire, on the ridge
Of some dark mountain; or than those which seem
Humbly to hang, like twinkling winter lamps,
Among the branches of the leafless trees.

INFLUENCE OF NATURAL OBJECTS

IN CALLING FORTH AND STRENGTHENING THE IMAGINATION IN BOYHOOD AND EARLY YOUTH.

WISDOM and Spirit of the Universe!
Thou Soul, that art the Eternity of thought!
And givest to forms and images a breath
And everlasting motion! not in vain,
By day or star-light, thus from my first dawn
Of childhood didst thou intertwine for me
The passions that build up our human soul
Not with the mean and vulgar works of man,
But with high objects, with enduring things,
With life and nature; purifying thus
The elements of feeling and of thought,
And sanctifying by such discipline
Both pain and fear,—until we recognise
A grandeur in the beatings of the heart.
Nor was this fellowship vouchsafed to me
With stinted kindness.   In November days,
When vapours rolling down the valleys made
A lonely scene more lonesome; among woods
At noon; and mid the calm of summer nights,
When, by the margin of the trembling Lake,
Beneath the gloomy hills, I homeward went
In solitude, such intercourse was mine:

'Twas mine among the fields both day and night,
And by the waters, all the summer long.
And in the frosty season, when the sun
Was set, and, visible for many a mile,
The cottage windows through the twilight blazed,
I heeded not the summons :—happy time
It was indeed for all of us ; for me
It was a time of rapture !—Clear and loud
The village clock tolled six—I wheeled about,
Proud and exulting like an untired horse
That cares not for his home.—All shod with steel
We hissed along the polished ice, in games
Confederate, imitative of the chase
And woodland pleasures,—the resounding horn,
The pack loud-bellowing, and the hunted hare.
So through the darkness and the cold we flew,
And not a voice was idle : with the din
Meanwhile the precipices rang aloud ;
The leafless trees and every icy crag
Tinkled like iron ; while the distant hills
Into the tumult sent an alien sound
Of melancholy, not unnoticed, while the stars,
Eastward, were sparkling clear, and in the west
The orange sky of evening died away.

Not seldom from the uproar I retired
Into a silent bay,—or sportively
Glanced sideway, leaving the tumultuous throng,
To cut across the reflex of a Star ;
Image, that, flying still before me, gleamed
Upon the glassy plain : and oftentimes,
When we had given our bodies to the wind,
And all the shadowy banks on either side
Came sweeping through the darkness, spinning still
The rapid line of motion, then at once

Have I, reclining back upon my heels,
Stopped short; yet still the solitary cliffs
Wheeled by me—even as if the earth had rolled
With visible motion her diurnal round!
Behind me did they stretch in solemn train,
Feebler and feebler, and I stood and watched
Till all was tranquil as a summer sea.

"THERE WAS A BOY."

THERE was a Boy; ye knew him well, ye Cliffs
And islands of Winander!—many a time,
At evening, when the earliest stars began
To move along the edges of the hills,
Rising or setting, would he stand alone,
Beneath the trees, or by the glimmering lake;
And there, with fingers interwoven, both hands
Pressed closely palm to palm and to his mouth
Uplifted, he, as through an instrument,
Blew mimic hootings to the silent owls,
That they might answer him.—And they would shout
Across the watery vale, and shout again,
Responsive to his call,—with quivering peals,
And long halloos, and screams, and echoes loud
Redoubled and redoubled; concourse wild
Of mirth and jocund din! And, when it chanced
That pauses of deep silence mocked his skill,
Then, sometimes, in that silence, while he hung
Listening, a gentle shock of mild surprise
Has carried far into his heart the voice
Of mountain torrents; or the visible scene

Would enter unawares into his mind
With all its solemn imagery, its rocks,
Its woods, and that uncertain heaven, received
Into the bosom of the steady lake.

This Boy was taken from his Mates, and died
In childhood, ere he was full twelve years old.
Fair is the spot, most beautiful the Vale
Where he was born : the grassy Churchyard hangs
Upon a slope above the village-school ;
And, through that Church-yard when my way has led
At evening, I believe that oftentimes
A long half-hour together I have stood
Mute—looking at the grave in which he lies !

YEW-TREES.

THERE is a Yew-tree, pride of Lorton Vale,
Which to this day stands single, in the midst
Of its own darkness, as it stood of yore,
Not loth to furnish weapons for the Bands
Of Umfraville or Percy ere they marched
To Scotland's heaths ; or those that crossed the sea
And drew their sounding bows at Azincour,
Perhaps at earlier Crecy, or Poictiers.
Of vast circumference and gloom profound
This solitary Tree !—a living thing
Produced too slowly ever to decay ;
Of form and aspect too magnificent
To be destroyed.   But worthier still of note
Are those fraternal Four of Borrowdale,
Joined in one solemn and capacious grove ;
Huge trunks !—and each particular trunk a growth

Of intertwisted fibres serpentine
Up-coiling, and inveterately convolved,—
Nor uninformed with Phantasy, and looks
That threaten the profane ;—a pillared shade,
Upon whose grassless floor of red-brown hue,
By sheddings from the pining umbrage tinged
Perennially—beneath whose sable roof
Of boughs as if for festal purpose decked
With unrejoicing berries—ghostly shapes
May meet at noontide ; Fear and trembling Hope,
Silence and Foresight, Death the Skeleton
And Time the Shadow ; there to celebrate,
As in a natural temple scattered o'er
With altars undisturbed of mossy stone,
United worship ; or in mute repose
To lie, and listen to the mountain flood
Murmuring from Glaramara's inmost caves.

LINES,

COMPOSED A FEW MILES ABOVE TINTERN ABBEY, ON
REVISITING THE BANKS OF THE WYE DURING A TOUR.

JULY 13, 1798.

FIVE years have past ; five summers, with the length
Of five long winters ! and again I hear
These waters, rolling from their mountain-springs
With a sweet inland murmur.[1]—Once again
Do I behold these steep and lofty cliffs,
That on a wild secluded scene impress
Thoughts of more deep seclusion ; and connect
The landscape with the quiet of the sky.
The day is come when I again repose
Here, under this dark sycamore, and view
These plots of cottage-ground, these orchard-tufts,
Which at this season, with their unripe fruits,
Are clad in one green hue, and lose themselves
Among the woods and copses, nor disturb
The wild green landscape.   Once again I see
These hedgerows, hardly hedgerows, little lines
Of sportive wood run wild : these pastoral farms,
Green to the very door ; and wreaths of smoke
Sent up, in silence, from among the trees !
With some uncertain notice, as might seem
Of vagrant dwellers in the houseless woods,
Or of some Hermit's cave, where by his fire
The Hermit sits alone.
                    These beauteous Forms,
Through a long absence, have not been to me

[1] The river is not affected by the tides a few miles above Tintern.

As is a landscape to a blind man's eye :
But oft, in lonely rooms, and 'mid the din
Of towns and cities, I have owed to them,
In hours of weariness, sensations sweet,
Felt in the blood, and felt along the heart ;
And passing even into my purer mind,
With tranquil restoration :—feelings too
Of unremembered pleasure : such, perhaps,
As have no slight or trivial influence
On that best portion of a good man's life,
His little, nameless, unremembered acts
Of kindness and of love.   Nor less, I trust,
To them I may have owed another gift,
Of aspect more sublime ; that blessed mood,
In which the burthen of the mystery,
In which the heavy and the weary weight
Of all this unintelligible world,
Is lightened :—that serene and blessed mood,
In which the affections gently lead us on,—
Until, the breath of this corporeal frame
And even the motion of our human blood
Almost suspended, we are laid asleep
In body, and become a living soul :
While with an eye made quiet by the power
Of harmony, and the deep power of joy,
We see into the life of things.
                          If this
Be but a vain belief, yet, oh ! how oft,
In darkness, and amid the many shapes
Of joyless daylight ; when the fretful stir
Unprofitable, and the fever of the world,
Have hung upon the beatings of my heart,
How oft, in spirit, have I turned to thee,
O sylvan Wye !   Thou wanderer thro' the woods,
How often has my spirit turned to thee !

And now, with gleams of half-extinguished thought,
With many recognitions dim and faint,
And somewhat of a sad perplexity,
The picture of the mind revives again :
While here I stand, not only with the sense
Of present pleasure, but with pleasing thoughts
That in this moment there is life and food
For future years.   And so I dare to hope,
Though changed, no doubt, from what I was when first
I came among these hills ; when like a roe
I bounded o'er the mountains, by the sides
Of the deep rivers, and the lonely streams,
Wherever nature led : more like a man
Flying from something that he dreads, than one
Who sought the thing he loved.   For nature then
(The coarser pleasures of my boyish days,
And their glad animal movements all gone by)
To me was all in all.—I cannot paint
What then I was.   The sounding cataract
Haunted me like a passion : the tall rock,
The mountain, and the deep and gloomy wood,
Their colours and their forms, were then to me
An appetite ; a feeling and a love,
That had no need of a remoter charm,
By thought supplied, or any interest
Unborrowed from the eye.—That time is past,
And all its aching joys are now no more,
And all its dizzy raptures.   Not for this
Faint I, nor mourn nor murmur ; other gifts
Have followed, for such loss, I would believe,
Abundant recompence.   For I have learned
To look on nature, not as in the hour
Of thoughtless youth ; but hearing oftentimes
The still, sad music of humanity,
Nor harsh nor grating, though of ample power

To chasten and subdue.   And I have felt
A presence that disturbs me with the joy
Of elevated thoughts : a sense sublime
Of something far more deeply interfused,
Whose dwelling is the light of setting suns,
And the round ocean and the living air,
And the blue sky, and in the mind of man :
A motion and a spirit, that impels
All thinking things, all objects of all thought,
And rolls through all things.   Therefore am I still
A lover of the meadows and the woods,
And mountains ; and of all that we behold
From this green earth ; of all the mighty world
Of eye and ear, both what they half create,[1]
And what perceive ; well pleased to recognise
In nature and the language of the sense,
The anchor of my purest thoughts, the nurse,
The guide, the guardian of my heart, and soul
Of all my moral being.

           Nor perchance,
If I were not thus taught, should I the more
Suffer my genial spirits to decay :
For thou art with me, here, upon the banks
Of this fair river ; thou, my dearest Friend,
My dear, dear Friend, and in thy voice I catch
The language of my former heart, and read
My former pleasures in the shooting lights
Of thy wild eyes.   Oh ! yet a little while
May I behold in thee what I was once,
My dear, dear Sister ! and this prayer I make,
Knowing that Nature never did betray
The heart that loved her ; 'tis her privilege,
Through all the years of this our life, to lead

---

[1] This line has a close resemblance to an admirable line of Young,
the exact expression of which I do not recollect.

From joy to joy : for she can so inform
The mind that is within us, so impress
With quietness and beauty, and so feed
With lofty thoughts, that neither evil tongues,
Rash judgments, nor the sneers of selfish men,
Nor greetings where no kindness is, nor all
The dreary intercourse of daily life,
Shall e'er prevail against us, or disturb
Our cheerful faith, that all which we behold
Is full of blessings.   Therefore let the moon
Shine on thee in thy solitary walk ;
And let the misty mountain winds be free
To blow against thee : and in after years,
When these wild ecstasies shall be matured
Into a sober pleasure, when thy mind
Shall be a mansion for all lovely forms,
Thy memory be as a dwelling-place
For all sweet sounds and harmonies ; oh ! then,
If solitude, or fear, or pain, or grief,
Should be thy portion, with what healing thoughts
Of tender joy wilt thou remember me,
And these my exhortations !   Nor, perchance
If I should be where I no more can hear
Thy voice, nor catch from thy wild eyes these gleams
Of past existence, wilt thou then forget
That on the banks of this delightful stream
We stood together ; and that I, so long
A worshipper of Nature, hither came
Unwearied in that service : rather say
With warmer love, oh ! with far deeper zeal
Of holier love.   Nor wilt thou then forget,
That after many wanderings, many years
Of absence, these steep woods and lofty cliffs,
And this green pastoral landscape, were to me
More dear, both for themselves and for thy sake !

ADDRESS TO MY INFANT DAUGHTER DORA,

ON BEING REMINDED THAT SHE WAS A MONTH OLD
THAT DAY, SEPTEMBER 16.

———— HAST thou then survived—
Mild offspring of infirm humanity,
Meek Infant ! among all forlornest things
The most forlorn—one life of that bright star,
The second glory of the Heavens ?—Thou hast ;
Already hast survived that great decay,
That transformation through the wide earth felt,
And by all nations.   In that Being's sight
From whom the race of human kind proceed,
A thousand years are but as yesterday ;
And one day's narrow circuit is to Him
Not less capacious than a thousand years.
But what is time ?   What outward glory ? Neither
A measure is of Thee, whose claims extend
Through "heaven's eternal year."—Yet hail to Thee,
Frail, feeble Monthling !—by that name, methinks,
Thy scanty breathing-time is portioned out
Not idly.—Hadst thou been of Indian birth,
Couched on a casual bed of moss and leaves,
And rudely canopied by leafy boughs,
Or to the churlish elements exposed
On the blank plains,—the coldness of the night,
Or the night's darkness, or its cheerful face
Of beauty, by the changing Moon adorned,
Would, with imperious admonition, then
Have scored thine age, and punctually timed
Thine infant history, on the minds of those

Who might have wandered with thee.—Mother's love,
Nor less than mother's love in other breasts,
Will, among us warm-clad and warmly-housed
Do for thee what the finger of the heavens
Doth all too often harshly execute
For thy unblest coevals, amid wilds
Where fancy hath small liberty to grace
The affections, to exalt them or refine;
And the maternal sympathy itself,
Though strong, is, in the main, a joyless tie
Of naked instinct, wound about the heart.
Happier, far happier, is thy lot and ours!
Even now—to solemnise thy helpless state,
And to enliven in the mind's regard
Thy passive beauty—parallels have risen,
Resemblances, or contrasts, that connect,
Within the region of a father's thoughts,
Thee and thy mate and sister of the sky.
And first; thy sinless progress, through a world
By sorrow darkened and by care disturbed,
Apt likeness bears to hers, through gathered clouds,
Moving untouched in silver purity,
And cheering oft-times their reluctant gloom.
Fair are ye both, and both are free from stain:
But thou, how leisurely thou fill'st thy horn
With brightness! leaving her to post along,
And range about, disquieted in change,
And still impatient of the shape she wears.
Once up, once down the hill, one journey, Babe,
That will suffice thee; and it seems that now
Thou hast fore-knowledge that such task is thine;
Thou travellest so contentedly, and sleep'st
In such a heedless peace.   Alas! full soon
Hath this conception, grateful to behold,
Changed countenance, like an object sullied o'er

By breathing mist ; and thine appears to be
A mournful labour, while to her is given
Hope, and a renovation without end.
—That smile forbids the thought ; for on thy face
Smiles are beginning, like the beams of dawn,
To shoot and circulate ; smiles have there been seen ;
Tranquil assurances that Heaven supports
The feeble motions of thy life, and cheers
Thy loneliness : or shall those smiles be called
Feelers of love, put forth as if to explore
This untried world, and to prepare thy way
Through a strait passage intricate and dim ?
Such are they ; and the same are tokens, signs,
Which, when the appointed season hath arrived,
Joy, as ner holiest language, shall adopt ;
And Reason's godlike power be proud to own.

LINES

Left upon a Seat in a Yew-tree, which stands near the Lake of Esthwaite, on a desolate Part of the Shore, commanding a beautiful Prospect.

NAY, Traveller! rest. This lonely Yew-tree stands
Far from all human dwelling: what if here
No sparkling rivulet spread the verdant herb?
What if the bee love not these barren boughs?
Yet, if the wind breathe soft, the curling waves,
That break against the shore, shall lull thy mind
By one soft impulse saved from vacancy.
———————— Who he was
That piled these stones, and with the mossy sod
First covered o'er, and taught this aged Tree
With its dark arms to form a circling bower,
I well remember.—He was one who owned
No common soul. In youth by science nursed,
And led by nature into a wild scene
Of lofty hopes, he to the world went forth
A favoured Being, knowing no desire
Which Genius did not hallow,—'gainst the taint
Of dissolute tongues, and jealousy, and hate,
And scorn,—against all enemies prepared,
All but neglect. The world, for so it thought,
Owed him no service; wherefore he at once
With indignation turned himself away,
And with the food of pride sustained his soul
In solitude.—Stranger! these gloomy boughs
Had charms for him; and here he loved to sit,
His only visitants a straggling sheep,
The stone-chat, or the glancing sand-piper:

And on these barren rocks, with fern and heath
And juniper and thistle sprinkled o'er,
Fixing his downcast eye, he many an hour
A morbid pleasure nourished, tracing here
An emblem of his own unfruitful life :
And, lifting up his head, he then would gaze
On the more distant scene,—how lovely 'tis
Thou see'st,—and he would gaze till it became
Far lovelier, and his heart could not sustain
The beauty, still more beauteous ! Nor, that time,
When nature had subdued him to herself,
Would he forget those beings, to whose minds,
Warm from the labours of benevolence,
The world and human life appeared a scene
Of kindred loveliness : then he would sigh
With mournful joy, to think that others felt
What he must never feel : and so, lost Man !
On visionary views would fancy feed,
Till his eye streamed with tears.   In this deep vale
He died,—this seat his only monument.

If Thou be one whose heart the holy forms
Of young imagination have kept pure,
Stranger ! henceforth be warned ; and know that pride,
        Howe'er disguised in its own majesty,
Is littleness ; that he who feels contempt
For any living thing, hath faculties
Which he has never used ; that thought with him
Is in its infancy.   The man whose eye
Is ever on himself doth look on one,
The least of Nature's works, one who might move
The wise man to that scorn which wisdom holds
Unlawful, ever.   O be wiser, Thou !
Instructed that true knowledge leads to love,

K

> True dignity abides with him alone
> Who, in the silent hour of inward thought,
> Can still suspect, and still revere himself,
> In lowliness of heart.

FRENCH REVOLUTION,

AS IT APPEARED TO ENTHUSIASTS AT ITS
COMMENCEMENT.

OH! pleasant exercise of hope and joy!
For mighty were the auxiliars, which then stood
Upon our side, we who were strong in love!
Bliss was it in that dawn to be alive,
But to be young was very heaven!—Oh! times,
In which the meagre, stale, forbidding ways
Of custom, law, and statute, took at once
The attraction of a country in Romance!
When Reason seemed the most to assert her rights
When most intent on making of herself
A prime enchantress—to assist the work,
Which then was going forward in her name!
Not favoured spots alone, but the whole earth,
The beauty wore of promise—that which sets
(As at some moment might not be unfelt
Among the bowers of paradise itself)
The budding rose above the rose full blown.
What temper at the prospect did not wake
To happiness unthought of?   The inert
Were roused, and lively natures rapt away!
They who had fed their childhood upon dreams,
The playfellows of fancy, who had made

All powers of swiftness, subtilty and strength
Their ministers,—who in lordly wise had stirred
Among the grandest objects of the sense,
And dealt with whatsoever they found there
As if they had within some lurking right
To wield it ; they, too, who, of gentle mood,
Had watched all gentle motions, and to these
Had fitted their own thoughts, schemers more mild,
And in the region of their peaceful selves ;—
Now was it that *both* found, the Meek and Lofty
Did both find helpers to their heart's desire,
And stuff at hand, plastic as they could wish ;
Were called upon to exercise their skill,
Not in Utopia, subterranean Fields,
Or some secreted Island, Heaven knows where !
But in the very world, which is the world
Of all of us,—the place where in the end
We find our happiness, or not at all !

THE SIMPLON PASS.

——————Brook and road
Were fellow-travellers in this gloomy Pass,
And with them did we journey several hours
At a slow step.   The immeasurable height
Of woods decaying, never to be decayed,
The stationary blasts of waterfalls,
And in the narrow rent, at every turn,
Winds thwarting winds bewildered and forlorn,
The torrents shooting from the clear blue sky,
The rocks that muttered close upon our ears,
Black drizzling crags that spake by the wayside

As if a voice were in them, the sick sight
And giddy prospect of the raving stream,
The unfettered clouds and region of the heavens,
Tumult and peace, the darkness and the light—
Were all like workings of one mind, the features
Of the same face, blossoms upon one tree,
Characters of the great Apocalypse,
The types and symbols of Eternity,
Of first, and last, and midst, and without end.

FRAGMENT FROM *THE RECLUSE*.

ON Man, on Nature, and on Human Life,
Musing in solitude, I oft perceive
Fair trains of imagery before me rise,
Accompanied by feelings of delight
Pure, or with no unpleasing sadness mixed ;
And I am conscious of affecting thoughts
And dear remembrances, whose presence soothes
Or elevates the Mind, intent to weigh
The good and evil of our mortal state.
—To these emotions, whencesoe'er they come,
Whether from breath of outward circumstance,
Or from the Soul—an impulse to herself,
I would give utterance in numerous verse.
Of Truth, of Grandeur, Beauty, Love, and Hope—
And melancholy Fear subdued by Faith ;
Of blessed consolations in distress ;
Of moral strength, and intellectual power ;
Of joy in widest commonalty spread ;
Of the individual Mind that keeps her own
Inviolate retirement, subject there

To Conscience only, and the law supreme
Of that Intelligence which governs all ;
I sing :—"fit audience let me find though few !"

So prayed, more gaining than he asked, the Bard,
Holiest of Men.—Urania, I shall need
Thy guidance, or a greater Muse, if such
Descend to earth or dwell in highest heaven !
For I must tread on shadowy ground, must sink
Deep—and, aloft ascending, breathe in worlds
To which the heaven of heavens is but a veil.
All strength—all terror, single or in bands,
That ever was put forth in personal form ;
Jehovah—with his thunder, and the choir
Of shouting Angels, and the empyreal thrones—
I pass them unalarmed.   Not Chaos, not
The darkest pit of lowest Erebus,
Nor aught of blinder vacancy, scooped out
By help of dreams, can breed such fear and awe
As fall upon us often when we look
Into our Minds, into the Mind of Man,
My haunt, and the main region of my song.
—Beauty—a living Presence of the earth,
Surpassing the most fair ideal Forms
Which craft of delicate Spirits hath composed
From earth's materials—waits upon my steps ;
Pitches her tents before me as I move,
An hourly neighbour.   Paradise, and groves
Elysian, Fortunate Fields—like those of old
Sought in the Atlantic Main—why should they be
A history only of departed things,
Or a mere fiction of what never was ?
For the discerning intellect of Man,
When wedded to this goodly universe
In love and holy passion, shall find these

A simple produce of the common day.
I, long before the blissful hour arrives,
Would chant, in lonely peace, the spousal verse
Of this great consummation :—and, by words
Which speak of nothing more than what we are,
Would I arouse the sensual from their sleep
Of Death, and win the vacant and the vain
To noble raptures ; while my voice proclaims
How exquisitely the individual Mind
(And the progressive powers perhaps no less
Of the whole species) to the external World
Is fitted :—and how exquisitely, too,
Theme this but little heard of among Men,
The external World is fitted to the Mind ;
And the creation (by no lower name
Can it be called) which they with blended might
Accomplish :—this is our high argument.
—Such grateful haunts forgoing, if I oft
Must turn elsewhere—to travel near the tribes
And fellowships of men, and see ill sights
Of madding passions mutually inflamed ;
Must hear Humanity in fields and groves
Pipe solitary anguish ; or must hang
Brooding above the fierce confederate storm
Of sorrow, barricadoed evermore
Within the walls of Cities ; may these sounds
Have their authentic comment,—that even these
Hearing, I be not downcast or forlorn !
—Descend, prophetic Spirit ! that inspirest
The human Soul of universal earth,
Dreaming on things to come ; and dost possess
A metropolitan Temple in the hearts
Of mighty Poets ; upon me bestow
A gift of genuine insight ; that my Song
With star-like virtue in its place may shine,

Shedding benignant influence,—and secure,
Itself, from all malevolent effect
Of those mutations that extend their sway
Throughout the nether sphere !—And if with this
I mix more lowly matter ; with the thing
Contemplated, describe the Mind and Man
Contemplating, and who, and what he was,
The transitory Being that beheld
This Vision,—when and where, and how he lived ;—
Be not this labour useless.   If such theme
May sort with highest objects, then, dread Power,
Whose gracious favour is the primal source
Of all illumination, may my Life
Express the image of a better time,
More wise desires, and simpler manners ;—nurse
My Heart in genuine freedom :—all pure thoughts
Be with me ;—so shall thy unfailing love
Guide, and support, and cheer me to the end !

THE OLD CUMBERLAND BEGGAR.

The class of Beggars, to which the Old Man here described belongs,
will probably soon be extinct. It consisted of poor, and, mostly,
old and infirm persons, who confined themselves to a stated
round in their neighbourhood, and had certain fixed days, on
which, at different houses, they regularly received alms, sometimes in money, but mostly in provisions.

I saw an aged Beggar in my walk ;
And he was seated, by the highway side,
On a low structure of rude masonry
Built at the foot of a huge hill, that they
Who lead their horses down the steep rough road
May thence remount at ease.   The aged Man
Had placed his staff across the broad smooth stone
That overlays the pile ; and, from a bag
All white with flour, the dole of village dames,
He drew his scraps and fragments, one by one ;
And scanned them with a fixed and serious look
Of idle computation.   In the sun,
Upon the second step of that small pile,
Surrounded by those wild unpeopled hills,
He sat, and ate his food in solitude :
And ever, scattered from his palsied hand,
That, still attempting to prevent the waste,
Was baffled still, the crumbs in little showers
Fell on the ground ; and the small mountain birds,
Not venturing yet to peck their destined meal,
Approached within the length of half his staff.

Him from my childhood have I known ; and then
He was so old, he seems not older now ;

He travels on, a solitary Man,
So helpless in appearance, that for him
The sauntering horseman-traveller does not throw
With careless hand his alms upon the ground,
But stops,—that he may safely lodge the coin
Within the old Man's hat; nor quits him so,
But still, when he has given his horse the rein,
Watches the aged Beggar with a look
Sidelong—and half-reverted. She who tends
The toll-gate, when in summer at her door
She turns her wheel, if on the road she sees
The aged Beggar coming, quits her work,
And lifts the latch for him that he may pass.
The post-boy, when his rattling wheels o'ertake
The aged Beggar in the woody lane,
Shouts to him from behind; and, if thus warned
The old Man does not change his course, the boy
Turns with less noisy wheels to the roadside,
And passes gently by—without a curse
Upon his lips, or anger at his heart.
He travels on, a solitary Man;
His age has no companion. On the ground
His eyes are turned, and, as he moves along,
They move along the ground; and, evermore,
Instead of common and habitual sight
Of fields with rural works, of hill and dale,
And the blue sky, one little span of earth
Is all his prospect. Thus, from day to day,
Bow-bent, his eyes for ever on the ground,
He plies his weary journey; seeing still,
And seldom knowing that he sees, some straw,
Some scattered leaf, or marks which, in one track,
The nails of cart or chariot-wheel have left
Impressed on the white road,—in the same line,
At distance still the same. Poor Traveller!

His staff trails with him ; scarcely do his feet
Disturb the summer dust ; he is so still
In look and motion, that the cottage curs,
Ere he have passed the door, will turn away,
Weary of barking at him.   Boys and girls,
The vacant and the busy, maids and youths,
And urchins newly breeched—all pass him by ;
Him even the slow-paced waggon leaves behind.

But deem not this Man useless.—Statesmen ! ye
Who are so restless in your wisdom, ye
Who have a broom still ready in your hands
To rid the world of nuisances ; ye proud,
Heart-swoln, while in your pride ye contemplate
Your talents, power, and wisdom, deem him not
A burthen of the earth !   'Tis Nature's law
That none, the meanest of created things,
Of forms created the most vile and brute,
The dullest or most noxious, should exist
Divorced from good—a spirit and pulse of good,
A life and soul, to every mode of being
Inseparably linked.   While thus he creeps
From door to door, the Villagers in him
Behold a record which together binds
Past deeds and offices of charity,
Else unremembered, and so keeps alive
The kindly mood in hearts which lapse of years
And that half-wisdom half-experience gives,
Make slow to feel, and by sure steps resign
To selfishness and cold oblivious cares.
Among the farms and solitary huts,
Hamlets and thinly-scattered villages,
Where'er the aged Beggar takes his rounds,
The mild necessity of use compels
To acts of love ; and habit does the work

Of reason; yet prepares that after-joy
Which reason cherishes. And thus the soul,
By that sweet taste of pleasure unpursued,
Doth find herself insensibly disposed
To virtue and true goodness. Some there are,
By their good works exalted, lofty minds
And meditative, authors of delight
And happiness, which to the end of time
Will live, and spread, and kindle : even such minds
In childhood, from this solitary Being,
Or from like wanderer, haply have received
(A thing more precious far than all that books
Or the solicitudes of love can do !)
That first mild touch of sympathy and thought,
In which they found their kindred with a world
Where want and sorrow were. The easy man
Who sits at his own door,—and, like the pear
That overhangs his head from the green wall,
Feeds in the sunshine ; the robust and young,
The prosperous and unthinking, they who live
Sheltered, and flourish in a little grove
Of their own kindred ;—all behold in him
A silent monitor, which on their minds
Must needs impress a transitory thought
Of self-congratulation, to the heart
Of each recalling his peculiar boons,
His charters and exemptions ; and, perchance,
Though he to no one give the fortitude
And circumspection needful to preserve
His present blessings, and to husband up
The respite of the season, he at least—
And 'tis no vulgar service—makes them felt.

Yet further.——Many, I believe, there are
Who live a life of virtuous decency,

Men who can hear the Decalogue and feel
No self-reproach ; who of the moral law
Established in the land where they abide
Are strict observers ; and not negligent,
In acts of love to those with whom they dwell,
Their kindred, and the children of their blood.
Praise be to such, and to their slumbers peace !
—But of the poor man ask, the abject poor ;
Go, and demand of him, if there be here
In this cold abstinence from evil deeds,
And these inevitable charities,
Wherewith to satisfy the human soul ?
No—Man is dear to Man ; the poorest poor
Long for some moments in a weary life
When they can know and feel that they have been,
Themselves, the fathers and the dealers-out
Of some small blessings ; have been kind to such
As needed kindness, for this single cause,
That we have all of us one human heart.
—Such pleasure is to one kind being known,
My neighbour, when with punctual care, each week
Duly as Friday comes, though pressed herself
By her own wants, she from her store of meal
Takes one unsparing handful for the scrip
Of this old Mendicant, and, from her door
Returning with exhilarated heart,
Sits by her fire, and builds her hope in heaven.

Then let him pass, a blessing on his head !
And while in that vast solitude to which
The tide of things has borne him, he appears
To breathe and live but for himself alone,
Unblamed, uninjured, let him bear about
The good which the benignant law of Heaven
Has hung around him : and, while life is his,

Still let him prompt the unlettered Villagers
To tender offices and pensive thoughts.
—Then let him pass, a blessing on his head!
And, long as he can wander, let him breathe
The freshness of the valleys; let his blood
Struggle with frosty air and winter snows;
And let the chartered wind that sweeps the heath
Beat his gray locks against his withered face.
Reverence the hope whose vital anxiousness
Gives the last human interest to his heart!
May never HOUSE, misnamed of INDUSTRY,
Make him a captive! for that pent-up din,
Those life-consuming sounds that clog the air,
Be his the natural silence of old age!
Let him be free of mountain solitudes;
And have around him, whether heard or not,
The pleasant melody of woodland birds.
Few are his pleasures: if his eyes have now
Been doomed so long to settle on the earth
That not without some effort they behold
The countenance of the horizontal sun,
Rising or setting, let the light at least
Find a free entrance to their languid orbs.
And let him, *where* and *when* he will, sit down
Beneath the trees, or by the grassy bank
Of highway side, and with the little birds
Share his chance-gathered meal; and, finally,
As in the eye of Nature he has lived,
So in the eye of Nature let him die!

ANIMAL TRANQUILLITY AND DECAY.

A SKETCH.

THE little hedgerow birds,
That peck along the road, regard him not.
He travels on, and in his face, his step,
His gait, is one expression ; every limb,
His look and bending figure, all bespeak
A man who does not move with pain, but moves
With thought.—He is insensibly subdued
To settled quiet : he is one by whom
All effort seems forgotten ; one to whom
Long patience hath such mild composure given,
That patience now doth seem a thing of which
He hath no need.   He is by nature led
To peace so perfect, that the young behold
With envy, what the Old Man hardly feels.

NUTTING.

——————————————It seems a day
(I speak of one from many singled out)
One of those heavenly days which cannot die ;
When, in the eagerness of boyish hope,
I left our Cottage-threshold, sallying forth
With a huge wallet o'er my shoulders slung,
A nutting-crook in hand, and turned my steps
Toward the distant woods, a Figure quaint,
Tricked out in proud disguise of cast-off weeds
Which for that service had been husbanded,
By exhortation of my frugal Dame ;
Motley accoutrement, of power to smile
At thorns, and brakes, and brambles,—and, in truth,
More ragged than need was !   Among the woods,
And o'er the pathless rocks, I forced my way
Until, at length, I came to one dear nook
Unvisited, where not a broken bough
Drooped with its withered leaves, ungracious sign
Of devastation, but the hazels rose
Tall and erect, with milk-white clusters hung,
A virgin scene !—A little while I stood,
Breathing with such suppression of the heart
As joy delights in ; and, with wise restraint
Voluptuous, fearless of a rival, eyed
The banquet,—or beneath the trees I sate
Among the flowers, and with the flowers I played ;
A temper known to those, who, after long
And weary expectation, have been blest
With sudden happiness beyond all hope.—
Perhaps it was a bower beneath whose leaves
The violets of five seasons re-appear

And fade, unseen by any human eye;
Where fairy water-breaks do murmur on
For ever,—and I saw the sparkling foam,
And with my cheek on one of those green stones
That, fleeced with moss, beneath the shady trees,
Lay round me, scattered like a flock of sheep,
I heard the murmur and the murmuring sound,
In that sweet mood when pleasure loves to pay
Tribute to ease; and, of its joy secure,
The heart luxuriates with indifferent things,
Wasting its kindliness on stocks and stones,
And on the vacant air. Then up I rose,
And dragged to earth both branch and bough, with
     crash
And merciless ravage; and the shady nook
Of hazels, and the green and mossy bower,
Deformed and sullied, patiently gave up
Their quiet being: and, unless I now
Confound my present feelings with the past,
Even then, when from the bower I turned away
Exulting, rich beyond the wealth of kings,
I felt a sense of pain when I beheld
The silent trees and the intruding sky.—
Then, dearest Maiden! move along these shades
In gentleness of heart; with gentle hand
Touch—for there is a spirit in the woods.

TO JOANNA.

AMID the smoke of cities did you pass
The time of early youth; and there you learned,
From years of quiet industry, to love
The living beings by your own fireside,
With such a strong devotion, that your heart
Is slow toward the sympathies of them
Who look upon the hills with tenderness,
And make dear friendships with the streams and
    groves.
Yet we, who are transgressors in this kind,
Dwelling retired in our simplicity
Among the woods and fields, we love you well,
Joanna! and I guess, since you have been
So distant from us now for two long years,
That you will gladly listen to discourse,
However trivial, if you thence are taught
That they, with whom you once were happy, talk
Familiarly of you and of old times.

    While I was seated, now some ten days past,
Beneath those lofty firs, that overtop
Their ancient neighbour, the old steeple tower,
The Vicar from his gloomy house hard by
Came forth to greet me; and when he had asked,
" How fares Joanna, that wild-hearted Maid!
And when will she return to us?" he paused:
And, after short exchange of village news,
He with grave looks demanded, for what cause,
Reviving obsolete idolatry,
I, like a Runic Priest, in characters
Of formidable size had chiselled out

Some uncouth name upon the native rock,
Above the Rotha, by the forest side.
—Now, by those dear immunities of heart
Engendered betwixt malice and true love,
I was not loth to be so catechised,
And this was my reply :—" As it befel,
One summer morning we had walked abroad
At break of day, Joanna and myself.
—'Twas that delightful season when the broom,
Full-flowered, and visible on every steep,
Along the copses runs in veins of gold.
Our pathway led us on to Rotha's banks ;
And when we came in front of that tall rock
Which looks toward the East, I there stopped short,
And traced the lofty barrier with my eye
From base to summit ; such delight I found
To note in shrub and tree, in stone and flower,
That intermixture of delicious hues,
Along so vast a surface, all at once,
In one impression, by connecting force
Of their own beauty, imaged in the heart.
—When I had gazed perhaps two minutes' space,
Joanna, looking in my eyes, beheld
That ravishment of mine, and laughed aloud.
The Rock, like something starting from a sleep,
Took up the Lady's voice, and laughed again :
That ancient Woman seated on Helm-Crag
Was ready with her cavern ; Hammer-Scar,
And the tall Steep of Silver-How, sent forth
A noise of laughter ; southern Loughrigg heard
And Fairfield answered with a mountain tone :
Helvellyn far into the clear blue sky
Carried the Lady's voice,—old Skiddaw blew
His speaking trumpet ;—back out of the clouds
Of Glaramara southward came the voice ;

And Kirkstone tossed it from his misty head.
—Now whether (said I to our cordial friend,
Who in the hey-day of astonishment
Smiled in my face) this were in simple truth
A work accomplished by the brotherhood
Of ancient mountains, or my ear was touched
With dreams and visionary impulses
To me alone imparted, sure I am
That there was a loud uproar in the hills :
And, while we both were listening, to my side
The fair Joanna drew, as if she wished
To shelter from some object of her fear.
—And hence, long afterwards, when eighteen moons
Were wasted, as I chanced to walk alone
Beneath this rock, at sunrise, on a calm
And silent morning, I sat down, and there,
In memory of affections old and true,
I chiselled out in those rude characters
Joanna's name upon the living stone.
And I, and all who dwell by my fireside,
Have called the lovely rock, ' JOANNA'S ROCK.' "

NOTE.—In Cumberland and Westmorland are several Inscrip-
tions, upon the native rock, which, from the wasting of Time, and
the rudeness of the Workmanship, have been mistaken for Runic.
They are without doubt Roman.

The Rotha, mentioned in this poem, is the River which, flowing
through the lakes of Grasmere and Rydale, falls into Wynander.
On Helm-Crag, that impressive single Mountain at the head of the
Vale of Grasmere, is a rock which from most points of view bears a
striking resemblance to an Old Woman cowering. Close by this
rock is one of those Fissures or Caverns, which in the language of
the country are called Dungeons. Most of the Mountains here
mentioned immediately surround the Vale of Grasmere ; of the others,
some are at a considerable distance, but they belong to the same
cluster.

THE FIR-GROVE PATH.

WHEN, to the attractions of the busy World
Preferring studious leisure, I had chosen
A habitation in this peaceful Vale,
Sharp season followed of continual storm
In deepest winter; and, from week to week,
Pathway, and lane, and public road, were clogged
With frequent showers of snow. Upon a hill
At a short distance from my Cottage, stands
A stately Fir-grove, whither I was wont
To hasten; for I found, beneath the roof
Of that perennial shade, a cloistral place
Of refuge, with an unincumbered floor.
Here, in safe covert, on the shallow snow,
And, sometimes, on a speck of visible earth,
The redbreast near me hopped; nor was I loth
To sympathise with vulgar coppice Birds
That, for protection from the nipping blast,
Hither repaired.—A single beech-tree grew
Within this grove of firs; and, on the fork
Of that one beech, appeared a thrush's nest;
A last year's nest, conspicuously built
At such small elevation from the ground
As gave sure sign that they, who in that house
Of nature and of love had made their home
Amid the fir-trees, all the summer long
Dwelt in a tranquil spot. And oftentimes,
A few sheep, stragglers from some mountain-flock,
Would watch my motions with suspicious stare,
From the remotest outskirts of the grove,—
Some nook where they had made their final stand,
Huddling together from two fears—the fear

Of me and of the storm.   Full many an hour
Here did I lose.   But in this grove the trees
Had been so thickly planted, and had thriven
In such perplexed and intricate array,
That vainly did I seek, between their stems,
A length of open space, where to and fro
My feet might move without concern or care ;
And, baffled thus, before the storm relaxed,
I ceased the shelter to frequent,—and prized,
Less than I wished to prize, that calm recess.

The snows dissolved, and genial Spring returned
To clothe the fields with verdure.   Other haunts
Meanwhile were mine ; till, one bright April day,
By chance retiring from the glare of noon
To this forsaken covert, there I found
A hoary path-way traced between the trees,
And winding on with such an easy line
Along a natural opening, that I stood
Much wondering how I could have sought in vain
For what was now so obvious.   To abide,
For an allotted interval of ease,
Beneath my cottage roof, had newly come
From the wild sea a cherished Visitant ;
And with the sight of this same path—begun,
Begun and ended, in the shady grove,
Pleasant conviction flashed upon my mind
That, to this opportune recess allured,
He had surveyed it with a finer eye,
A heart more wakeful ; and had worn the track
By pacing here, unwearied and alone,
In that habitual restlessness of foot
With which the Sailor measures o'er and o'er
His short domain upon the vessel's deck,
While she is travelling through the dreary sea.

When thou hadst quitted Esthwaite's pleasant shore,
And taken thy first leave of those green hills
And rocks that were the play-ground of thy Youth,
Year followed year, my Brother! and we two,
Conversing not, knew little in what mould
Each other's minds were fashioned; and at length,
When once again we met in Grasmere Vale,
Between us there was little other bond
Than common feelings of fraternal love.
But thou, a School-boy, to the sea hadst carried
Undying recollections; Nature there
Was with thee; she, who loved us both, she still
Was with thee; and even so didst thou become
A *silent* Poet; from the solitude
Of the vast sea didst bring a watchful heart
Still couchant, an inevitable ear,
And an eye practised like a blind man's touch.
—Back to the joyless Ocean thou art gone;
Nor from this vestige of thy musing hours
Could I withhold thy honoured name, and now
I love the fir-grove with a perfect love.
Thither do I withdraw when cloudless suns
Shine hot, or wind blows troublesome and strong:
And there I sit at evening, when the steep
Of Silver-how, and Grasmere's peaceful Lake,
And one green Island, gleam between the stems
Of the dark firs, a visionary scene!
And, while I gaze upon the spectacle
Of clouded splendour, on this dream-like sight
Of solemn loveliness, I think on thee,
My Brother, and on all which thou hast lost.
Nor seldom, if I rightly guess,—while Thou,
Muttering the Verses which I muttered first
Among the mountains, through the midnight watch
Art pacing thoughtfully the Vessel's deck

In some far region,—here, while o'er my head,
At every impulse of the moving breeze,
The fir-grove murmurs with a sea-like sound,
Alone I tread this path ;—for aught I know,
Timing my steps to thine ; and, with a store
Of undistinguishable sympathies,
Mingling most earnest wishes for the day
When we, and others whom we love, shall meet
A second time, in Grasmere's happy Vale.

NOTE.—This wish was not granted ; the lamented Person not
long after perished by shipwreck, in discharge of his duty as Com-
mander of the Honourable East India Company's Vessel, the Earl
of Abergavenny.

A FAREWELL.

COMPOSED IN THE YEAR 1802.

FAREWELL, thou little Nook of mountain-ground,
Thou rocky corner in the lowest stair
Of that magnificent temple which doth bound
One side of our whole vale with grandeur rare ;
Sweet garden-orchard, eminently fair,
The loveliest spot that man hath ever found,
Farewell !—we leave thee to Heaven's peaceful care,
Thee, and the Cottage which thou dost surround.

Our boat is safely anchored by the shore,
And there will safely ride when we are gone :
The flowering shrubs that deck our humble door
Will prosper, though untended and alone :
Fields, goods, and far-off chattels we have none :
These narrow bounds contain our private store
Of things earth makes, and sun doth shine upon ;
Here are they in our sight—we have no more.

Sunshine and shower be with you, bud and bell!
For two months now in vain we shall be sought;
We leave you here in solitude to dwell
With these our latest gifts of tender thought;
Thou, like the morning, in thy saffron coat,
Bright gowan, and marsh-marigold, farewell!
Whom from the borders of the Lake we brought,
And placed together, near our rocky Well.

We go for One to whom ye will be dear;
And she will prize this Bower, this Indian shed,
Our own contrivance, building without peer!
—A gentle Maid, whose heart is lowly bred,
Whose pleasures are in wild fields gathered,
With joyousness, and with a thoughtful cheer,
Will come to you,—to you herself will wed,—
And love the blessed life that we lead here.

Dear Spot! which we have watched with tender heed,
Bringing thee chosen plants and blossoms blown
Among the distant mountains, flower and weed,
Which thou hast taken to thee as thy own,
Making all kindness registered and known;
Thou for our sakes, though Nature's Child indeed,
Fair in thyself and beautiful alone,
Hast taken gifts which thou dost little need.

And O most constant, yet most fickle Place,
That hast thy wayward moods, as thou dost show
To them who look not daily on thy face;
Who, being loved, in love no bounds dost know,
And sayest, when we forsake thee, "Let them go!
Thou easy-hearted Thing, with thy wild race
Of weeds and flowers, till we return be slow,
And travel with the year at a soft pace.

Help us to tell her tales of years gone by,
And this sweet spring, the best beloved and best;
Joy will be flown in its mortality;
Something must stay to tell us of the rest.
Here, thronged with primroses, the steep rock's breast
Glittered at evening like a starry sky;
And in this bush our Sparrow built her nest,
Of which I sang one song that will not die.

O happy Garden! whose seclusion deep
Hath been so friendly to industrious hours;
And to soft slumbers, that did gently steep
Our spirits, carrying with them dreams of flowers,
And wild notes warbled among leafy bowers;
Two burning months let summer overleap,
And, coming back with Her who will be ours,
Into thy bosom we again shall creep.

STANZAS

WRITTEN IN MY POCKET-COPY OF THOMSON'S CASTLE OF INDOLENCE.

WITHIN our happy Castle there dwelt One [1]
Whom without blame I may not overlook;
For never sun on living creature shone
Who more devout enjoyment with us took:
Here on his hours he hung as on a book;
On his own time here would he float away,
As doth a fly upon a summer brook;
But go to-morrow—or belike the day—
Seek for him,—he is fled; and whither none can say.

[1] S. T. Coleridge.

Thus often would he leave our peaceful home,
And find elsewhere his business or delight ;
Out of our Valley's limits did he roam :
Full many a time, upon a stormy night,
His voice came to us from the neighbouring height :
Oft did we see him driving full in view
At mid-day when the sun was shining bright ;
What ill was on him, what he had to do,
A mighty wonder bred among our quiet crew.

Ah ! piteous sight it was to see this Man
When he came back to us, a withered flower,—
Or, like a sinful creature, pale and wan.
Down would he sit ; and without strength or power
Look at the common grass from hour to hour :
And oftentimes, how long I fear to say,
Where apple-trees in blossom made a bower,
Retired in that sunshiny shade he lay ;
And, like a naked Indian, slept himself away.

Great wonder to our gentle Tribe it was
Whenever from our Valley he withdrew ;
For happier soul no living creature has
Than he had, being here the long day through.
Some thought he was a lover, and did woo :
Some thought far worse of him, and judged him wrong :
But Verse was what he had been wedded to ;
And his own mind did like a tempest strong
Come to him thus, and drove the weary Wight along.

With him there often walked in friendly guise,
Or lay upon the moss by brook or tree,
A noticeable man with large gray eyes,
And a pale face that seemed undoubtedly
As if a blooming face it ought to be ;

Heavy his low-hung lip did oft appear
Deprest by weight of musing Phantasy ;
Profound his forehead was, though not severe ;
Yet some did think that he had little business here .

Sweet heaven forefend ! his was a lawful right ;
Noisy he was, and gamesome as a boy ;
His limbs would toss about him with delight
Like branches when strong winds the trees annoy.
Nor lacked his calmer hours device or toy
To banish listlessness and irksome care ;
He would have taught you how you might employ
Yourself ; and many did to him repair,—
And certes not in vain ; he had inventions rare.

Expedients, too, of simplest sort he tried :
Long blades of grass, plucked round him as he lay,
Made—to his ear attentively applied—
A Pipe on which the wind would deftly play ;
Glasses he had, that little things display,
The beetle panoplied in gems and gold,
A mailèd angel on a battle day ;
The mysteries that cups of flowers enfold,
And all the gorgeous sights which fairies do behold.

He would entice that other Man to hear
His music, and to view his imagery :
And, sooth, these two did love each other dear,
As far as love in such a place could be ;
There did they dwell—from earthly labour free,
As happy spirits as were ever seen ;
If but a bird, to keep them company,
Or butterfly sate down, they were, I ween,
As pleased as if the same had been a Maiden Queen.

TRIBUTE

TO THE MEMORY OF A DOG.

LIE here, without a record of thy worth,
Beneath a covering of the common earth!
It is not from unwillingness to praise,
Or want of love, that here no Stone we raise;
More thou deserv'st; but *this* Man gives to Man,
Brother to Brother, *this* is all we can.
Yet they to whom thy virtues made thee dear
Shall find thee through all changes of the year:
This Oak points out thy grave; the silent Tree
Will gladly stand a monument of thee.

I grieved for thee, and wished thy end were past;
And willingly have laid thee here at last:
For thou hadst lived till every thing that cheers
In thee had yielded to the weight of years;
Extreme old age had wasted thee away,
And left thee but a glimmering of the day;
Thy ears were deaf, and feeble were thy knees,—
I saw thee stagger in the summer breeze,
Too weak to stand against its sportive breath,
And ready for the gentlest stroke of death.
It came, and we were glad; yet tears were shed;
Both Man and Woman wept when Thou wert dead;
Not only for a thousand thoughts that were,
Old household thoughts, in which thou hadst thy share;
But for some precious boons vouchsafed to thee,
Found scarcely any where in like degree!
For love, that comes to all—the holy sense,

Best gift of God—in thee was most intense ;
A chain of heart, a feeling of the mind,
A tender sympathy, which did thee bind
Not only to us Men, but to thy Kind :
Yea, for thy Fellow-brutes in thee we saw
The soul of Love, Love's intellectual law :—
Hence, if we wept, it was not done in shame ;
Our tears from passion and from reason came,
And, therefore, shalt thou be an honoured name !

THE SMALL CELANDINE.

THERE is a Flower, the Lesser Celandine,
That shrinks, like many more, from cold and rain ;
And, the first moment that the sun may shine,
Bright as the sun itself, 'tis out again !

When hailstones have been falling, swarm on swarm,
Or blasts the green field and the trees distressed,
Oft have I seen it muffled up from harm,
In close self-shelter, like a thing at rest.

But lately, one rough day, this Flower I passed
And recognised it, though an altered form,
Now standing forth an offering to the blast,
And buffeted at will by rain and storm.

I stopped, and said with inly-muttered voice,
" It doth not love the shower, nor seek the cold :
This neither is its courage nor its choice,
But its necessity in being old.

" The sunshine may not cheer it, nor the dew ;
It cannot help itself in its decay ;
Stiff in its members, withered, changed of hue. '
And, in my spleen, I smiled that it was gray.

To be a Prodigal's Favourite—then, worse truth,
A Miser's Pensioner—behold our lot !
O Man, that from thy fair and shining youth
Age might but take the things Youth needed not !

BEGGARS.

SHE had a tall man's height or more ;
No bonnet screen'd her from the heat ;
A long drab-coloured cloak she wore,
A mantle, to her very feet
Descending with a graceful flow,
And on her head a cap as white as new-fallen snow.

Her skin was of Egyptian brown ;
Haughty, as if her eye had seen
Its own light to a distance thrown,
She towered—fit person for a Queen,
To head those ancient Amazonian files ;
Or ruling Bandit's wife among the Grecian Isles.

Before me begging did she stand,
Pouring out sorrows like a sea,
Grief after grief ;—on English land
Such woes, I knew, could never be ;
And yet a boon I gave her ; for the Creature
Was beautiful to see—a weed of glorious feature !

I left her, and pursued my way ;
And soon before me did espy
A pair of little Boys at play,
Chasing a crimson butterfly ;
The Taller followed with his hat in hand,
Wreathed round with yellow flowers the gayest of the land

The Other wore a rimless crown
With leaves of laurel stuck about ;
And, while both followed up and down,
Each whooping with a merry shout,
In their fraternal features I could trace
Unquestionable lines of that wild Suppliant's face.

Yet *they*, so blithe of heart, seemed fit
For finest tasks of earth or air :
Wings let them have, and they may flit
Precursors of Aurora's Car,
Scattering fresh flowers ; though happier far, I ween,
To hunt their fluttering game o'er rock and level green.

They dart across my path—and lo,
Each ready with a plaintive whine !
Said I, " Not half an hour ago
Your Mother has had alms of mine."
" That cannot be," one answered—" she is dead :"—
I looked reproof—they saw—but neither hung his head

" She has been dead, Sir, many a day"—
" Sweet Boys ! you're telling me a lie ;
It was your Mother, as I say !"
And, in the twinkling of an eye,
" Come ! come !" cried one, and without more ado,
Off to some other play the joyous Vagrants flew !

SEQUEL TO THE FOREGOING.

COMPOSED MANY YEARS AFTER.

WHERE are they now, those wanton Boys?
For whose free range the dædal earth
Was filled with animated toys,
And implements of frolic mirth ;
With tools for ready wit to guide ;
And ornaments of seemlier pride,
More fresh, more bright, than Princes wear
For what one moment flung aside,
Another could repair ;
What good or evil have they seen
Since I their pastime witnessed here,
Their daring wiles, their sportive cheer?
I ask—but all is dark between !

Spirits of beauty and of grace !
Associates in that eager chase ;
Ye, by a course to nature true,
The sterner judgment can subdue ;
And waken a relenting smile
When she encounters fraud or guile ;
And sometimes ye can charm away
The inward mischief, or allay,
Ye, who within the blameless mind
Your favourite seat of empire find !

They met me in a genial hour,
When universal nature breathed
As with the breath of one sweet flower,—
A time to overrule the power
Of discontent, and check the birth

Of thoughts with better thoughts at strife,
The most familiar bane of life
Since parting Innocence bequeathed
Mortality to Earth!
Soft clouds, the whitest of the year,
Sailed through the sky—the brooks ran clear;
The lambs from rock to rock were bounding;
With songs the budded groves resounding;
And to my heart is still endeared
The faith with which it then was cheered;
The faith which saw that gladsome pair
Walk through the fire with unsinged hair.
Or, if such thoughts must needs deceive,
Kind Spirits! may we not believe
That they, so happy and so fair,
Through your sweet influence and the care
Of pitying Heaven at least were free
From touch of *deadly* injury?
Destined, whate'er their earthly doom,
For mercy and immortal bloom!

MATTHEW.

In the School of Hawkshead is a Tablet, on which are inscribed, in gilt letters, the Names of the several Persons who have been Schoolmasters there since the Foundation of the School, with the Time at which they entered upon and quitted their Office. Opposite to one of those Names the Author wrote the following Lines.

IF Nature, for a favourite Child,
In thee hath tempered so her clay,
That every hour thy heart runs wild,
Yet never once doth go astray,

Read o'er these lines ; and then review
This tablet, that thus humbly rears
In such diversity of hue
Its history of two hundred years.

—When through this little wreck of fame,
Cipher and syllable ! thine eye
Has travelled down to Matthew's name,
Pause with no common sympathy.

And, if a sleeping tear should wake,
Then be it neither checked nor stayed :
For Matthew a request I make
Which for himself he had not made.

Poor Matthew, all his frolics o'er,
Is silent as a standing pool ;
Far from the chimney's merry roar,
And murmur of the village school.

The sighs which Matthew heaved were sighs
Of one tired out with fun and madness ;
The tears which came to Matthew's eyes
Were tears of light, the dew of gladness.

Yet, sometimes, when the secret cup
Of still and serious thought went round,
It seemed as if he drank it up—
He felt with spirit so profound.

—Thou soul of God's best earthly mould !
Thou happy Soul ! and can it be
That these two words of glittering gold
Are all that must remain of thee ?

THE TWO APRIL MORNINGS.

WE walked along, while bright and red
Uprose the morning sun ;
And Matthew stopped, he looked and said,
"The will of God be done!"

A village Schoolmaster was he,
With hair of glittering gray ;
As blithe a man as you could see
On a spring holiday.

And on that morning, through the grass
And by the steaming rills,
We travelled merrily, to pass
A day among the hills.

"Our work," said I, "was well begun ;
Then, from thy breast what thought,
Beneath so beautiful a sun,
So sad a sigh has brought ?"

A second time did Matthew stop ;
And fixing still his eye
Upon the eastern mountain-top,
To me he made reply :

"Yon cloud with that long purple cleft
Brings fresh into my mind
A day like this which I have left
Full thirty years behind.

"And just above yon slope of corn
Such colours, and no other,
Were in the sky, that April morn,
Of this the very brother.

"With rod and line I sued the sport
Which that sweet season gave,
And, coming to the church, stopped short
Beside my daughter's grave.

"Nine summers had she scarcely seen,
The pride of all the vale;
And then she sang;—she would have been
A very nightingale.

"Six feet in earth my Emma lay;
And yet I loved her more,
For so it seemed, than till that day
I e'er had loved before.

"And, turning from her grave, I met,
Beside the churchyard yew,
A blooming girl, whose hair was wet
With points of morning dew.

"A basket on her head she bare;
Her brow was smooth and white:
To see a child so very fair,
It was a pure delight!

"No fountain from its rocky cave
E'er tripped with foot so free;
She seemed as happy as a wave
That dances on the sea.

"There came from me a sigh of pain
Which I could ill confine ;
I looked at her, and looked again :
—And did not wish her mine."

Matthew is in his grave, yet now,
Methinks, I see him stand,
As at that moment, with a bough
Of wilding in his hand.

THE FOUNTAIN.

A CONVERSATION.

WE talked with open heart, and tongue
Affectionate and true,
A pair of Friends, though I was young,
And Matthew seventy-two.

We lay beneath a spreading oak,
Beside a mossy seat ;
And from the turf a fountain broke,
And gurgled at our feet.

"Now, Matthew !" said I, " let us match
This water's pleasant tune
With some old Border-song, or Catch,
That suits a summer's noon ;

" Or of the Church-clock and the chimes
Sing here beneath the shade,
That half-mad thing of witty rhymes
Which you last April made ! "

In silence Matthew lay, and eyed
The spring beneath the tree ;
And thus the dear old man replied,
The gray-haired man of glee :

"Down to the vale this water steers,
How merrily it goes !
'Twill murmur on a thousand years,
And flow as now it flows.

" And here, on this delightful day,
I cannot choose but think
How oft, a vigorous man, I lay
Beside this Fountain's brink.

" My eyes are dim with childish tears,
My heart is idly stirred,
For the same sound is in my ears
Which in those days I heard.

" Thus fares it still in our decay :
And yet the wiser mind
Mourns less for what age takes away
Than what it leaves behind.

" The Blackbird in the summer trees.
The Lark upon the hill,
Let loose their carols when they please,
Are quiet when they will.

" With Nature never do *they* wage
A foolish strife ; they see
A happy youth, and their old age
Is beautiful and free :

" But we are pressed by heavy laws ;
And often, glad no more,
We wear a face of joy, because
We have been glad of yore.

" If there be one who need bemoan
His kindred laid in earth,
The household hearts that were his own,
It is the man of mirth.

" My days, my Friend, are almost gone,
My life has been approved,
And many love me ; but by none
Am I enough beloved."

" Now both himself and me he wrongs,
The man who thus complains !
I live and sing my idle songs
Upon these happy plains,

" And, Matthew, for thy Children dead
I'll be a son to thee ! "
At this he grasped my hand, and said,
" Alas ! that cannot be."

We rose up from the fountain-side ;
And down the smooth descent
Of the green sheep-track did we glide ;
And through the wood we went ;

And, ere we came to Leonard's-rock,
He sang those witty rhymes
About the crazy old church-clock,
And the bewildered chimes.

A POET'S EPITAPH.

ART thou a Statesman, in the van
Of public business trained and bred?
—First learn to love one living man;
Then may'st thou think upon the dead.

A Lawyer art thou?—draw not nigh!
Go, carry to some fitter place
The keenness of that practised eye,
The hardness of that sallow face.

Art thou a Man of purple cheer?
A rosy Man, right plump to see?
Approach; yet, Doctor, not too near.
This grave no cushion is for thee.

Or art thou one of gallant pride,
A Soldier, and no man of chaff?
Welcome!—but lay thy sword aside,
And lean upon a peasant's staff.

Physician art thou? One, all eyes,
Philosopher! a fingering slave,
One that would peep and botanize
Upon his mother's grave?

Wrapt closely in thy sensual fleece,
O turn aside,—and take, I pray,
That he below may rest in peace,
That abject thing, thy soul, away!

A Moralist perchance appears ;
Led, Heaven knows how ! to this poor sod :
And he has neither eyes nor ears ;
Himself his world, and his own God ;

One to whose smooth-rubbed soul can cling
Nor form, nor feeling, great or small ;
A reasoning, self-sufficing thing,
An intellectual All-in-all !

Shut close the door ; press down the latch ;
Sleep in thy intellectual crust ;
Nor lose ten tickings of thy watch
Near this unprofitable dust.

But who is He, with modest looks,
And clad in homely russet brown ?
He murmurs near the running brooks
A music sweeter than their own.

He is retired as noontide dew,
Or fountain in a noon-day grove :
And you must love him, ere to you
He will seem worthy of your love.

The outward shows of sky and earth,
Of hill and valley, he has viewed ;
And impulses of deeper birth
Have come to him in solitude.

In common things that round us lie
Some random truths he can impart ;—
The harvest of a quiet eye
That broods and sleeps on his own heart.

But he is weak ; both Man and Boy,
Hath been an idler in the land ;
Contented if he might enjoy
The things which others understand.

—Come hither in thy hour of strength ;
Come, weak as is a breaking wave !
Here stretch thy body at full length ;
Or build thy house upon this grave !

LINES

Composed at Grasmere, during a walk one Evening, after a stormy day, the Author having just read in a Newspaper that the dissolution of Mr. Fox was hourly expected.

LOUD is the Vale ! the Voice is up
With which she speaks when storms are gone ;
A mighty Unison of streams !
Of all her Voices, One !

Loud is the Vale ;—this inland Depth
In peace is roaring like the Sea ;
Yon star upon the mountain-top
Is listening quietly.

Sad was I, even to pain deprest,
Importunate and heavy load ! [1]
The Comforter hath found me here,
Upon this lonely road ;

And many thousands now are sad—
Wait the fulfilment of their fear ;
For he must die who is their stay,
Their glory disappear.

A Power is passing from the earth
To breathless Nature's dark abyss ;
But when the Mighty pass away
What is it more than this,

That Man, who is from God sent forth,
Doth yet again to God return ? —
Such ebb and flow must ever be,
Then wherefore should we mourn ?

[1] Importuna e grave salma.—MICHAEL ANGELO.

ELEGIAC STANZAS,

SUGGESTED BY A PICTURE OF PEELE CASTLE, IN A STORM,

PAINTED BY SIR GEORGE BEAUMONT.

I WAS thy neighbour once, thou rugged Pile!
Four summer weeks I dwelt in sight of thee:
I saw thee every day; and all the while
Thy Form was sleeping on a glassy sea.

So pure the sky, so quiet was the air!
So like, so very like, was day to day!
Whene'er I looked, thy Image still was there;
It trembled, but it never passed away.

How perfect was the calm! it seemed no sleep;
No mood, which season takes away, or brings:
I could have fancied that the mighty Deep
Was even the gentlest of all gentle things.

Ah! THEN, if mine had been the Painter's hand,
To express what then I saw; and add the gleam,
The light that never was, on sea or land,
The consecration, and the Poet's dream;

I would have planted thee, thou hoary Pile,
Amid a world how different from this!
Beside a sea that could not cease to smile;
On tranquil land, beneath a sky of bliss.

A Picture had it been of lasting ease,
Elysian quiet, without toil or strife;
No motion but the moving tide, a breeze,
Or merely silent Nature's breathing life.

Such, in the fond illusion of my heart,
Such Picture would I at that time have made :
And seen the soul of truth in every part,
A stedfast peace that might not be betrayed.

So once it would have been,—'tis so no more;
I have submitted to a new control :
A power is gone, which nothing can restore;
A deep distress hath humanised my Soul.

Not for a moment could I now behold
A smiling sea, and be what I have been :
The feeling of my loss will ne'er be old;
This, which I know, I speak with mind serene.

Then, Beaumont, Friend! who would have been the Friend,
If he had lived, of Him whom I deplore,
This work of thine I blame not, but commend;
This sea in anger, and that dismal shore.

O 'tis a passionate Work—yet wise and well,
Well chosen is the spirit that is here;
That Hulk which labours in the deadly swell,
This rueful sky, this pageantry of fear!

And this huge Castle, standing here sublime,
I love to see the look with which it braves,
Cased in the unfeeling armour of old time,
The lightning, the fierce wind, and trampling waves.

Farewell, farewell the heart that lives alone,
Housed, in a dream, at distance from the Kind!
Such happiness, wherever it be known,
Is to be pitied; for 'tis surely blind.

But welcome fortitude, and patient cheer,
And frequent sights of what is to be borne!
Such sights, or worse, as are before me here.—
Not without hope we suffer and we mourn.

GLEN-ALMAIN; OR, THE NARROW GLEN.

IN this still place, remote from men,
Sleeps Ossian, in the NARROW GLEN;
In this still place, where murmurs on
But one meek Streamlet, only one:
He sang of battles, and the breath
Of stormy war, and violent death;
And should, methinks, when all was past,
Have rightfully been laid at last
Where rocks were rudely heaped, and rent
As by a spirit turbulent;
Where sights were rough, and sounds were wild,
And every thing unreconciled;
In some complaining, dim retreat,
For fear and melancholy meet;
But this is calm; there cannot be
A more entire tranquillity.

Does then the Bard sleep here indeed?
Or is it but a groundless creed?
What matters it?—I blame them not
Whose fancy in this lonely spot
Was moved; and in such way expressed
Their notion of its perfect rest.
A convent, even a Hermit's cell,
Would break the silence of this Dell:
It is not quiet, is not ease;
But something deeper far than these:
The separation that is here
Is of the grave; and of austere
Yet happy feelings of the dead:
And, therefore, was it rightly said
That Ossian, last of all his race,
Lies buried in this lonely place.

WRITTEN ON A BLANK LEAF OF MACPHERSON'S OSSIAN.

OFT have I caught, upon a fitful breeze,
Fragments of far-off melodies,
With ear not coveting the whole,
A part so charmed the pensive soul.
While a dark storm before my sight
Was yielding, on a mountain height
Loose vapours have I watched, that won
Prismatic colours from the sun;
Nor felt a wish that Heaven would show
The image of its perfect bow.

What need, then, of these finished Strains?
Away with counterfeit Remains!
An abbey in its lone recess,
A temple of the wilderness,
Wrecks though they be, announce with feeling
The majesty of honest dealing.
Spirit of Ossian! if imbound
In language thou may'st yet be found,
If aught (intrusted to the pen
Or floating on the tongues of men,
Albeit shattered and impaired)
Subsist thy dignity to guard,
In concert with memorial claim
Of old gray stone, and high-born name,
That cleaves to rock or pillared cave,
Where moans the blast, or beats the wave,
Let Truth, stern arbitress of all,
Interpret that original,
And for presumptuous wrongs atone;
Authentic words be given, or none!

Time is not blind;—yet He, who spares
Pyramid pointing to the Stars,
Hath preyed with ruthless appetite
On all that marked the primal flight
Of the poetic ecstasy
Into the land of mystery.
No tongue is able to rehearse
One measure, Orpheus! of thy verse;
Musæus, stationed with his lyre
Supreme among the Elysian quire,
Is, for the dwellers upon earth,
Mute as a Lark ere morning's birth.
Why grieve for these, though past away
The music, and extinct the lay?

When thousands, by severer doom,
Full early to the silent tomb
Have sunk, at Nature's call; or strayed
From hope and promise, self-betrayed;
The garland withering on their brows;
Stung with remorse for broken vows;
Frantic—else how might they rejoice!
And friendless, by their own sad choice.

Hail, Bards of mightier grasp! on you
I chiefly call, the chosen Few,
Who cast not off the acknowledged guide,
Who faltered not, nor turned aside;
Whose lofty Genius could survive
Privation, under sorrow thrive;
In whom the fiery Muse revered
The symbol of a snow-white beard,
Bedewed with meditative tears
Dropped from the lenient cloud of years.

Brothers in Soul! though distant times
Produced you, nursed in various climes.
Ye, when the orb of life had waned,
A plenitude of love retained;
Hence, while in you each sad regret
By corresponding hope was met,
Ye lingered among human kind,
Sweet voices for the passing wind;
Departing sunbeams, loth to stop,
Though smiling on the last hill top;

Such to the tender-hearted Maid
Even ere her joys begin to fade;
Such, haply, to the rugged Chief
By Fortune crushed, or tamed by grief;

Appears, on Morven's lonely shore,
Dim-gleaming through imperfect lore,
The Son of Fingal; such was blind
Mæonides of ample mind;
Such Milton, to the fountain-head
Of glory by Urania led!

THE WISHING-GATE.

In the vale of Grasmere, by the side of the highway leading to
Ambleside, is a gate, which, time out of mind, has been called
the Wishing-gate, from a belief that wishes formed or indulged
there have a favourable issue.

HOPE rules a land for ever green:
All powers that serve the bright-eyed Queen
Are confident and gay;
Clouds at her bidding disappear;
Points she to aught?—the bliss draws near,
And Fancy smooths the way.

Not such the land of wishes—there
Dwell fruitless day-dreams, lawless prayer,
And thoughts with things at strife;
Yet how forlorn, should *ye* depart,
Ye superstitions of the *heart*,
How poor were human life!

When magic lore abjured its might,
Ye did not forfeit one dear right,
One tender claim abate ;
Witness this symbol of your sway,
Surviving near the public way,
The rustic Wishing-gate !

Inquire not if the faery race
Shed kindly influence on the place,
Ere northward they retired ;
If here a warrior left a spell,
Panting for glory as he fell ;
Or here a saint expired.

Enough that all around is fair,
Composed with Nature's finest care,
And in her fondest love ;
Peace to embosom and content,
To overawe the turbulent,
The selfish to reprove.

Yea ! even the Stranger from afar,
Reclining on this moss-grown bar,
Unknowing, and unknown,
The infection of the ground partakes,
Longing for his Beloved—who makes
All happiness her own.

Then why should conscious Spirits fear
The mystic stirrings that are here,
The ancient faith disclaim ?
The local Genius ne'er befriends
Desires whose course in folly ends,
Whose just reward is shame.

Smile if thou wilt, but not in scorn,
If some, by ceaseless pains outworn,
Here crave an easier lot ;
If some have thirsted to renew
A broken vow, or bind a true,
With firmer, holier knot.

And not in vain, when thoughts are cast
Upon the irrevocable past,
Some penitent sincere
May for a worthier future sigh,
While trickles from his downcast eye
No unavailing tear.

The Worldling, pining to be freed
From turmoil, who would turn or speed
The current of his fate,
Might stop before this favoured scene,
At Nature's call, nor blush to lean
Upon the Wishing-gate.

The Sage, who feels how blind, how weak.
Is man, though loth such help to *seek*,
Yet, passing, here might pause,
And yearn for insight to allay
Misgiving, while the crimson day
In quietness withdraws ;

Or when the church-clock's knell profound
To Time's first step across the bound
Of midnight makes reply ;
Time pressing on with starry crest,
To filial sleep upon the breast
Of dread eternity !

TO THE LADY FLEMING,

ON SEEING THE FOUNDATION PREPARING FOR THE
ERECTION OF RYDAL CHAPEL, WESTMORELAND.

BLEST is this Isle—our native Land ;
Where battlement and moated gate
Are objects only for the hand
Of hoary Time to decorate ;
Where shady hamlet, town that breathes
Its busy smoke in social wreaths,
No rampart's stern defence require,
Nought but the heaven-directed spire,
And steeple tower (with pealing bells
Far-heard)—our only citadels.

O Lady ! from a noble line
Of chieftains sprung, who stoutly bore
The spear, yet gave to works divine
A bounteous help in days of yore
(As records mouldering in the Dell
Of Nightshade[1] haply yet may tell) ;
Thee kindred aspirations moved
To build, within a vale beloved,
For Him upon whose high behests
All peace depends, all safety rests.

---

[1] Bekangs Ghyll—or the dell of Nightshade—in which stands St
Mary's Abbey in Low Furness.

How fondly will the woods embrace
This Daughter of thy pious care,
Lifting her front with modest grace
To make a fair recess more fair ;
And to exalt the passing hour ;
Or soothe it with a healing power
Drawn from the Sacrifice fulfilled
Before this rugged soil was tilled,
Or human habitation rose
To interrupt the deep repose !

Well may the villagers rejoice !
Nor heat, nor cold, nor weary ways,
Will be a hindrance to the voice
That would unite in prayer and praise ;
More duly shall wild wandering Youth
Receive the curb of sacred truth,
Shall tottering Age, bent earthward, hear
The Promise, with uplifted ear ;
And all shall welcome the new ray
Imparted to their Sabbath-day.

Nor deem the Poet's hope misplaced,
His fancy cheated—that can see
A shade upon the future cast
Of Time's pathetic sanctity ;
Can hear the monitory clock
Sound o'er the lake with gentle shock
At evening, when the ground beneath
Is ruffled o'er with cells of death ;
Where happy generations lie,
Here tutored for eternity.

Lives there a man whose sole delights
Are trivial pomp and city noise,
Hardening a heart that loathes or slights
What every natural heart enjoys ?
Who never caught a noon-tide dream
From murmur of a running stream ;
Could strip, for aught the prospect yields
To him, their verdure from the fields ;
And take the radiance from the clouds
In which the sun his setting shrouds.

A soul so pitiably forlorn,
If such do on this earth abide,
May season apathy with scorn,
May turn indifference to pride ;
And still be not unblest—compared
With him who grovels, self-debarred
From all that lies within the scope
Of holy faith and Christian hope ;
Yea, strives for others to bedim
The glorious Light too pure for him.

Alas ! that such perverted zeal
Should spread on Britain's favoured ground ;
That public order, private weal,
Should e'er have felt or feared a wound
From champions of the desperate law
Which from their own blind hearts they **draw ;**
Who tempt their reason to deny
God, whom their passions dare defy,
And boast that they alone are free
Who reach this dire extremity!

But turn we from these "bold bad" men ;
The way, mild Lady ! that hath led
Down to their "dark opprobrious den,"
Is all too rough for Thee to tread.
Softly as morning vapours glide
Down Rydal-cove from Fairfield's side,
Should move the tenor of *his* song
Who means to charity no wrong ;
Whose offering gladly would accord
With this day's work, in thought and word.

Heaven prosper it ! may peace, and love,
And hope, and consolation, fall,
Through its meek influence, from above,
And penetrate the hearts of all ;
All who, around the hallowed Fane,
Shall sojourn in this fair domain ;
Grateful to Thee, while service pure,
And ancient ordinance, shall endure,
For opportunity bestowed
To kneel together, and adore their God

TO THE REV. DR. WORDSWORTH.

(WITH THE SONNETS TO THE RIVER DUDDON, AND
OTHER POEMS.)

THE minstrels played their Christmas tune
To-night beneath my cottage-eaves ;
While, smitten by a lofty moon,
The encircling laurels, thick with leaves,
Gave back a rich and dazzling sheen,
That overpowered their natural green.

Through hill and valley every breeze
Had sunk to rest with folded wings :
Keen was the air, but could not freeze
Nor check the music of the strings ;
So stout and hardy were the band
That scraped the chords with strenuous hand.

And who but listened ?—till was paid
Respect to every Inmate's claim :
The greeting given, the music played,
In honour of each household name,
Duly pronounced with lusty call,
And "merry Christmas" wished to all !

O Brother ! I revere the choice
That took thee from thy native hills ;
And it is given thee to rejoice :
Though public care full often tills
(Heaven only witness of the toil)
A barren and ungrateful soil.

Yet, would that Thou, with me and mine,
Hadst heard this never-failing rite ;
And seen on other faces shine
A true revival of the light
Which Nature and these rustic Powers,
In simple childhood, spread through ours !

For pleasure hath not ceased to wait
On these expected annual rounds ;
Whether the rich man's sumptuous gate
Call forth the unelaborate sounds,
Or they are offered at the door
That guards the lowliest of the poor.

How touching, when, at midnight, sweep
Snow-muffled winds, and all is dark,
To hear—and sink again to sleep !
Or, at an earlier call, to mark,
By blazing fire, the still suspense
Of self-complacent innocence ;

The mutual nod,—the grave disguise
Of hearts with gladness brimming o'er ;
And some unbidden tears that rise
For names once heard, and heard no more ;
Tears brightened by the serenade
For infant in the cradle laid.

Ah ! not for emerald fields alone,
With ambient streams more pure and bright
Than fabled Cytherea's zone
Glittering before the Thunderer's sight,
Is to my heart of hearts endeared
The ground where we were born and reared !

Hail, ancient Manners ! sure defence,
Where they survive, of wholesome laws ;
Remnants of love whose modest sense
Thus into narrow room withdraws ;
Hail, Usages of pristine mould,
And ye that guard them, Mountains old !

Bear with me, Brother ! quench the thought
That slights this passion, or condemns ;
If thee fond Fancy ever brought
From the proud margin of the Thames,
And Lambeth's venerable towers,
To humbler streams, and greener bowers.

Yes, they can make, who fail to find,
Short leisure even in busiest days ;
Moments, to cast a look behind,
And profit by those kindly rays
That through the clouds do sometimes steal,
And all the far-off past reveal.

Hence, while the imperial City's din
Beats frequent on thy satiate ear,
A pleased attention I may win
To agitations less severe,
That neither overwhelm nor cloy,
But fill the hollow vale with joy !

EVENING VOLUNTARIES.

I.

NOT in the lucid intervals of life
That come but as a curse to party-strife;
Not in some hour when Pleasure with a sigh
Of languor puts his rosy garland by;
Not in the breathing-times of that poor slave
Who daily piles up wealth in Mammon's cave—
Is Nature felt, or can be : nor do words,
Which practised talent readily affords,
Prove that her hand has touched responsive chords;
Nor has her gentle beauty power to move
With genuine rapture and with fervent love
The soul of Genius, if he dare to take
Life's rule from passion craved for passion's sake;
Untaught that meekness is the cherished bent
Of all the truly great and all the innocent.

But who *is* innocent?   By grace divine,
Not otherwise, O Nature! we are thine,
Through good and evil thine, in just degree
Of rational and manly sympathy.
To all that Earth from pensive hearts is stealing,
And Heaven is now to gladdened eyes revealing,
Add every charm the universe can show
Through every change its aspects undergo—
Care may be respited, but not repealed;
No perfect cure grows on that bounded field.
Vain is the pleasure, a false calm the peace,
If He, through whom alone our conflicts cease,
Our virtuous hopes without relapse advance,
Come not to speed the Soul's deliverance;
To the distempered Intellect refuse
His gracious help. or give what we abuse.

II.

ON A HIGH PART OF THE COAST OF CUMBERLAND.

Easter Sunday, April 7,

THE AUTHOR'S SIXTY-THIRD BIRTH-DAY.

THE Sun, that seemed so mildly to retire,
Flung back from distant climes a streaming fire,
Whose blaze is now subdued to tender gleams,
Prelude of night's approach with soothing dreams.
Look round ;—of all the clouds not one is moving :
'Tis the still hour of thinking, feeling, loving.
Silent, and stedfast as the vaulted sky,
The boundless plain of waters seems to lie :—
Comes that low sound from breezes rustling o'er
The grass-crowned headland that conceals the shore?
No ; 'tis the earth-voice of the mighty sea,
Whispering how meek and gentle he *can* be !

Thou Power supreme ! who, arming to rebuke
Offenders, dost put off the gracious look,
And clothe thyself with terrors like the flood
Of ocean roused into his fiercest mood ;
Whatever discipline thy Will ordain
For the brief course that must for me remain,
Teach me with quick-eared spirit to rejoice
In admonitions of thy softest voice !
Whate'er the path these mortal feet may trace,
Breathe through my soul the blessing of thy grace,
Glad, through a perfect love, a faith sincere
Drawn from the wisdom that begins with fear ;
Glad to expand ; and, for a season, free
From finite cares, to rest absorbed in Thee !

TO MARY WORDSWORTH.

O DEARER far than light and life are dear.
Full oft our human foresight I deplore ;
Trembling, through my unworthiness, with fear
That friends, by death disjoined, may meet no more !

Misgivings, hard to vanquish or control,
Mix with the day, and cross the hour of rest ;
While all the future, for thy purer soul,
With "sober certainties" of love is blest.

If a faint sigh, not meant for human ear,
Tell that these words thy humbleness offend,
Cherish me still—else faltering in the rear
Of a steep march : uphold me to the end.

Peace settles where the Intellect is meek,
And love is dutiful in thought and deed ;
Through Thee communion with that Love I seek ;
The faith Heaven strengthens where *he* moulds the creed.

TO A CHILD.

WRITTEN IN HER ALBUM.

SMALL service is true service while it lasts :
Of humblest Friends, bright Creature ! scorn not one ;
The Daisy, by the shadow that it casts,
Protects the lingering dew-drop from the Sun.

EXTEMPORE EFFUSION UPON THE DEATH OF JAMES HOGG.

NOVEMBER, 1835.

WHEN first, descending from the moorlands
I saw the Stream of Yarrow glide
Along a bare and open valley,
The Ettrick Shepherd was my guide.

When last along its banks I wandered,
Through groves that had begun to shed
Their golden leaves upon the pathways,
My steps the Border-minstrel led.

The mighty Minstrel breathes no longer,
Mid mouldering ruins low he lies ;
And death upon the braes of Yarrow,
Has closed the Shepherd-poet's eyes :

Nor has the rolling year twice measured,
From sign to sign, its stedfast course,
Since every mortal power of Coleridge
Was frozen at its marvellous source ;

The rapt One, of the godlike forehead,
The heaven-eyed creature sleeps in earth
And Lamb, the frolic and the gentle,
Has vanished from his lonely hearth.

Like clouds that rake the mountain-summits,
Or waves that own no curbing hand,
How fast has brother followed brother,
From sunshine to the sunless land!

Yet I, whose lids from infant slumber
Were earlier raised, remain to hear
A timid voice, that asks in whispers,
" Who next will drop and disappear?"

Our haughty life is crowned with darkness,
Like London with its own black wreath,
On which with thee, O Crabbe! forth-looking,
I gazed from Hampstead's breezy heath.

As if but yesterday departed,
Thou too art gone before; but why,
O'er ripe fruit, seasonably gathered,
Should frail survivors heave a sigh?

Mourn rather for that holy Spirit,
Sweet as the spring, as ocean deep;
For Her [1] who, ere her summer faded,
Has sunk into a breathless sleep.

No more of old romantic sorrows,
For slaughtered Youth or love-lorn Maid!
With sharper grief is Yarrow smitten,
And Ettrick mourns with her their Poet dead.

[1] Mrs. Hemans.

DEVOTIONAL INCITEMENTS.

"Not to the earth confined,
Ascend to heaven."

WHERE will they stop, those breathing Powers,
The Spirits of the new-born flowers?
They wander with the breeze, they wind
Where'er the streams a passage find;
Up from their native ground they rise
In mute aërial harmonies;
From humble violet, modest thyme,
Exhaled, the essential odours climb,
As if no space below the sky
Their subtle flight could satisfy:
Heaven will not tax our thoughts with pride
If like ambition be *their* guide.

Roused by this kindliest of May-showers,
The spirit-quickener of the flowers,
That with moist virtue softly cleaves
The buds, and freshens the young leaves,
The birds pour forth their souls in notes
Of rapture from a thousand throats—
Here checked by too impetuous haste,
While there the music runs to waste,
With bounty more and more enlarged,
Till the whole air is overcharged.
Give ear, O Man! to their appeal,
And thirst for no inferior zeal,
Thou, who canst *think*, as well as feel.

M

Mount from the earth ; aspire ! aspire !
So pleads the town's cathedral quire,
In strains that from their solemn height
Sink, to attain a loftier flight ;
While incense from the altar breathes
Rich fragrance in embodied wreaths ;
Or, flung from swinging censer, shrouds
The taper-lights, and curls in clouds
Around angelic Forms, the still
Creation of the painter's skill,
That on the service wait concealed
One moment, and the next revealed.
—Cast off your bonds, awake, arise,
And for no transient ecstasies !
What else can mean the visual plea
Of still or moving imagery—
The iterated summons loud,
Not wasted on the attendant crowd,
Nor wholly lost upon the throng
Hurrying the busy streets along ?

Alas ! the sanctities combined
By art to unsensualise the mind
Decay and languish : or, as creeds
And humours change, are spurned like weeds :
The priests are from their altars thrust ;
Temples are levelled with the dust ;
And solemn rites and awful forms
Founder amid fanatic storms.
Yet evermore, through years renewed
In undisturbed vicissitude
Of seasons balancing their flight
On the swift wings of day and night,
Kind Nature keeps a heavenly door
Wide open for the scattered Poor.

Where flower-breathed incense to the skies
Is wafted in mute harmonies ;
And ground fresh-cloven by the plough
Is fragrant with a humbler vow ;
Where birds and brooks from leafy dells
Chime forth unwearied canticles,
And vapours magnify and spread
The glory of the sun's bright head—
Still constant in her worship, still
Conforming to the eternal Will,
Whether men sow or reap the fields,
Divine monition Nature yields,
That not by bread alone we live,
Or what a hand of flesh can give ;
That every day should leave some part
Free for a sabbath of the heart :
So shall the seventh be truly blest,
From morn to eve, with hallowed rest.

INSCRIPTION FOR A STONE

IN THE GROUNDS OF RYDAL MOUNT.

In these fair vales hath many a Tree
  At Wordsworth's suit been spared
And from the builder's hand this Stone
For some rude beauty of its own,
  Was rescued by the Bard.
So let it rest ; and time will come
  When here the tender-hearted
May heave a gentle sigh for him,
  As one of the departed.

INDEX OF FIRST LINES.

INDEX OF FIRST LINES.

THE END.

PRINTED BY R. & R. CLARK. LTD., EDINBURGH

The Golden Treasury Series

MACMILLAN & CO LTD